Memories *of* Wind *and* Waves

KODANSHA INTERNATIONAL
Tokyo · New York · London

Memories
of Wind and Waves
A Self-Portrait of Lakeside Japan

Dr. Junichi Saga

TRANSLATED BY
Juliet Winters Carpenter

ILLUSTRATED BY
Dr. Susumu Saga

Publication of this book was assisted
by a generous grant provided by Ms.
Kan Yamaguchi of Tsuchiura City,
Japan. A select number of interesting
works in English on Asian themes
have been given such assistance.

The photograph on page 139 is by Tomiji Hagiwara. The illustrations on pages 58, 79, 83, 124, and 241 are reprinted with the
kind permission of the Kasumigaura Citizens' Association. The
map on the endpapers is by Noriko Murotani.

Distributed in the United States by Kodansha America, Inc.,
575 Lexington Avenue, New York, NY 10022, and in the United
Kingdom and continental Europe by Kodansha Europe Ltd.,
95 Aldwych, London WC2B 4JF. Published by Kodansha International Ltd., 17-14 Otowa 1-chome, Bunkyo-ku, Tokyo 112-
8652, and Kodansha America, Inc. Copyright © 2002 by Junichi
Saga. All rights reserved. Printed in Japan.

Originally published in Japanese under the title *Kasumigaura
fudoki* (Tokyo: Joyo Shinbunsha, 1995).

First edition, 2002
ISBN 4-7700-2758-3
02 03 04 05 06 10 9 8 7 6 5 4 3 2 1

Library of Congress CIP data available

CONTENTS

4. Town Life   205

TRANSLATOR'S PREFACE

Years ago, as a hospital intern in Honolulu, Dr. Junichi Saga decided to visit the local library to see what information was available on Japan. He found plenty of works detailing the finer points of the tea ceremony, haiku, ukiyo-e, and Noh drama, but nothing that remotely suggested the everyday lives of men and women like those he grew up with in his birthplace, Tsuchiura. Dissatisfied with this lopsided portrayal of Japan, Saga conceived a need for other kinds of books to remedy the imbalance. Fortunately for us, he took the situation into his own hands. *Memories of Wind and Waves*, first published in 1995 under the title *Kasumigaura fudoki* (A topographical record of Kasumigaura) is a set of colorful reminiscences that evokes the joys and hardships of life for fishermen and others on the shores of Lake Kasumigaura in early twentieth-century Ibaraki Prefecture.

Dr. Saga used a tape recorder to first record the words of these hardy men and women—all of them his own patients and friends—after work at the local clinic, and then painstakingly transcribed, rewrote, and reorganized them for clarity and cohesion. The process took years. The result, like his earlier, prize-winning *Memories of Silk and Straw*, is an intimate self-portrait of a Japan fast vanishing from living memory.

It cannot be stressed enough how valuable and important a service Dr. Saga has done us. The thirty-odd voices here are, as he points out, among our last surviving links with Japan's long feudal period that ended with the overthrow of the Tokugawa shogunate in 1868. The network of memories he has preserved helps to close the lacuna between the traditional Japan of the past and the progressive Japan of today. The world these people inhabited, in a rural backwater only an hour's train ride from Tokyo, continued virtually unchanged for centuries; but in their lifetimes they saw that world turned upside down.

Over the last half-century Japan has been on a dizzying ride, experiencing widespread poverty, then the horrors of militarism and wartime devastation, before achieving its present status as a peaceful economic superpower. The storytellers are largely unsentimental in their perspective, and unabashed in

their appreciation and enjoyment of the significant material improvements in their lives. At the same time, in the midst of relative abundance and ease they are nostalgic for the small, good things of the past: gathering on a freezing hilltop with family and neighbors to worship the full moon; swimming and playing in the pure, clear waters of the lake; racing to be first to a fishing spot; or just strolling around carefree at a festival, buying treats as delicious as they were infrequent.

Along with the overall tenor of life, the look of the towns and the landscape have of course been transformed as well. The town of Tsuchiura depicted in these pages is truly a little "city of water" crisscrossed with rivers and canals, where every household had one or more boats tied up out back as a means of getting around. The Tsuchiura that I saw a couple of years ago had swelled to more than 115,000 in population, and was virtually indistinguishable from any other town its size in Japan. The rivers have been mostly paved over and turned into roads. Much of the surrounding wetlands too has been filled in and converted to farmland. And, as has happened all across Japan, the characteristic low, wooden houses and shops of earlier times have given way to high-rise condominiums and office buildings of glass and concrete.

Just west of Tsuchiura today is Tsukuba Academic New Town, a planned community built a quarter of a century ago on the southern slope of Mount Tsukuba; it houses two leading universities, as well as some forty-five state and private high-tech research institutes. To the east lies Lake Kasumigaura, the second-largest lake in Japan. Once connected to the sea, it was gradually cut off as a result of steps taken three centuries ago to save Edo (today's Tokyo) from flooding by rechanneling the River Tone. Unfortunately this bold project, while sparing the nation's capital, resulted in frequent disastrous flooding in and around Tsuchiura. In any case, the lake has been entirely freshwater since the mid-1970s.

About seven miles to the south of Tsuchiura there used to be the Kasumi-gaura naval airforce base, a pilot–training school established in the 1920s that became the largest and most prestigious air base in the country. Here the kamikaze pilots of World War II received their training; in a nearby restaurant the attack on Pearl Harbor was planned. The influx of large numbers of young men facing their own imminent demise had a significant impact on Tsuchiura, leading quickly to a matching influx of geisha and prostitutes for the men's diversion. The last two narratives, by former geisha in their eighties, hark back to those days. Today the base is closed and the amusement quarter just a memory.

During my visit to Tsuchiura, Dr. Saga took me to the homes of some of the surviving fishermen represented in the pages of this book. It was a signal honor to enter their spic-and-span houses, whether traditional or newly built, and be introduced to the storytellers in person, taking in the warmth of their hospitality, seeing the strength of their family bonds, and observing the easy communication between them and the good doctor. I looked on in fascination as the conversations grew animated, with him teasing, prompting, and asking question after question. He responded with enthusiasm to everything they said, focusing on new revelations with palpable interest or amazement. The depth of his friendship and respect for them, and the strength of his commitment to learning all he could of their histories, was no less remarkable than the profound love and trust they clearly bore him. No wonder the book contains such a wealth of information, I thought: who else but Dr. Saga could have spent so much time this way, entering so sympathetically into the minutiae of these people's lives and eliciting such rich and telling detail?

I must confess that I mostly sat and watched Dr. Saga interacting with his cronies, scarcely joining in the conversation, for another reason: mesmerized by the sound of the local dialect, it was all I could do to follow what was being said. Although they grew up barely forty miles from Tokyo, country folk in Tsuchiura and the surrounding area were not exposed in their youth to the equalizing influence of national television, movies, and magazines. Their speech, like their lifestyle, accordingly retains much of its old, idiosyncratic features. Transcribed on paper, the dialect was not too difficult to work out, but as spoken by these old-timers it became startlingly incomprehensible: one more sign of the region's strong collective identity, and one more tie to the past.

These memoirs contain descriptions of dozens of occupations that people once pursued on and around Lake Kasumigaura. The storytellers themselves, twenty-two men and eleven women, represent a cross-section of life in that place and time. Besides fishermen of all kinds—including some who lived as water nomads, roaming the lake in little roofed boats—the men include boat-builders, ship carpenters, a riverboat captain and a ferryman. A few were the sons of prosperous tradesmen, at least one was of samurai stock, and one was a schoolteacher. Others were mired in poverty, forced to work at both fishing and farming to scrape by. Of the women, two were town geishas and the rest worked alongside their husbands, fishing, repairing nets, loading cargo, or farming; some earned extra income by weaving straw bags, or even hired themselves out as day laborers.

Childhood was short, and not always easy. One fifth-grade boy who came from a family of weavers and dyers would dash from school to catch the steamer for Tsuchiura, run errands in the city, stay overnight alone in an inn, then get up at the crack of dawn to be at his desk in school on the stroke of eight.

Though well on in years, the fishermen and their wives appeared to be in robust health. In general, the strength and vitality of these men and women, physical and mental, could be another surprise to any who are accustomed to thinking of Japanese people as diminutive and self-effacing. The first storyteller, Hama Suzuki, compares today's men unfavorably to her father, who she declares was "a far cry from the limp, skinny excuses for men you see nowadays!" She herself comes across as a fireball who was never shy about speaking her mind (except once, when confronted by the jilted fiancé who scorned her for marrying a riverboat captain). But then, by tradition the people of Ibaraki are supposed to share a certain hotness of blood and bellicosity. It is a trait made endearing in Suzuki by her good humor, honesty, loyalty, and seemingly endless capacity for punishing physical labor. All in all, along with vivid details of life on a riverboat, she offers up an engaging picture of strong, resilient Japanese womanhood—one greatly at odds, needless to say, with the stereotypical image of docile, doll-faced flower arrangers.

Because so many of the storytellers fished the lake or lived on boats year-round, or farmed the land nearby, they gained an intimate knowledge of nature that seems almost uncanny today—hard-won, expert knowledge that was applied with remarkable patience and ingenuity. One story tells of "Catfish Kyubei," who learned to catch catfish and carp in the middle of winter by the simple expedient of swimming underwater, naked except for a strategically placed bit of straw; once his body was chilled to the same temperature as the fish's, he had only to insert his thumb in their half-open mouths and drag them up to the surface. Grandfather Sakurai could pin together the wings of a sparrow in mid-flight with one well-aimed blow dart, while his grandson Takamasa learned by heart the exact shapes, colors, textures, and peculiarities of dozens of huge, treacherous underwater rocks, so that he could navigate through and around them to reach the best fishing grounds. Fishermen learned how to tell with dead certainty what fish were biting where, what they would feed on, and how best to get them to market. They learned how to read the play of wind and light on waves and to detect warning signs in clouds, knowing full well that misreading those messages could be fatal. And they learned, despite intense rivalries, to cooperate and look out for their neighbors when things were bad.

Two themes come up repeatedly. "People today would never believe how hard life was," we are assured over and over, and we can only marvel at tales of backbreaking labor performed barefoot on a barely sufficient diet and stolen snatches of sleep. At the same time, people were often keenly aware of the beauty around them. Memories of early morning fishing in bitter cold are made lyrical with recollections of the moon lying silver in the water and the sky turning slowly to crimson. A young girl is so moved by the pathos of sunset that she climbs on a high pile of firewood each night to sing a song to the disappearing sun. This capacity to feel the attractions of nature, and to respond to them wholeheartedly, is to me one of the most compelling aspects of the narratives. It is a tribute to the spirit of the people of Ibaraki, and by extension of all Japan, that they kept a lively appreciation of beauty in nature despite the suffering they endured.

Today, for Ibaraki residents as for people all around Japan, life has become easier in countless ways, and no one would say this is bad. The lower living standards and lower expectations of the past can have no attraction. But at the same time it seems that if so much of the unsullied beauty and purity of nature has been lost, not only in Japan but elsewhere—and even more, if human awareness of and receptivity to the beauty around us has been dulled, and our sense of its importance diminished—then the price of affluence has been very high indeed.

It is a source of unceasing pain to Dr. Saga that so many of the people who opened their lives and hearts to him have died in recent years, one after another, without living to see this book completed. I share his sadness, and yet more than anything I am grateful to him, and them, for making it possible for all of us to share in their stories and their world.

AUTHOR'S PREFACE

Years after my first book on Tsuchiura came out and the English version, titled *Memories of Silk and Straw: A Self-Portrait of Small-Town Japan* (Kodansha International, 1987), was published, a terrible time in my life began: the men and women whom I had known for so many years began all at once to die. Even as I was busy collecting their stories, there would be the occasional sad news of someone's death—but then one day, quite suddenly, they began dying in droves. Like actors in a play who take their several turns on stage and, moments later, disappear all at once with the final curtain, they were gone, as if some great invisible curtain had fallen in front of me and closed their world off to me forever. But the reality of death is far worse than any such metaphor can convey: after a play, the vanished actors can be seen again at the curtain call, whereas my friends are nowhere to be found.

For a long time I supposed that my purpose in gathering so many life stories and making them into a book was to convey an era of history. That is why for years on end I went about listening to and recording what elderly people around me had to say, spending countless days with them. Once the book came out, my purpose would be fulfilled; yes, shallow as it now sounds, that is what I once believed.

The truth was otherwise. Without my ever realizing it, my life had become interwoven with theirs. Day after day I would sit in their homes till late at night, listening to their life stories and leaving finally with the promise, "I'll be back tomorrow!" For more than a dozen years we shared many a heartfelt moment; we ate at the same table; we knew and trusted each other. By sharing funny anecdotes and marvelous experiences, by confessing things never told to anyone else, we became closer than family. In winter we would sit companionably for hours on end around the *kotatsu*, eating tangerines, engrossed in conversation; at other times, like a prosecutor gathering evidence, I would pose question after question, sharing with my informants the joy of seeing a long-forgotten world spring back to life before our eyes.

I spent more than sixteen such years with Mitsu Oshima, and my conversations with Tai Terakado, from the same neighborhood, went on for more than seventeen years. Then one day it was over.

I was utterly dismayed. I felt just like Urashima Taro,[1] the Japanese Rip van Winkle. I'd gone in search of the jeweled box of the fairy tale, going out of my way to track and record the stories of an earlier generation, those who lived before me—only to find that I'd settled all unknowing into that other world, spending months and years of my life there, and awakening one day to find myself borne away on an invisible string and stranded alone on a desert shore.

Writing lost all attraction for me. I didn't know what to do. Several years went by, filled with the tedious routine of a small-town doctor. Then one day I received an unexpected phone call.

"How've you been, doc? Long time no see." It was the half-forgotten voice of a fisherman named Susumu Fujii.

"Yes, it's been a long time," I replied. "Are you well?"

"Not bad, except I can't move from the waist down."

"What happened?"

"Well—come by and take a look sometime, would you?"

I raced over in my car and found him in bed in his old house with a view of the lake.

"Hey there, doc," he said. "I'm in pretty bad shape. Look at this." He produced a cord next to his pillow and gripped it in both his hands. By pulling on it with all his might, he was able to lift himself slowly to a sitting position, like raising an ancient, half-decayed tree trunk with a crane. Through a crack between sliding doors, I could see his fishing net lying piled on the floor.

"It's all over for me. But tell me, doc, how are things with you? What have you been up to lately?" He looked at me intently.

Not long afterwards, I began to publish *Kasumigaura fudoki* serially in a newspaper, determined to finish writing up all the memoirs relating to Lake Kasumigaura while Susumu Fujii was alive. My first book had included some mention of the lake, but never had I written anything focused exclusively on the people making their living on and around it. Now I scribbled like one possessed.

It wasn't long before I found myself once again the resident of a strange new world. Fishermen, riverboat captains and their wives, farmers' wives who used to fish for shrimp—one after another I searched them out and took down their reminiscences. All were past eighty-five, and some were well into their nineties; but in every case, their stories came pouring out as if a dam had burst, as if they had been waiting patiently for me to come. For over six months I wrote every day. The hundredth episode ran in the paper and still I wasn't finished. Never before had the rivers and the lake seemed so richly alive; my heartbeat quickened as I wrote.

But this time, after the last episode ran, there was truly no one left. One day even Mr. Fujii himself, my friend who had such a loud voice, and who spent his life rowing the length and breadth of the lake, slipped away forever.

Out of the window of the study where I am writing this manuscript I can see an eight-story building, and beyond it the snakelike coils of an expressway built to link Tsuchiura with a new academic center. All of that used to be a river—one of a network of waterways down which goods from across the lake were transported to town and then stacked in people's storehouses. That vanished river, that water's edge, once rang with the shouts of men hauling in their nets as couples on houseboats waited among the reeds for night to fall. It wasn't so very long ago, and yet that era, that scenery, and the life-breath of those people have all vanished like phantoms.

This book is both a tribute to the too-swift passing of time and an echo from the lives of the men and women who experienced that once-vivid era. They have responded to this final curtain call, letting us hear once again the nostalgic sound of their voices.

Tsuchiura no sato (My hometown, Tsuchiura), the original version of *Memories of Silk and Straw: A Self-Portrait of Small-Town Japan*, was published in 1981 and translated by an Englishman named Garry O. Evans. The appearance of that translation was preceded by a number of twists and turns, too many to recount here; let me just say that without the encouragement and cooperation of Kazuko Hirose, his wife Teiko, and Professor Yasuhiko Doi, the project would never have gotten off the ground. Fortunately, in 1985 the translation came to the attention of Stephen Shaw, senior editor at Kodansha International, and two years later the English version came out. Mr. Shaw's backing was truly a godsend.

Now, thirteen years later, this companion volume has been rendered into English by Professor Juliet W. Carpenter of Doshisha Women's College. It boggles my mind to think of the immense difficulty, even for a translator with as much experience as Professor Carpenter, of rendering into English a book filled with as many special problems and dialectal peculiarities as this one. I would like to take this opportunity to express my deepest respect and gratitude to her.

At every step of the way, Stephen Shaw has once again taken the lead in planning the publication of this book, and Machiko Moriyasu and Elizabeth Floyd have acted as the hands-on editors. I have no words to express my thanks to them.

I would also like to offer my sincere thanks to Kan Yamaguchi. Thanks to her generosity, the "Kan Yamaguchi Series" has already produced three splendid English translations; it is a great honor that my book should be the fourth.

Finally, I wish to offer respect and gratitude to my father. He lived a life of unswerving dedication to his calling as a small-town doctor, but in his later years he also took up painting. *Tsuchiura no sato* contained over 150 of his watercolors, and nearly all the illustrations in this book too are his, each one drawn with the intense focus and painstaking attention to detail of a surgeon in mid-operation. They are valuable not only for the accuracy with which they record history, but for their success in recapturing the indefinable spirit of the past. Each illustration aptly portrays some aspect of life around Tsuchiura in the twentieth century; looking them over it is hard to believe that the beauties of nature and even some of the towns and villages they depict have actually vanished from the earth. My father must have loved this world tremendously. I hope that his illustrations—like the stories told by these many storytellers—will live on in readers' hearts.

1

TAKASE RIVERBOATS

A Captain's Wife

Mrs. Hama Suzuki (1906–1997)

I only married the captain because the matchmaker was such a smooth talker. "A captain's sitting pretty, just like a landowner—he makes money just sailing up and down the river." That was all my parents needed to hear. They were desperate to marry me off. Farmer, captain—anybody making a decent living would have done. Why? That's a long story, one that brings back a lot of memories. Just listen.

My folks were rice farmers in Aso. I was the biggest tomboy you ever saw, but I was a good daughter to them. After the fall harvest, every morning we'd get up at the crack of dawn and tromp out to the hills to gather fuel for winter. I was eleven or twelve when I started. Farmers were all dirt poor, no one owned their own land, but people didn't mind if you carried away dead wood or picked pine needles off the ground. So every morning before breakfast I'd go out to gather needles, make them into a big ball, and lug it home in a basket on my back.

From the hilltops you could see all the white sails on the lake. You could see boats using huge nets, fishermen going about their business, and women on the shore spreading the day's catch out to dry, hundreds of fish on straw mats. It was a grand sight. The beach sparkled. It was wide and white, and stretched on forever.

We kids played there by Lake Kasumigaura too. Did we ever! I'll never forget it. In summer we'd run around stark naked, swimming and fishing and playing on the sand. You could catch clams by the bucketful, and sea mussels. All you had to do was wade out knee-deep and stir the sand with your foot, and you could catch all you wanted. Kids today wouldn't believe the fun we had.

You wouldn't believe how clean the beach was either. Fine-grained sand without a speck of dirt in it, and water in the shoals as clear as clear could be. Any time you got thirsty, you'd just put your mouth down in it and take a drink. If you lived on the beach you didn't need a well. Only one house in three had a well back then. People used lake water for laundry, for baths, for everything.

All the houses by the lake belonged to fishermen. Mostly they used sailboats, but two men fished with large *daitoku* nets. Shozaemon and Gonbei, their names were. Those two had real clout. They bossed dozens of men who brought in the daily catch, and streams of peddlers who came around every day looking for fresh-caught fish. The two of them were like millionaires. Workers were given all they could eat and drink. When people got too hungry they'd say, "Well, let's go work on the *daitoku*." Times were good.

Farmers from all around would pitch in. Farming didn't pay by the day but this did, and that was a great attraction. Whenever he could my pa helped out too. Pa was a fine-looking man. When he pulled, the sweat would pour off him and his muscles shone. A far cry from the limp, skinny excuses for men you see today! He wore a loincloth, and a towel twisted around his head. He was burned black all over from the sun, his face and shoulders and back especially.

To pull in a *daitoku* net, they used winches called *kagura* set up all along the beach. The net would be out from sundown, all night long until dawn. Fishermen would pile the net into a boat, take it out and lower it into the water, then swish it around. On shore, more men would line up eight in a row and winch it in, digging in their feet and working up a sweat while their muscles bulged. Little by little they'd haul the net in. *Daitoku* nets were huge, made of hemp, a thousand feet or more across. While the men worked, the women chanted in rhythm:

> Here it comes, in it comes,
> Look there, see it come, look see look look
> *Essa hoisa*, haul it in, pull it in,

That's it, that's the way.
Aso and Ukijima, famous in Kihara—
Barefoot in winter, a loincloth in summer.
Take a melon rind, pickle it in vinegar.
Essa hoisa, haul it in, pull it in.

When the net got close to shore then everybody would grab hold, men and girls and women too, and pull for all they were worth, chanting together at the tops of their lungs. I can still hear it.

Don't just hold it now, give a pull now!
Aso and Ushibori, famous in Itako—
Pull it in, that's the way, pull it in, harder.

The beach people were a rough crowd and if you slacked off they'd yell at you. You had to stay on your toes. It was something to see.

The part of the net holding the littlest fish was called the *shido*, and by the time that came in, we'd all be in a sweat. The fish were put into baskets right away. The women would sort them while the men loaded the empty nets back onto the boat and went out for another go. This kept on all night, three times a night. We thought nothing of staying up all night. Nobody stopped for a minute's sleep. No sir! Back then, that was the only way to do business. You had to go without sleep.

There were plenty of fish for the taking. You could even throw a net right from shore and get a good catch. Around 1920, a pailful of *wakasagi* [pond smelt] sold for about five sen.[1] The workers got paid in *wakasagi* mostly. Other times we'd get coins. A grown man earned one yen for a day's work. That was big money!

Youth

Before I knew it I was fourteen. Then my mother said girls have to learn to sew, and she sent me to sewing school. The teacher was Mrs. Miyoshi, the wife of someone who was descended from a samurai family. It's different nowadays, but back then the old ways still hung on. This was a very old family that had three storehouses full of rice and a moat around the house, just like a castle. Later there was a Miyoshi Button Factory in Tsuchiura built by the same family. Anyway, all the fishermen's daughters and farmers' daughters went to her to learn sewing and manners.

Lessons were fifty sen a month. I earned all the money myself by gathering pine needles. There was a kiln in town, and for every ball of needles I took there, I'd get six sen. My parents never gave me any money—I earned every bit on my own.

Then one day I rebelled. You know why? My older sister went to Tokyo to work in a fine home, and when she came back for a visit I couldn't believe my eyes. Her hair, her kimono, her obi and accessories, her footwear—it was nothing like the way country girls dressed, I can tell you that. She had a silk purse with more bills in it than I'd ever laid eyes on. So I said to myself, Hama, what are you doing wasting your life in this dump? My brother was in Tokyo too, working for a contractor, and I was dying to go. But my parents said no. They wouldn't hear of me going off to Tokyo before I was even twenty. I was crushed. To forget about it, I'd sneak off with my friend Maki and sing one of the popular songs of the day: "I miiiiss you, I loooong for you."

Then in 1923 the Great Kanto Earthquake hit Tokyo and turned it to ashes. We lost hope for my brother and sister, but one day my brother came home and said Tokyo was a boomtown. It had burned to the ground and now everybody was rebuilding. I thought, this I've got to see. I talked it over with Maki, and we wrapped our belongings up in a *furoshiki* wrapping cloth and

ran away. We were seventeen.

We took the train to Ueno, but we didn't know up from down. We had no idea where to go to get work. Then right in front of us we saw a two-story wooden building with a sign in gold lettering, "Tamagawa Inn." The fence had a help-wanted poster. We walked straight in and called out: "Anybody here?"

"What do you want?"

"We want to be maids."

"You do, eh? Come this way."

The head maid came out and asked us our ages and our names. We told her we were twenty, and we gave fake names. She didn't care. She was probably happy to get two strong country girls to work for her. She brought out aprons and told us to put them on and start carrying food to the banquet room. I carried five trays, and then I'd had enough. "Maki," I said, "this is no way to see Tokyo. Let's get out of here."

We folded up the aprons and laid them down in the kitchen, picked up our bundles, and snuck out the back. Nobody came after us, which was a relief, but what were we going to do now?

My brother had said something about a place called Kameido that was always lively and had a famous shrine, so we decided to go there. When we did, we found burned rubble everywhere, with just a house or two standing. It was a shock to see how bad the destruction from the earthquake was. We walked around till we came to a pretty little café all lighted up. The sign said "Kinokuniya." I thought, oh boy, this is it, the real Tokyo. So in we went.

Give us work, we said again, and the owner, who was a stout middle-aged woman, seemed to take a liking to us. "You're on," she said. "You can start right now." She brought out nice white aprons for us, and we put them on over our kimonos, powdered our faces, and went out to greet the customers. First thing we hear is loud music coming from a big gramophone: "I miiiiss

A hostess with customers at a café

you, I loooong for you, all my fear is gone." Beautiful lights hung down from the ceiling, and there were embroidered curtains at the windows. Behind the counter was a boy with a bow tie, and rows of glass cups were lined up against the wall. It was my dream come true.

Well, I may have been a hayseed, but I was young and pretty and I worked hard, so the owner liked me and the customers did too. I raked in ten yen a day in tips. Yes, I did—why would an old lady like me lie about a thing like that?

Times were good back then, better even than in 1964 when the Olympics came to Tokyo. The whole city was waiting to be rebuilt, so there was work galore for carpenters, plasterers, lumber dealers, steeplejacks, joiners, and anybody else who had anything to do with house-building. Workers were rolling in dough, even those who weren't so skilled. Master carpenters were lining their pockets. And at night they'd all come to our café for some fun. I'd tease them a little and they'd press money in my hand. I knew enough to look out for myself, so I swore those city fellers would never get the better of me. I took their money, but I never took *them* seriously. They liked me all the better for that, and the place was jam-packed every night.

The hit song then was "The Boatman's Song." Everywhere you went, you'd hear the lyrics: "I am withered grass on a dry riverbed."

> Dying and living, it's all the same—
> Just like the flow of the water.
> You and me, we'll end our days
> Riverboat captains on the River Tone.

I didn't have a good voice, but when I sang along with the record a hush used to come over the room, and then everybody would burst into applause.

The wind blows cold
On withered grass like us.
When my tears fall hot,
Then moon, you dip them up.

A lot of the men used to make eyes at me. One was a watchmaker, and he really liked me. He was thirty years old. He came every day and always left me a big tip. Bought me kimonos too, till I had enough to fill a great big wicker basket. His wife had died, and he had a notion to marry me next. He asked me out on a date, but the owner wouldn't hear of it. She felt responsible, you see. Finally she said I could go, but only if the cook and the waiter came along as bodyguards, and he agreed, so that's what we did. Pretty funny when you think about it.

Anyway, after three months I'd saved one hundred yen. And you know what I did? I sent it home. Farmers back then were dirt poor. I figured my folks needed it more than I did, so I sent it to them, and next thing I know my brother's there to take me home. I was such a baby I couldn't understand how he knew where I was, but of course the postmark gave it away. He came stomping in and the owner couldn't do a thing. He dragged me out, and that was that. Maki didn't go, though. She'd gotten herself knocked up. I never knew anything was going on, but she was pregnant and said she'd live with her man, so she stayed behind.

My folks must have been crazy with worry. I'd run off to the city and been gone for three months, and then out of the blue I sent home a small fortune. Of course they figured I'd been selling my body. I'd done no such thing, so it made me spitting mad. Here I'd saved every tip I ever earned and sent it home just to make their miserable lives a little easier, and they went and accused me of a thing like that! Oh, it made my blood boil.

"All right, I want my money back," I told them. "Hand it over." I went right out and bought myself muslin kimonos, sandals, rings, you name it—I spent every last bit on myself.

It was spring when I went back, time for rice planting and weeding. I helped do the work, but after a taste of Tokyo how could I go back to farm life? I made up my mind that as soon as the rice was harvested I'd take off again, and I did. Packed up my things in a *furoshiki* wrapper and ran away.

This time I picked Asakusa. I went to a hotel called the "Kirakuya," behind the famous statue of Kannon. It was a first-rate place. A man had to be somebody to get in the door. The owner was a widow, thirty years old, and she liked me right off. At first I worked in the kitchen, but she said I was wasted there and moved me out to be with the customers. Sent me to a hairdresser, where I had my hair done up the old-fashioned way. Then I put on a kimono with a pretty design all along the skirt and went to wait on guests in one of the party rooms.

There were geisha, of course, and *taikomochi*—men whose only job was to flatter the customers and pander to them. They could keep it up for hours. There were famous actors too, kabuki actors I think they were. They'd take turns standing up in the middle of the room and acting out various scenes, having competitions to see who was better. It was more fun than I'd ever dreamed of. But there was more to it than I thought. You know why those actors were there? Because rich married women would buy them, that's why. Those women would sneak in before the party got going, and later, when it was over and everybody'd gone home, they'd each get their favorite actor for the night. In the morning they'd call for rickshaws and go home. What did I do? I served those people their dinners, laid out their futons at night, and folded them up again in the morning. I got good and sick of it too.

Is this why you left home, Hama, I asked myself, to do *this*? By the third day I'd had enough and went to the owner and told her so. She saw I meant it, so

The main street in Asakusa

from then on I did kitchen jobs and laundry. I tucked up my kimono, tied back my sleeves, and wrapped a kerchief around my head. Before anybody was up, it was my job to light the fire in the cooking stove and do the cleaning. First the entryway and halls, then every corner of the kitchen till it sparkled. After that came the laundry. From the well out back I could see the temple building where the Kannon statue was. I'd say a good morning to her, my hands pressed together like this, and then start singing loudly: "I miiiiss you, I loooong for you." I scrubbed so hard I nearly wore a hole in that washtub.

The owner was tickled pink with the way I worked. But wouldn't you know, after three months my brother found me again. I told him, "Look here. I'm working hard, and I'm not doing anything to be ashamed of, so why don't you go away and leave me alone?" But he wouldn't listen. The owner argued with him, but he stuck to his guns and in the end I had to go back.

This time my parents and all my relatives put their heads together and talked over what to do with me. My aunt said the only thing to do was marry me off, that once I was married I wouldn't be so wild. So without one word to me they picked the captain of a *takase* riverboat to be my husband. The betrothal money arrived in no time. That shook me up. I was eighteen and I wanted to have fun, and here they were, marrying me off to some fellow I'd never seen or heard of. It was too much.

But the captain was all for it. The go-between came and told us how well-off he was. One trip from Tsuchiura to Tokyo and back a month was enough for him to live in style, he said—and not only that, his family ran a big store on main street in the port town of Itako, selling cakes and sugar, and if he ever got tired of his boat he could always go back there and work.

It was all a lie, every word, but my aunt and my folks didn't know better. They ate it up. I had my doubts, though. Secretly I decided to run away again.

There was a fellow named Shinji in the neighborhood, a boy I used to gather firewood with. He grew up to be a rice farmer. I went to him and I said, "Shinji, I don't want to marry this captain, what'll I do?" Shinji said, "Let's elope, you and me. I don't want to be a farmer forever. I'll never be happy till I go to Tokyo and make a name for myself, so come away with me. We can set up house together there."

I said yes, and we swore we'd do it, and even set the date. But before we could go, my folks caught on. I'd run away so many times before, they were keeping an eye on me—and then they heard I'd been whispering with Shinji. They didn't waste a minute. They went around to all the neighbors and relatives and told them I was about to run away again, and would they please come talk some sense into me.

That was a jolt. All those people came crowding into our little house, and this is what they said. "Hama, look. No matter how much you don't want to marry this riverboat captain, you've got to get married someday and the betrothal money has already come. If you elope now, your family will lose face. For their sakes you've *got* to go through with it, even if it's only for three days."

My parents prostrated themselves in front of me and begged. What could I do? If I refused, they'd have had to pack up and move away from there in shame. Okay, I said, I'll do it. I'll marry him for three days.

Shinji was fit to be tied. "Traitor!" he yelled. "I was going to stake everything on you. How could you change your mind like that? I'll never forgive you!" He ran away that very night, and later he joined the navy.

One time after the war started I was unloading charcoal off the boat, black from head to toe, and along came a handsome sailor and stopped right in front of me. It was winter, so he was wearing a sort of cape, and his shoes were shining as he stood looking down at me. Out of my way, sailor, I thought, I've got work to do. I looked up to tell him off. Wouldn't you know, it was Shinji. He stared at me and then he sneered, "Look at you! On a cold day like this you've

Takase riverboats

got nothing but a *hanten* jacket to keep you warm, and your face is coal-black. I was going to elope with you, but you went back on your word. This is what you get for it. Look at me. I'm an officer in the Japanese Imperial Navy. If you'd married me, you'd have had an easy life, but you picked a riverboat captain instead, so go ahead—crawl around in the dirt and suffer for the rest of your life."

That night I cried my eyes out. I was good and mad, and I remembered the old days, and the tears came pouring out. I got no sleep that night. But as it turned out, Shinji was sent south after that and died in action. I heard his widow had a terrible time and barely managed to hang on by selling used books door to door.

Marriage

Anyhow, that's how I became the wife of a riverboat captain at the age of nineteen. We lived on the boat from day one. There was no honeymoon. Besides us, there were his parents and his younger brother too. Five people on one little boat. In the prow there was a small room below—just two tatami mats and a bit of wood floor. In the stern there was a room only half that size. His parents and his brother had the front and we had the tiny room aft. All I took with me was a little dresser and a wicker basket. Even if I'd wanted to take more, where was I going to put it? But my mother-in-law was always griping that I came with nothing. My father-in-law spent all his time lying around and drinking. As soon as he finished one bottle, he sent me out to buy him another. Some family I married into, I thought.

What really got me, though, was that there was no toilet. I'd never dreamed of living without such a thing. The first night I was in big trouble. You can imagine. Here I am, my bladder tight as a drum, and no place to go. So I ask my new husband what to do. He says, "Go over the side of the boat." I couldn't believe my ears. Even for a tomboy like me, that was too much.

"I can't do that!" I said, steaming mad.

"Then what *are* you going to do?" he says. "There's no other choice. Complaining won't help."

I was mad enough to cry, but that wouldn't help either. Finally I couldn't stand it any more and I stuck my bottom over the edge and relieved myself. At that moment I hated the go-between and my aunt with a passion for making me wind up in such a place. Peeing was bad enough, but the other was worse. I could have died with embarrassment then.

That set me thinking. What kind of people would make a young girl stick her bum out over the water, when who knew who was looking, and relieve herself? The hell with this, I said to myself, I'm through. From then on all I did was watch for a chance to escape.

It wasn't only the lack of a toilet that I hated, though. It was also the lack of a bath. As *takase* go, ours was pretty big—it could hold five hundred sacks of rice—but there was no place on board to put a bathtub. There was one place along the river where they set up a *takase* as a public bath, and for a small price you could have a nice hot soak. All the captains' families would gather there. There was a room where you could relax and have something to drink while you waited your turn. The tub was inside on a wooden floor, and the water came from the river so you could use all you wanted.

Everywhere else you had to walk to a farmhouse and ask if you could use their bath—but people were so poor, they begrudged the extra firewood. They used reeds or willow branches instead, but that didn't give enough heat. The only way to get the water hot was to use less, so there was never enough for a good soak all the way to your shoulders. You'd sit in a half-full tub and shiver in the cold air. Finally, whenever we had to use somebody else's bath, I'd take firewood with me. But as a woman my turn came last, and by then the water

A midwife with a baby

would be filthy. Think of it—this was after farmers black with dirt had all taken their baths. It wasn't bath water any more, just a kind of sludge. God, I hated it.

One spring night about six months after I got married, when the boat docked at Ushibori I thought, "Now's my chance!" and away I ran, as fast as my legs would carry me, tearing barefoot down the road in the middle of the night till I got to my old house in Aso. You could have knocked my parents over with a feather. Here was their married daughter, coming home in the middle of the night with her hair all wild from running.

"I don't care what you say, I'm not going back!" I said. "You said you'd be happy if I stayed married for three days, and I stuck it out for six whole months. You can't ask for more."

My mother listened quietly, and all she said was, "What about that baby in your belly?"

"Baby?"

"You heard me. Didn't you know? Take a good look at yourself."

This was news to me. A baby in my belly. I put a hand on my stomach.

"Now you listen here," she told me. "I know it's hard for you. But if you leave there now, it'll only be worse. And the baby will suffer more than you do. You've got to work for the sake of the baby now. If you do, someday things will go the way you want. Just hang on till then."

In the morning I went back to the boat. And I worked hard. I carried anything—potatoes, rice, straw, firewood, anything. Right up till the day before I gave birth, I helped load and unload the boat. When the time came, I sent for a midwife and had the baby right on board. There was a woman called Momotaro Midwife, and she helped all the captains' wives give birth. The name comes from the folk tale about Momotaro, the boy who was born from a giant peach. He grew up to be big and strong, and so did all the babies she brought into the world, I guess.

Three days later I was on my feet, cooking and cleaning as usual. I couldn't take twenty-one days off, the way farmers' wives do. Who was going to look after me if I did? My mother-in-law was indifferent.

I pushed myself after that. Wait and see, I thought, one of these days I'll buy some land and build a house with a roof where I can relieve myself in peace and soak in a hot tub all I want.

My husband just couldn't see it. A captain spends his whole life on his boat. Living on land would be crazy, he told me. I was a farmer's daughter so maybe I didn't know this, but someone like him whose ancestors had all been boatmen couldn't imagine living on shore.

"Fine," I said. "If that's what you want, live here till your teeth fall out. But I won't. I'm not having my daughter grow up on a boat where she's got to stick her rear end over the side to take a dump." When the baby cried I'd think, go on and cry. At least I won't make you go through what I did. You can go to a girls' school or do anything you want. And when it comes time for you to marry, you'll have a pile of fine silk kimonos. You won't be crying then.

This is a folk song the boatmen sang:

> The rain comes down and the wood gets wet,
> The baby bawls, and the dinner burns.

That's just how it was too. If it started to rain when you were loading firewood or rice on board, you couldn't let the cargo get wet, so you'd lower the mast and use it for a crossbeam, line up cedar planks along it, and spread a big straw mat on top to form an instant roof. While you were doing that, the baby on your back would get wet in the rain and start to bawl. If you had something on the stove, you couldn't pay attention, so the dinner would burn. You needed more than one body to get all the work done.

Men in Those Days

Mostly we carried gravel. Back then there was a gravel company in Tsuchiura, founded by Gihei Okamoto. The workers would dig up gravel from the lake bed with the latest equipment and pile it by the mouth of the river. We'd take on a load and carry it to a work site, wherever the Ministry of the Interior was improving the River Tone or repairing the riverbanks. Okamoto had dozens of people working for him, and when we came in they'd load us up with the gravel the ministry had ordered. When we got to the site, my husband and his brother and I did the unloading. God knows how many trips we made back and forth. Even in the last month of pregnancy, I unloaded gravel.

I have some special memories of Gihei Okamoto. He was quite a business-man. Besides gravel, he sold fertilizers, coal, grain, and who knows what. He knew everyone. He used to invite big Tokyo bankers and trading company executives for outings on Lake Kasumigaura in his houseboat. It had glass sliding doors and a kitchen and a toilet. He'd cross the lake with his guests and several geisha and their attendants on board. There I'd be, sweating like a pig while I hauled his gravel, and right in front of me that houseboat would glide by with its geisha in fine kimonos playing hand-drums and plucking the shamisen. It used to make me so jealous. It seemed to me they lived at the height of luxury. All I could think was, could their lives possibly be any more different from mine?

Okamoto married the daughter of the president of Ikegaya Steel, and there were about fifteen black limousines at his wedding. People were amazed. He built a fancy mansion, the kind you might see in Kyoto's Gion-cho, with solid copper roofing that shone red in the sun. People called it Okamoto's

Copper Palace. He was a powerful man, and his gravel company was going strong, but then something went wrong and all of a sudden it collapsed. He went bankrupt. Then, what do you know—all of a sudden his friends don't want anything to do with him. People can be so cruel.

In the end he and his mistress got in a boat and escaped secretly at night. And what do you think happened? Their boat was right next to ours. The gods put it there. I looked over and there he was, the great man Gihei Okamoto, looking pretty pathetic in a tiny boat face to face with his mistress. I reached in my pocket and pulled out two yen and handed it to him. "Mr. Okamoto," I said, "I hauled gravel for your company for many years. I hope you won't take offense at this, but I'd like to offer you this money in farewell if I may." Well, the tears poured down his cheeks. "Thank you, thank you so much," he said. "The people I trained and supported for years have all turned their backs on me, and only a stranger like you has a kind word. I'll never forget this." He and his mistress went to Choshi and lived out their lives there.

Anyway, men in those days played around all they wanted, with never a thought for their wives and children. Women put up with a lot.

Here's another boatman's song:

> Captain dear, I love you.
> Never mind when you're coming into port—
> When are coming back to me?
> When will I see you again?

He's been to see a woman in a brothel, you see, and she's sorry to see him go. Every harbor had its whorehouses, its bars, and its teahouses. The men would go in and blow all their hard-earned money. Lie with their head in a woman's lap, with never a thought for their wives and kids at home crying.

The busiest place of all was Itako. That town was a red-light district from way back, and in the twenties and thirties it was still going strong. There were some great big brothels, three stories high. I remember the "Tamaya," the "Fukuya," and the "Ayame." One of them, I think it was the Fukuya, had a pair of gold killer whales up on top. Not solid gold of course—they must have been gilded. Still, they were a sight, shining in the sun just like on Nagoya Castle. When the boat stopped there, you could see the women going down the alleyways, their faces and necks coated with white powder. They wore their obis tied up high in front, over the bust. They were from up north, sold by their families into a life of night after night with no-good men. You had to feel sorry for the poor things. There certainly were a lot of them. Who knows how many?

It wasn't only boat captains who fooled around. If they had the chance, farmers too would get in boats and row right over to Itako, or go on horseback, or even walk if they had to. Men were proud of it too.

Gambling was another thing that was popular. The boatmen would all gather on one boat, lower the mast and put a sheet over it, and sit there huddled by the light of a lamp. A dozen men or so, sitting with their tongues hanging out, gambling till they were flat broke. Utter foolishness. Any winnings anyone ever got, they spent on women, as happy-go-lucky as if they were made of money. So they always wound up with empty pockets. They never learned. When it was our turn to host a gambling session I wanted to give them all a piece of my mind, but they were friends so you couldn't just turn them out.

One time there was a police raid. The morning after a gambling party on a river in Tsuchiura, a dozen policemen came barging in with their shoes on. My husband and my parents-in-law looked sick. Then the questioning started: "Last night there was gambling here. Tell us the names of the men and their boats."

I went forward, and I let them have it. "Just who do you think you are?" I said. "This is my home, I'll have you know. The floor's wood, not tatami, but I polish it every day, and it's so clean you could eat off it. Who said you could come in here with your dirty shoes on? The nerve of some people!" They were surprised, all right. "Get out of here, all of you," I said. "Go someplace else."

The leader of the police smiled as sweet as you please and took off his shoes, and then all the rest of them did too. "Ma'am," he says, "I respect what you're saying, but you know there was gambling here last night, and we can't overlook that."

"Oh, there was, was there?" says I. "Now, who told you a thing like that? I'm on this boat day in and day out and I've never seen any gambling here, but then I can't swear for what goes on when I'm asleep. If you want to look into it, take my husband away to the police station and ask him all the questions you want." My husband turned pale. "You wouldn't be here if you didn't have proof, so maybe he did do something wrong. Better get the whole thing straightened out right now. If he's guilty, go right ahead and throw him in the slammer for a year or two. Be my guest."

"You don't care if we take him with us?"

"Take him anywhere you want, but you're not taking this boat. You might as well take the food right out of our mouths. We've got to get a load of cargo all the way to Choshi by tomorrow. If we're late, customers lose faith in us and we end up starving. So if you mean to impound this boat, you'd better be willing to provide for us from now on. Otherwise you'll never get your hands on this boat, so help me God."

"Now, ma'am," he says to me, "you know we'd never do a thing like that. We just want your husband to come with us so we can ask him about the gambling." So they took him away and never examined the boat. My parents-in-law were beside themselves. With their son in jail for a year we'll starve for real, they're thinking, so what possessed me? They were in a tizzy.

"Don't worry," I said. "Who'd give a man a year in jail just for doing a little gambling with his buddies?" Sure enough, my husband was back that night with his tail between his legs.

"Well?" I said.

"They knocked me around with a bamboo sword a time or two, that's all," he said.

"You didn't give them any names, did you?" I said.

"Hell no. You think I want to get myself killed? Anyway, the police couldn't get over you. That's some spitfire you've got for a wife, they said, you sure better be nice to her."

After that, I wouldn't let him gamble on our boat. He did it on other boats, though.

Saving for a House

I couldn't wait to leave the boat and live in a house on land. The desire got stronger in me every year. For one thing, loading the boat was tough. It's not easy to fill the hold of a thirty-ton *takase*. Not that I had to do it by myself, of course. Sometimes we hired help, but that cost money so usually my husband, his brother, and I did it ourselves. In the end it was just my husband and me. Between the boat and the shore was a plank about eight yards long and a yard wide, and staggering up it with a loaded yoke across your shoulders—90 pounds on one side, 110 on the other—wasn't easy. Try it sometime. One slip and you're in the water, *kersplash*! Keep it up all day and you get so worn out, you're too tired to stand up. But still there's dinner to get on.

I grew crops too. To save money I decided to grow at least enough rice to feed the family. I rented a parcel of land by the dock and plowed it and

planted and fertilized it. To get fertilizer I went begging to restaurants in town, scooped up night soil from their privies and carried it in a yoke all the way to the dock. One time I tripped on my own feet and dumped a load of night soil right in front of an inn. There was a big uproar. All the guests ran away. I had to push the mess down into the river with my hands and then wash off the road. Everybody felt sorry for me and they all came out and helped, and finally things got back to normal. My husband never knew. He never helped me with the rice or anything else.

Takase captains took time off when it rained, or if there was no wind. If the wind was too strong or was blowing the wrong way, they took the day off too. It drove me crazy. My husband would lie around drinking, and that was no way to get us a house on shore. So when the boat was grounded, I'd put the baby on my back and go off to work as a day laborer for one yen a day. I'd lay her on a mat while I worked. I did it whenever the boat needed repairing too, and that was often. We carried heavy loads, and the river was full of shallows where the boat scraped on the river bottom. It ruined the hull. You had to get a ship-wright to redo it, but generally it took a month; having the whole thing redone took six months. That's half a year we would sit twiddling our thumbs. In the end we decided the *takase* boat wasn't worth it, and we used our savings to get a used steamer instead—another thirty-ton boat, but with a hot-bulb engine. That was about 1935. My husband loved it, but I'd rather have used the money to buy land for a house.

Anyway, thanks to all my hard work, I was able to set some money aside. But honest to God, men are just hopeless about some things. Next thing I knew, my husband had fallen for a young geisha and spent all my hard-earned savings on her.

There were drinking places all over Tsuchiura in those days. One night when we docked, my husband got dressed up in a serge suit and went out. I waved him off, but then I looked in the savings box and my eyes popped out of my head. There was a hundred yen gone—a huge fortune back then. And he was about to hand it over to some floozy. I was madder than a hornet.

I went on shore and asked around and found he'd gone into a drinking place with a woman named Kinryu. All right, buster, I thought, look out. I went back to the boat and coated my face and neck with white powder, put on a muslin kimono and my best obi and went back to that *machiai*. There were dozens of shoes lined up in the entrance. While I was standing there the owner came out.

"Pardon me," I said, "but is the captain of the *Suki Maru* here?"

She looked me up and down and said, "No, there's nobody here like that."

I gave her a look. "Oh no? Well, do you see these shoes here? They happen to be my husband's. Excuse me, if you don't mind, I'm coming in." I marched right in and looked in the guest rooms. The downstairs room was filled with naval officers having a drinking party. I went upstairs and heard a drunken voice coming from the room at the end of the hall. I knew it was him the minute I heard it. I slid the door open a crack and, sure enough, there he was with his arm around a fat woman, drinking saké and living it up. Of all the god-damn nerve! I thought for a minute and then went back downstairs where the naval officers were.

"Sorry to barge in when you're enjoying yourselves, gentlemen," I said, "but hear me out. I'm the wife of the captain of the *Suki Maru*. We've had a little luck and some money has come our way. As a token of thanks for the service you render our country, we'd like to pay for your dinner tonight. What do you say?"

They clapped their hands and thanked me. So I said, "You know, this room is a little cramped and the view isn't much. Why don't we move upstairs?" And I gave the owner ten yen. She had no idea what I was up to, but she wasn't

Tsuchiura's red-light district

about to turn down ten yen, so she led us upstairs to a nice big room with an alcove, right next door to my husband.

"All right, gentlemen," I said, "go ahead and enjoy yourselves." I told the owner to bring in a geisha to liven things up. Well, before you know it, she's playing the shamisen and everyone's clapping, and things are definitely getting lively. I called for more saké. Then I said, "You know, there are so many of us, it's pretty crowded in here. Why don't we take down these sliding doors? The party next door can join right in with us." And I took down the doors myself. "Sir," I said to my husband, "we're having a party for these officers. Won't you join us?"

My husband was thunderstruck. One minute he's canoodling with a woman and the next thing he knows, a crowd of rowdy officers is looking in at him, and his wife is standing in the next room. His eyes opened wide as saucers. The fat, ugly little raccoon dog he was with had her mouth wide open too.

"My, what a fine suit you're wearing," I said. "My husband has a blue serge suit exactly like that. I bought it for him in Choshi for twenty yen, but he thinks so much of it he's never worn it once. It certainly looks good on you."

He had a sour look on his face, but he didn't say a word. I didn't care, so the party went on.

Then my husband and the fatty tried to sneak out. I heard him call for the bill so I excused myself to the officers, reminding them that the evening was on me, paid the owner twenty yen, and left.

My husband and the fatty were just turning the corner. A light rain was falling. I followed them. They were walking along sharing an umbrella, their heads together. He had his arm around her and was saying, "She's a regular bitch. She's famous for it. I can't do a thing about it. You don't know what it's like being married to a bitch like that."

That was too much. I rolled up my sleeves, tucked up my kimono so my underskirt was showing, and butted my way right between them. We were standing between a fish shop, with piles of empty fish crates, and a ditch along the side of the road.

"Sorry, Kinryu," I said, "time's up. I'll take him from here."

She took one look at me, gave a little scream, and jumped back so fast she nearly fell over.

"Don't worry," I said calmly. "I'm not going to hurt you. But this is my husband, and if you ever come near him again, you'll be sorry. Now get out of here."

She hightailed it. Ran off in the rain without even putting up her umbrella. I watched her disappear around the corner and then I grabbed my husband by the lapels and yelled, "You bastard, just see what I do to you!" He was a strong man, but after all the work I did every day, carrying hundreds of loads of coal and sand, I was no weakling either. And he'd been drinking, so he was no match for me. I got a good hold and then I spun him around and knocked him right in the ditch. He started sputtering and yelling bloody murder. That just made me madder. What did *he* have to yell bloody murder about? So I picked up a fish crate and smashed it over his head as hard as I could. It broke in pieces, and he let out a howl. "Now you've done it, you damn bitch!" he said, and he squatted down in the ditch with his hands on his head. The blood ran down between his fingers. The red light from the lanterns nearby made it look even redder. That finally put a scare into me.

Lord, I've split his head open and killed him, I thought. I didn't know if I should leave him there and run for a doctor, or what. Then I reached out and felt his head, and I'll be damned if it wasn't just a little scratch. That was the last straw.

"How can you carry on about a tiny scratch like that!" I yelled. "You make me sick. You took money I went without sleep to earn, one hundred yen of it, and gave it to that fatso. You put on the serge suit I bought you to have your little fling, and you think you can get off with a couple of knocks on the head?" I shrieked at him and hit him again and again.

It was late at night, but in no time a crowd gathered to gawk at us. My husband was crawling around on his knees with his hands over his head. Then five or six other riverboat captains came bursting through the crowd and pulled me off him.

"What are you doing here, woman?" they said. "Your boat's all loaded and you're leaving for Choshi in the morning. This is no time to be fighting."

"I don't care," I said. "I'm through. I'm leaving him. We'll split everything fifty-fifty. I'll take one kid and he can have the other. I'll take half the cargo and split the boat in half too. What else can I do?"

"Now, you know you can't do that."

"Oh yes I can. Give me a hammer and I'll smash that boat in half, no matter how long it takes."

I meant it too. After all the work I'd done, wearing myself to the bone, for him to do this to me just about killed me. It was over. I was raring to go right out and bust up that boat. Well, he must have gathered as much, because he came over and bowed down with his hands flat on the ground in front of me.

"Wife, I was wrong," he says. "Forgive me."

"What are you talking about," I sniffed. "You know you don't mean a word of it. Why should I believe you?"

"I do mean it. I apologize from the bottom of my heart."

"You do?"

"I do."

"Is that so. Look, there's a whole crowd of witnesses. Your friends are here. Do you swear before all these people that you're sorry?"

"I do. I'm sorry."

"All right then, maybe I'll forgive you—on one condition. From now on I want control over all the money. Agreed?"

"Agreed."

"Don't forget," I told him. "Everybody's listening. Oh, and you can drink all the saké you want, but no more gambling. Is that understood?"

So from then on all the money we earned from the *Suki Maru* was under my control.

So Many Changes

After that things calmed down, and we finally did buy a little house by the river where his parents and the kids could live, and he and I had the boat to ourselves. Then just when I thought things were looking up, something awful happened: my husband lost his eyesight.

During the war prices went through the roof, and there wasn't any saké to be had. But men who liked their drink had to have it. My husband's buddies claimed they'd found some and brought it over. He was thrilled and took a big swig. I was out in the field then, getting some work done between air raids, and when I got back I found him rolling around on the floor in agony.

It was methyl alcohol. A lot of men drank it and died, and my husband came close too. At first I didn't know why. I just saw he was suffering, and I cradled his head and said, "What is it? What's happened?"

Finally he opened his eyes and he said, "Is that you? Why is it so dark today?" That's weird, I thought. It was a fine day, the sun blazing away.

"What are you talking about? It's bright out."

"No, no, it's cloudy. Looks like rain. Why, I can hardly see your face."

That sent a shock through me. I'd heard of people going blind and mute from bad alcohol. Even though the air raid siren was still sounding, I jumped up and ran barefoot all the way to the hospital by the station. The doctor[2] came tearing back with me as the sirens wailed. He saved my husband's life, but his eyesight was gone. This was fifteen days before the end of the war.

Everyone else was packing up and leaving town to get away from the incendiary bombs the Americans were dropping every night, but I couldn't. How could I go off and leave him there? I spread a straw mat in a lighter and lay him on it, put the two little ones on board, and rowed to a hiding-place in the rushes. I was afraid the American bombers would find us, so I covered the top with a cloth and we'd huddle under it till morning in holy terror, without a wink of sleep.

After the war ended I tried to get medicine for him, but there wasn't any. The only thing I knew to do was pray. Night after night I went to a shrine and walked back and forth a hundred times. There was no work on the river, so in the daytime I tended the vegetables and weeded the rice, in between cooking, cleaning and looking after the little ones. My two older boys had gone into the city to work, but the little ones knew what was going on, and they helped out too. And at night, back I'd go to the shrine to pray.

Someone told me the best way to get your prayer answered was to cut your hair. I took a pair of scissors and cut it all off, and wrapped a thin towel around my head. When my little girl saw me in the bath, she cried.

But nothing worked. He never got his sight back. It was hard, coming right at the end of the war when we were hoping for better times. Nothing ever got to me like that. I broke down and cried. What was going to keep us from starving to death? I thought and thought, and I came up with one answer: the black market.

Everybody ate black market rice back then, no exception. People would take the train into the countryside and bring back rice, eggs, fish, potatoes, and anything else they could get their hands on. I wasn't interested in a small-scale operation, though. I planned on carrying fifty or sixty sacks of rice at a

time. I knew I could buy rice on islands in the River Tone, where farmers were hoarding it, and sell it on the black market. I went out at night to negotiate with the rice farmers. They knew me, so we came to an agreement right away. They set one condition, though: if the police found out, they would get my boat as security. Also I had to promise never to tell where the rice came from.

In all I made twenty-eight trips, handling twenty-five hundred sacks of rice. It was good money. I made nearly three thousand yen before word got out and the police called me in. Did I know anything about black market trade in rice on the river, they wanted to know.

"I've got a blind husband and a pack of kids," I said. "There's no more work on the river so I have to scratch out a living in the fields. How would I know anything about black market rice?"

They let me go that night, but I knew they were onto me, so I sent word to the farmers that I was through. There wasn't enough money to retire on, so after that I carried rice to Shinjuku in Tokyo, one sack at a time, twice a day. I'd get up at two-thirty a.m., make rice and miso soup for my husband and kids' breakfast, make lunches for everybody, and get on the four a.m. train, catching snatches of sleep when I could. By the time I got back, it was ten. Then I'd go back with the second sack. When I got home it was three p.m.— time to work in the fields. The moon watched over me while I worked. I'd get in at eleven p.m., and my husband would snap, "Where've you been all this time? Out with some other man, is that it?" He didn't mean what he was saying, but it was hard on him, being alone all day. Then I'd do the laundry, grab a little sleep, and get up at two. That went on for years.

I always had my health. That and a lot of friends to share my troubles. As long as you're alive, you'll have troubles. I don't mind—I've had my fun too. Now it's all behind me, the children are grown, and my husband and I spend our days together in peace, so all's well that ends well.

Ohori, the Center of River Traffic

Mr. Kunizo Suzuki (b. 1904)

Takase *Boats*

I was twenty-two when I moved near Lake Kasumigaura in 1927 and started a shipyard of my own. Till then I worked in Ohori, on the River Tone. My father and my grandfather were shipwrights too, before me. I went to work for my father when I was twelve, straight out of primary school. Back then the River Tone and Lake Kasumigaura were part of one continuous transportation system, with Tokyo at one end, Choshi at the other, and Ohori smack in the middle. The village isn't what it used to be, but it had its glory days. I'm one of the last ones still around who knows what it was like.

Actually, Ohori was always a central player in water transportation, going back hundreds of years, because of its location. You've got to bear in mind that from Ohori to the River Edo, the Tone runs shallow. So, according to my grandfather, *takase* riverboats heading up to the capital with the yearly tax rice used to stop off in Ohori to transfer their cargo to barges. Without that heavy cargo weighing them down, the *takase* drew light in the water. Once past the canal, the river deepened again, so the rice would be loaded back on. That's how they transported the tax rice to the capital. It was a hell of a lot of work, but the domains needed the income, so they did what had to be done. There used to be several barge docks around Ohori for loading and unloading the rice. There were also a number of forwarding agents that handled rice for the general market.

The other thing Ohori was important for was rescue work. Heavy rains would change the flow of the river, making it so treacherous that boats would founder or capsize. Rescuers were based in Ohori because the river takes a slight bend there that slows the current. It bears little resemblance now to what it was like then, but in those days the Tone must have been, let's see, a good six hundred feet wide. Also, the riverbed by Ohori is sandy, while on the opposite side in Chiba it's rocky, so the boats had to put in at Ohori. There was no particular coastal anchorage, but the current slowed down so much that it was easier to stop there.

The *takase* riverboats always pulled a skiff behind them. The river was constantly changing, for one thing, and you never knew whether you'd be able to moor at a particular place. Sometimes it would be too crowded. Then the men would drop anchor a little ways off from the bank and ride to shore on the skiff. Every *takase* had one; they measured about seven yards long.

Takase were also made in Ohori. In my day the town had less than a hundred buildings, but there were three different shipwrights who made nothing but *takase*. Whether you were in the market for a new boat or wanted to patch up an old one, Ohori was the place to go. Everybody in town had some sort of connection with boats. The men were mostly *takase* captains who went to work on the river straight out of primary school, like I did, and learned the life firsthand. Some kept their wife and kids on board with them. There was space in the bow for four or five people, and another two or three could squeeze in the stern even when the boat was loaded with cargo. Those were the living quarters. If you didn't have your wife along, you had to do all the cooking and cleaning yourself, like I did.

Takase boats were expensive. Not at all easy to come by. Back then a new house went for around three hundred yen, and a brand-new *takase* would set you back ten times that much. Of course, unlike a house, a riverboat was something you could make a living from, by transporting goods. Still, owning one was way beyond most people's reach. Financing a *takase* generally meant taking out a big loan and struggling for years to pay it off.

"Roundabouts" and the Canal

People with no money or backers couldn't afford their own boats, so instead

Norimawashi

they served as deck hands—*norimawashi*, we called them, "roundabouts." Their job was to pole the *takase* boats the seven miles from Ohori to the canal. From there they'd get up on the bank and tow the boat another five miles through to the River Edo.

Why were they needed? Those first seven miles were full of shallows, so it would have been impossible to make it with sails alone. In general the river was much shallower than it is today. The current carried a lot of silt downstream. You might lie moored by a shoal for a couple of hours and then find that sand had built up under your hull till you were grounded, high and dry. The river's deeper now, thanks to dams and construction work, but back then one night of solid rain was all it took to drastically remap the river bottom. Yesterday's deep water could be today's shoals, and where there used to be shallows, the water might run deep—but unless you studied the river day in and day out, you couldn't tell the difference. Bends were especially treacherous. The Department of the Interior used to have charge of riparian works, but their methods were primitive by today's standards. They used to shore the banks by piling rubble on the riverbed and supporting it with pine stakes to protect it from the current, but those stakes were always breaking off, or getting hidden underwater—and God help you if you didn't remember where they were. Running up on a pile of rubble like that would smash any boat to pieces. That's where the *norimawashi* came in. Since they rode up and down that river day after day, they had it down cold. They were surefire guides, absolutely necessary to get the riverboats through safely. All the captains set great store by them. It was standard practice to stop at Ohori for the night on your way to Tokyo, hire a crew of hands, and be off early the next morning. It just goes to show how tricky those seven miles could be to navigate.

About six hands would ride from Ohori up to the lock at Funado. That's including kids of twelve or thirteen, fresh out of primary school; I helped out at that age too. Kids lacked strength, so they stood between older men. You'd take your pole and set one end in the shallows, the other in the pit of your arm; then you'd lean your full weight into it and push down with both arms while you walked aft along the edge of the boat. When you reached the stern, you'd turn round, walk back, and start all over again. That might sound simple, but with so many people involved everything had to be done just right. The movements of the poles and the way everybody walked had to be in synch or it was no good. The youngsters had to do their fair share or they got yelled at, same as anybody else. They were getting paid good money, after all.

A *takase* could haul 400 or 450 bales of rice—500 if the boat was big enough—and cords of firewood piled higher than a man's head. Back then nobody used gas for fuel, you see, not even in Tokyo. People used firewood in their kitchens—wood that came from the hills around Lake Kasumigaura. Lumber dealers had special lakefront areas reserved for loading firewood, and when a *takase* came in, the boatmen would go back and forth across the plank, loading wood by the armful. When they were loaded up, they'd wait for a good wind and then head for the Tone. If there was no wind you had to row—poles were no use there. In case of a dead calm, every *takase* came supplied with two sets of oars, fore and aft. Rowing was no easy job, especially when you had to cut straight across the center of the lake. Sailing in a gale was risky too; either way, getting a *takase* to the River Tone was tough. Once you entered the Tone, you had to go against a swift current; the water was still too deep for poling, and you couldn't make any headway rowing. The only thing to do was wait for a tailwind that would get you as far as Ohori; from there the river was shallower, so poling did the trick.

That firewood was damned heavy. The boats rode low in the water. Poling a heavy boat like that upstream for seven solid miles was backbreaking work. Men developed rock-hard calluses in the pit of each arm from the weight of the boat—and then long hair grew on the calluses. Naturally, the captain

worked shoulder to shoulder with the crew, poling right alongside them; I developed hairy calluses in my armpits and on my shoulders too.

The most difficult part of the trip was the canal entrance. Silt from the River Kinu up in Tochigi Prefecture used to pile up there especially. No sooner would a dredger go out and clear it than the channel would silt right up again. That made the water so shallow that a boat with a full load of heavy cargo couldn't get through. Little by little, cargo had to be transferred to the skiff, and then taken up on shore until the boat rode high enough to squeeze by. Before the canal was built, it must have been even worse. It was a great boon to river traffic when the canal opened.[3]

Fifty-ton boats would slowly pass one another in the canal. When a boat entered the canal, the captain took the helm, and one man with a pole stood aft to make sure the boat didn't come too close to the banks. Everyone else climbed up on shore, crouched down, and hauled on towropes. Back then, of course, only steamers had engines; every other kind of boat had to be towed through the canal, including *takase*.

After the boat left the canal and entered the River Edo, the deck hands would get off and wait for a riverboat heading back the other way. They'd tow it through the canal and then ride back down the Tone. On the return trip, boats were loaded with sugar, coal, oil, fertilizer, sweets, and clothing—that sort of cargo. Added together, it weighed less than half the cargo on the trip out, so the boats rode high in the water. And that's what many men did for a living, helping *takase* boats travel back and forth between Ohori and Tokyo.

Bathboats

Takase boats had no baths on board, so in Ohori there were special bathboats for boat captains and their families. They'd put a big roof over an old, retired *takase*, add a parlor and a bath, and take in customers. Operators heated river water by burning driftwood. There were three bathboats in Ohori. The most famous was "Nishinoya," and it lasted to the end, even after river transport had almost completely died out. There were also the "Jugoro Bath" and the "Gonbei Bath." They each raked in a lot of money. Old Gonbei had a beautiful mistress named O-Shige who did all the work while he lay around fanning himself. What a life!

The bathboats offered more than a hot soak. They sold sweets and a few household items, and the owners had another role too—that of job brokers. They let people know where the jobs were. If a boat came in needing hands, say, the bathboat owner would go around town the next day and tell the men where to report for work. It was a good system for everybody—it saved men the trouble of hunting for work, since the bath owners brought it right to their door. Bathboats were great centers of information, and the owners were in on all the latest goings-on up and down the river.

Dozens of riverboats would moor in Ohori every night. Relations between people on boats were special—everyone was family. Somebody'd lean over the side of the boat and holler, "We've got a mess of fresh fish, come on over!" Then folks in the next boat would grab their bowls and pile on over for dinner. That happened all the time. Rice, miso, soy sauce—all the necessities were shared equally. "I'm out of onions," someone would yell. "Right, here you go," someone would yell back, tie up a bunch of green onions, and toss it over. They might get a bag of sugar in return. Everybody was always helping each other out that way. Any boat on the return trip from Tokyo was bound to be running low on stores, so if you saw one you'd call out, "What do you need?"—and whatever it was, you'd chuck it over.

The bathboats were all different sizes. Even the smallest were a good fourteen or fifteen yards long and four across. Inside they had two eight-mat rooms, and a smaller room with a tub. Only one person at a time could fit in. While you waited your turn, you'd sip tea or saké and chew the fat. They sold saké right on board—and there was gambling too.

Riverboat captains loved to gamble. They certainly weren't alone; men from shore rowed out to the bathboats for a night of gambling too, the reason being that on shore you never knew when the police might come barging in, but on the bathboats you were pretty safe. Even then, it wasn't foolproof. Gamblers made the rounds, and they'd spread the word about where the gambling was good. One way or another the authorities would get wind of it and set up watch. Then sometimes they'd make a raid. I never heard of a bathboat in Ohori being raided, but it happened in Kawaguchi, I heard, with captains and day laborers being rounded up.

River captains were great womanizers too. There were geisha houses in Toride and all up and down the canal. It took nine hours to pole downriver from Ohori to the canal, so if you set out in the morning, you'd be there by evening and could spend the night in a geisha house. There were three or four of them at either end of the canal.

When a boat came in, the women would gather on the bank and turn on the charm: "Hey there, come on up for a visit, why don't you?" If you had your wife on board you had to look the other way, but single men couldn't resist. They'd tie their boats and be up like a flash. Spend the night listening to the shamisen and drinking, and maybe belt out a *naniwabushi* ballad or two if they had a good voice, having themselves a gay old time. Next day they'd wake up late, all bleary-eyed, but the women weren't finished with them yet. It'd be, "Stay another night, dearie, why not?" Sometimes it was three days before a man could get his boat out of that canal. Then on the way back, it'd be the same thing all over again. A man's favorite woman was like his wife. Every time she saw him, she'd be after him to come back up. I tell you, it was no easy thing to slip in and out of that canal unnoticed. I suppose some men did, but by and large riverboat captains figured there was more to life than working hard. They pretty much did as they liked.

The canal was surrounded as far as you could see on both sides by rice paddies, with a farmhouse here and there. The farmers and the captains got along beautifully. Farmers would make a special trip to a *takase* that had stopped for supper and tell the crew, "The bath's hot, come on over." If the cook looked to be short on vegetables, they'd bring over baskets loaded with onions or turnips, cabbages or cucumbers, whatever was in season, carrying them on their backs. Naturally, they didn't charge anything for the favor. In return, the captain would be sure to bring back sugar or sweets or some such treat from Tokyo. He'd give a call from the ship: "Hey there! We've got sugar! Come and get it!" Then the farmer would go down to the boat with a square basket on the end of a pole, and hold it up for someone to put the sugar in.

Life was so different then in the city and the country. In the country there was no white sugar or fancy cakes, so people set great store by what the boats brought in. They really looked up to the riverboat captains. Back then there wasn't anything like the information flow we have today, so people could hardly wait to see what the riverboats had brought back; that was their first look at what was new. Riverboat captains had the aura of being the bearers of culture, and that was how people saw them.

Fishing in the River

Takase boats on their way to Tokyo always stopped in Ohori to lay in a supply of drinking water. Tokyo water tasted bad. It was okay for washing or bathing, but not for drinking, so people would scoop up water from the River Tone

Setting a *koido* trap

around Ohori to take with them. Every boat had big barrels on board. You can't imagine how clean the water was back then—you could look over the side of the boat and see straight to the bottom.

When we washed rice, we'd pour the water off into the river, and *yamabe* [a kind of trout] would come swarming. The river used to be teeming with them. Using rice grains for bait, you could catch a hundred in a morning, easy. Or you might put a little leftover miso inside a glass globe about as big as a kid's head, drop it in the water, and pull it up again chock-full of *yamabe*. They'd be ready to suffocate, there were so many. You wouldn't have believed it! Plenty of eight-inch ones too, all you could want. You didn't need fancy equipment. All you had to do was put some mosquito netting over a shallow bowl, cut a little hole in the middle, put in a bit of miso or saké lees, and then lower it into the river. The fish would crowd in through that hole to get at the bait every time.

Pole-and-line angling was easy too. First you'd shape a mixture of wheat bran and mud into balls and throw it in the water as ground bait. Then you'd wrap a ball of steamed rice in rice bran, stick that on a hook, and dangle it in the water as the boat moved along. Wasn't seconds before you'd get a bite. It never failed.

There used to be an orthopedic surgeon in Toride who came to Ohori just to fish for *akahara*, which is something like a dace with a red belly. He had a private boat. The season for *akahara* was from May to July. To catch them, we took salted sardines and kneaded them with mud to make balls for ground bait; for regular bait we used jewel beetle grubs. When the grubs hatched they sprouted wings and flew off, and if you got stung, it would swell up and hurt like the dickens.

We caught a long thin fish called *sai* with a *nobenawa* [longline] or a round bamboo fish trap called a *koido*. We'd pack the *koido* with balls made of a mixture of mud and grain and sink them in the current. The mud would dissolve, leaving only the grains, and *sai* would swim inside to eat them. Then they'd get trapped and thrash around trying to get out. That would push more of the grain outside, which attracted more fish, and they'd swim inside too. That's how it worked. My grandfather used to fish that way. Sometimes he'd find little crabs mixed in with the catch.

The Tone used to be full of eels back then too. We'd go fishing for them at night—all night long, with mugwort smoking to keep the mosquitoes away. Our hooks weren't store-bought; we made them ourselves. If you beat brass wire with a hammer it would split in two; we'd use that to fashion a float, wrap sewing thread around it and attach it to a bamboo fishing pole. With one of those you could catch a good eight or nine pounds of fish in a few hours. We fished every night, April to October. In the morning a fellow called a *namashi* would come to buy our catch, carrying baskets suspended from a pole across his shoulders. A *namashi* was someone who specialized in eels and went around on foot buying them up; there were three in Ohori, as I recall.

When I was a boy, I made considerable money selling eels. One yen eighty sen for every eight pounds, which was darned good money. Bear in mind, boat hands earned less than a yen for a whole day's work. Retired captains used to catch eels for money too. An old man I knew once caught thirty pounds in a single evening. The demand was huge.

Kids back then were tough. We'd go anywhere to get eels. Baby elvers, called *dasuko*, were in season from May through August; they were tiny, but on a good day you might catch almost ninety pounds' worth. In the first three weeks of May you could stand on deck and watch them rise to the surface of the water. They'd come up in long dark swathes a foot long. Funny thing was, if they came up at ten a.m. one day, the next morning they'd be there again, at exactly the same time and place. Once you figured that out, you could

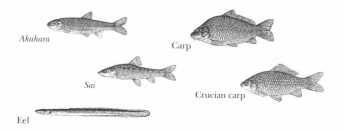

Akahara

Carp

Sai

Crucian carp

Eel

catch them every morning, for about half an hour.

Anyway, we fished for *dasuko* for all we were worth. They were good eating. After a while they'd disappear, and we'd grab nets and washbasins and go chasing after them down the river. Whenever you saw a school of elvers in the water, you'd go after them and scoop them up with your net, and that way you could fill a tub in a morning.

Once you'd caught those little ones they didn't survive long, though. They'd start to go slimy on you right away, and if they drank their own slime it killed them. It was hard keeping them alive. When they died, we'd heap them in a bowl raw and slurp them down, just like noodles except with bones that crunched; boy oh boy, they tasted good. What we couldn't eat, we boiled and kept for later. Eventually, fishing for *dasuko* was banned.

For catching carp and crucian carp, we used something called a "waiting net." That was a long, big net bag with a weight inside, attached to a three-foot-long bamboo pole. You'd drop it into the current and while you waited on shore, fish would swim in and get caught. I can still remember the tug on my pole when that happened—a satisfying feeling if there ever was one.

There was another type of fishing in Ohori called *gureami*, where you had to rely on a sixth sense. It involved setting out a net in dry rushes. The river bottom was a mixture of sand and rich sediment, and when the water was low enough, the riverbed could be planted as a field. The soil was so rich that you could grow great big beans without any fertilizer at all. Then when it rained, the rushes would fill back up with water, and with the water came carp. People around there had it all figured out—depending on how much it rained farther upstream, they'd figure on the river rising six or seven feet, say, and before it did they'd spread out their nets to catch the fish that were sure to come with it. When the catch was big, they shared it all around. We ate carp sliced raw, washed in cold water.

Flooding

You couldn't really raise crops in Ohori because there was too much flooding. There was no help for it, the village being right on the river. People would plant beans, and just as they were ready to harvest, they'd wind up under water. Once the water receded, they'd pull up the plants by the roots and set them in rice paddies. Then the bean plants would put out new shoots. We used to grind them up—beans and shoots—and eat them in our miso soup.

There was flooding two, three times a year. When that happened, families would take all their furnishings and put them up on a rack. That kept everything a good three feet off the floor—about the height of the middle shelf in a closet. You never knew when the next flood might come, so you had to be ready to scoop up your belongings at a moment's notice. In a two-room house, one room would be a living room and the other would have the racks. That wasn't all; the floorboards weren't nailed into place, so they could be easily torn up when the time came. When a flood came along, people would rush to pull up the tatami mats and put them in a safe place, and then they'd take out the floorboards and put them up too. Otherwise they got covered with mud, you see, and cleanup was ten times harder.

Flooding happened occasionally in June, and often from July to September. The wind from the east would pick up, black clouds would gather over the mountains, and people would stop to reckon how much rain we were in for. If it looked bad, I would moor my boat, cover it with rush matting, and hunker down. Townspeople put their bedding and tatami mats and everything else up on racks for safekeeping. After a heavy rain in Tochigi or Gunma, it used to take a full day before the water rose in Ohori. If it was a typhoon, of course, the water level went up faster. But that's just the way things were; dealing with it was second nature to us.

Every time your house got flooded, you could get a ration of "rescue-rice" from the government—I never knew if it was from the national government or the prefecture, but anyway it came to a measure and a half or two measures per person. You could keep on getting it up to a month after the waters went down. Back then it wasn't always easy to lay hands on enough rice for your family, so I bet there were those who thought Ohori had a pretty good deal going for itself.

In 1901 there was a worse flood than usual—water came up all the way to the second-story windows. A friend of mine had silkworms on the second floor of his house, with a three-foot hole for their droppings to go down. During the flood, they could reach down with a ladle through that hole and get water from below. All the one-story houses were under water, so everybody fled to houses with two stories like theirs.

The force of the floodwaters was unbelievable. One time a bridge came floating by that they said had been swept down all the way from Nikko. It was bright vermilion. Tree trunks floated past with the roots still attached. If one of those had ever rammed into a house, it would have been all over, but the big floods didn't follow the old riverbed; instead they roared down over the lowland, after the river improvements were put in, so Ohori was spared the worst. I can remember there were bamboo groves around the village, and stands of big trees—I see now those were a kind of breakwater, to protect houses from the full force of the water. Between floods, men would haul sand from the riverbed and use it to elevate the land around their houses. That helped. It diverted the flow of the floodwater. Otherwise, the entire town would have been carried off. During the floods, *takase* boats were moored to big trees with hemp-palm ropes. You might wonder if that was protection enough, but those ropes were strong. I could still use hemp-palm ropes that were woven in my old man's time, that's how strong they were.

Back then everybody was dirt poor. My dad told me that for a long time, a day's work wouldn't buy three cups of rice. On top of that, people had big families, so it was tough feeding everybody. Clothes were threadbare. Nobody had wooden *geta* clogs or woven *zori* sandals. We went barefoot even in winter, even in the snow. Funny thing was, my feet never felt cold. Sometimes I did get to wear *zori*, though. A captain would come to Ohori and sit on his boat smoking a pipe and weaving straw sandals. When they were done he'd say, "Here you go, sonny," and toss them to me. I was so happy I could have burst. But since the round trip to school was three and a half miles, they wore out in no time, and I always ended up barefoot again.

One thing I'll never forget is the lunches I used to take to school. I'd take fish when there was any to spare, but mostly it was boiled barley and rice covered with leftover miso soup from breakfast. Most of the soup would soak into the barley and rice, but the rest would gather in the bottom. So it wouldn't leak out on the way to school, I'd tip the lunchbox up and suck out the soup before putting on the lid. That's what I ate for lunch every day. Everybody was the same, even the children of captains. The captains made good money, but they spent it as fast as they made it, and anyway once they set out they weren't back for two weeks or a month. If there was no wind, or if the wind was too strong, they'd have to wait out the weather and then it might be two whole months before they came home. It was hard on their families, all right. That's why so many of the captains kept their families with them on board, but that was hard too, in its own way.

There were no toilets on board—you had to stick your bum over the side and go right into the water. That wasn't so bad if you were on the Tone or the

Edo, where there weren't many people around, but even if the boat was tied up in Fukagawa, say, right in the heart of Tokyo, you still had to go, of course. They used to say that when you could do your business in a place like that you were a real sailor. It was hardest on the young wives. And then after about 1925 rail transport began to boom, and water transport fell off. *Takase* captains couldn't afford to hire hands anymore, so from then on all the boats had wives on board, working with their husbands.

Talking of women reminds me—one evening a friend of mine stopped his *takase*, and his wife cooked rice for their supper. As they were about to eat, they looked at the rice and found long hairs in it. Not one or two either—a lot! They were puzzled, but they went ahead and ate the rice. Next morning, when my friend tried to raise the pole, he found the drowned body of a woman stuck on it. He called for help, and together he and his friends raised her out of the water. Then they got a monk and had him perform a proper service. Things like that were by no means unheard-of. People did everything in the water. Behind you somebody might be relieving himself, and in front of you somebody else could be dipping up drinking or cooking water. There was a saying that the water cleaned itself every three feet, and everybody believed it. By and large it was true, but not always.

The End of the Takase *Boats*

I left Ohori because by 1920 or so it was on the skids. Trucks were carrying more and more freight, and not only that, for some reason the Tone was getting increasingly shallow, almost drying up. The round trip from Ohori to Tokyo and back started taking two months instead of one, which made it all the harder to make ends meet. Then a new water route was completed in 1921, closing off the entrance to the upper reaches of the old river; the only access after that was on the lower Tone. That was the end. The last *takase* boat I made was in 1923. After that there was no more work to be had along the banks of the Tone.

I wondered where I could find work and set off with my tools in hand. Back then a man who wanted a boat would sometimes lay in all the materials first and then hire a live-in carpenter to build him one in his own front yard. There were opportunities like that around, so I went wherever I was needed and got paid by the job. Most of the time it wasn't *takase* boats I built, but something else called Edo barges. The prow was square and the bottom was flat. They were better suited to shallow rivers. I also built a lot of night-soil boats to carry night soil from Tokyo to the countryside. They were really important to the life of the towns around Tokyo.

It wasn't much fun for me to build night-soil boats, but I did it. Hard to imagine these days. Coming back from Tokyo they'd be piled high with night soil, and on the way up they were empty. People used to load them with vegetables to sell in Tokyo markets, and then take on a cargo of night soil to bring home. Folks today think of it as dirty, but back then people used human excrement as fertilizer in the fields and nobody thought it was dirty at all. It was the most natural thing in the world.

Sometimes I'd take an old boat apart and rebuild it. The shipowner would collect any old nails that came out, sell them at a junk shop, and use the proceeds to buy me food. A day's wages came to one yen twenty sen. Rice cost twenty sen a measure; for ten sen you could buy twelve pieces of tempura. Not bad, but a job like that ended in two or three months. Then I would come back to Ohori, but there wouldn't be any work. I eked out a living by fishing for eels and selling my catch.

That sort of life couldn't last forever. After a while I looked around Lake Kasumigaura and thought things there looked promising, so I packed up and

Toyoshima Cocoon Market

moved. There used to be a lot of shipbuilders in Tsuchiura at the mouth of the river back then: Ajiro, Dameya, Iizuka … Orders came in from Tokyo for barges and large sculling boats. The barges were pretty big, starting at a hundred tons. It was cheaper to make them in Tsuchiura than in Tokyo. Iizuka must have had twelve or thirteen men working for him in his heyday.

Around 1930, motor-powered boats came out, and all the villages started using them. That was a busy time for me. Plus boats called "courier boats" ran along the Tone. Farmers had no way to get to town and go shopping by themselves, so the riverboat captains would do it for them. They'd take a cargo of seasonal vegetables or silk cocoons for the cocoon exchange at Toyoshima Cocoon Market in Tsuchiura, load it on a trolley at the estuary, and take it to the shipping agent. Then on the way home they'd pick up whatever they'd been asked to get. In the old days that was all done in rowboats, but around 1930 a little engine called a *chaka* was invented, and pretty soon they were everywhere. Okijuku was only a stone's throw away so a rowboat did fine, but for places farther away like Ushiwata and Shitozaki, having an engine made all the difference. Orders for powerboats came piling in, and I filled them. I must have made four or five a year.

Then the fish dealers started to use *chaka* too. They used to row out to buy up the fishermen's catch, or go around on land by bicycle, but if it took too long the fish would start to spoil. The *chaka* let them go as far as they wanted. They could go all the way to Ushibori or Jurokushima to wait for the day's catch.

From 1932 on, power vessels were also used with sailing vessels. Until then, sailing boats had to be rowed into the wind, which required tremendous effort, but the power boats could tow several sailing vessels windward at one time. The *chaka* engine ignited with a magnet, and it ran on coal oil. It only had enough power to tow five boats at a time. More and more towing requests came in, though, so we started making boats with hot-bulb engines. Those ran

Cherry blossom–viewing

on heavy oil and could handle twenty boats at once.

From about that time till the end of the war, we also made something called a tunnel ship. Those ranged from several dozen tons to maybe a hundred. They had a unique feature in the propeller. Ships ride high in the water when their load is light, which can cause the propeller to spin uselessly. To prevent that, these ships all had a wooden plank in the stern that could be lowered behind the propeller, so that water would hit the plank and create an eddy. That made the propeller stop spinning uselessly and start to draw water. Once the ship was running normally again, the plank could be retracted. Thanks to that device, tunnel ships could navigate even shallow rivers with no problem.

So I worked for a while in Ajiro, but then I went into business for myself making boats on the River Sakura, by Naval Road. That area was a gorgeous sight back then. During cherry blossom season there'd be a tunnel of flowering branches that went on for miles and miles. At night it was all lit up with lanterns, and geisha would come out and dance in lines in the street. Behind them were shamisens and drums, and out on the river there'd be pleasure boats, with music and singing coming from there too. The area was full of excitement—all the more so with the naval academy being nearby. Sailors came round to Tsuchiura looking for a good time, so there were bars, cafés, teahouses, shooting galleries, back-alley hotels, you name it. The boat I had seated two or three people, but even with a fleet of twenty of these on the river they were always full. There was a constant line of people waiting their turn.

In wartime, my shipyard employed over 360 people. Some came to get out of the draft. There weren't any qualified shipwrights around then, so mostly the ships were built by amateurs. I hired a lot of house-builders, even some coopers. Anybody who could make anything at all used to come looking for work, from box-makers to joiners.

The military gave us a quota of so many tons per month. One time, to make a ship with, I even got the government to sell me the pine trees that were planted all along a national highway. I wonder whatever became of that ship.

2

FISHER FOLK
OF LAKE
KASUMIGAURA

Life on the Water

Mr. Takamasa Sakurai (1905–1993)

I've been rowing boats ever since I can remember—probably since age three. No, it's the truth. Even at that age I could make the boat go. It moved slowly, but it moved.

My maternal grandparents lived year-round in a fishing boat. Grandma's folks were farmers in Iwatsubo, and Grandpa Junosuke was adopted into the family to carry on the name. He did his part and worked on the farm, but eventually they turned everything over to their oldest son, got themselves a boat, and became fishers. They never looked back. They put a simple roof of straw on their boat, equipped it with cooking utensils and other necessities of life, and roamed around the lake, fishing mainly with fixed shore nets. That way of life was known as *watari* ["itinerant fishing"]. And from the time I was a baby, they took me with them. I lived with my parents only half the year. At night I'd sleep on the boat curled up next to Grandma, in her arms.

I didn't have any friends my own age. The other parents didn't want their kids playing with me, since they were afraid their kids would fall in the water and drown. I liked it fine on the boat with my grandparents, so I didn't play with village kids. Even after I started school, I'd spend my free time on the boat. At home I had to do chores like cleaning soot from lamp chimneys, which I hated. You cleaned them by using a stick with a cloth on the end, but I was always in a hurry to finish up and go play, so the thin glass would crack. I dreaded getting in trouble for that, so whenever I could I'd run off to Grandpa Junosuke's boat.

Grandpa wore his hair in the old *chonmage* style, shaved off in front with a topknot behind. They kept pomade, a razor, and a mirror on board, and when his hair started growing out in front, Grandma would ladle lake water on his scalp and shave it for him. I don't recall if we had bar soap back then or not, but maybe we did, because I can remember her hands working up a white froth on his head. Farmers' daughters washed their hair with clay, but clay wouldn't make bubbles, so that can't have been it. After she shaved him she'd comb out his topknot, part it and bring up the two sides just so, then pull it tight, bind it up with a paper cord, and put on pomade. Grandpa was the best-groomed fisherman you ever saw.

Grandma kept herself nice too. Every morning she combed her hair with a fine-tooth comb, and poufed it up in a becoming style. Once I asked Grandpa why he never did her hair for her, since she always did his for him. It didn't seem right. He said seriously, "I'd like to, but women's hair is hard. It's beyond me." He was a good husband, and I bet he really would have done it if he could.

Our clothes were always clean and freshly washed. "Taka," Grandma would say, "I'm going to wash your grandfather's loincloth now, so take off your things and I'll wash them too." Then she'd hang everything out to dry on a pole. We took baths at the fish dealer's, when we sold a batch of fish. In summer we rinsed ourselves off in the lake, but when it turned cold the dealers let us use their hot baths. That was only the dealers we did business with. There was a dealer named Kahei on the island of Ukishima who ran a bath, but we didn't do business with him, so Grandpa would tell me to hold off. "We'll be in Ushigome tomorrow," he'd say. "You can have your bath then."

Grandpa was a huge man, built kind of like a sumo wrestler. Not tall, but massive in the chest and hips. Even as a kid I thought he was impressive. I remember once he wore some old work clothes of my father's and the belt wasn't long enough to go around his hips. Nobody could come near him in strength. He was a hairy man too. When I was little, sometimes after he shaved he'd call me over to him and rub his chin against me; it would prickle and hurt, so I'd run to Grandma.

The kind of boat they lived in was called a *tomabune* and was a little bigger than a dinghy. From stem to stern it must have been eighteen feet. There

A *tomabune*

were four beams laid crosswise, evenly spaced from fore to aft. A pillar ran through the middle of the second one, with a ridgepole running between it and the bow. They rigged a makeshift roof over that and spread the bedding underneath. For the roof, they used cedar planks covered with tightly woven straw mats. No thatching grass was needed; the planks and straw mats gave perfect protection against rain and damp. There were eight mats. It was designed so the roof could be folded back on a nice day, to let in the sun and give more room to move around. You could fold the roof in half, but you couldn't get rid of it entirely. There wouldn't have been any place to store it on a boat so small, anyway. The aft portion of the boat had no roof at all. When it rained, we'd make a protective wall out of any wooden planks or barrels on board, cover that with straw matting, and take shelter there.

We slept in the small sheltered space under the roof. There wasn't room enough to stretch out all the way. It was small for a grown man and woman, just two and a half feet across and under six feet in length—plus they had me wedged between them, to boot. Looking back, I have to say it was a hell of a way for three people to sleep, but I never felt cramped at the time. Once we went to bed we were packed in so tight we could hardly move.

Mosquitoes in summer were fierce. When the boat was tied in the reeds, they were everywhere, in the sky and over the water. If you spat, you'd find mosquitoes mixed in—that's how bad it was. We used mosquito nets for protection, hanging them from the roof. Accidentally let an arm or a leg slip out during the night and you'd be eaten alive. It was something.

We were never cold in winter. The bottom of the boat had a covering made of split bamboo, to keep out the moisture. On top of that were mattresses of woven straw, and on top of them we laid old tatami mat facings. That kept the icy chill of the water from getting through. When we went to bed, we laid out flat bedding about the thickness of a floor cushion—just one for the three of us. That was all right, since it was wider than the boat. The edges curled up around us and helped keep off the cold from outside.

Besides that, Grandma and Grandpa each had nightclothes, and I'd snuggle up to one or the other of them. On top of it all was one thin quilt.

When the weather was good, they'd lay the bedding across the roof to air, then fold it up and stash it away by the prow. In the center of the boat was the stove, with a small space on one side where they kept the firewood and a little tea-chest on the other containing the bare necessities for housekeeping. Each of us had two bowls, one for rice and one for soup. There were also five or six teacups, for when company came over. Behind that space was the hold, where they stored the catch. There were two small holes in the sides of the boat there, one on either side. Usually they were plugged up, but when there was a catch, the plugs were taken out so that water could come in and keep the fish alive. Every time the boat swayed, water would splash over the fish and keep them from going bad. For smaller fish like smelt and sardines we covered the holes with netting so they wouldn't get away.

Life on the Boat

I heard my grandmother was a beauty when she was young. She and my grandfather were both mild-tempered. I never knew either of them to get in a quarrel with anyone else, much less each other.

One bright fall day I wanted to go swimming, but Grandma stopped me: "That water's so cold you'd freeze to death, child!" I got the sulks then, so to cheer me up she took a big shrimp thicker than a man's thumb, mashed it and mixed it with an egg, and cooked it in hot miso soup. That was the best thing I ever ate, and it warmed me all the way through. I went to bed in a good mood.

In the night I woke up all of a sudden. There was some kind of a funny

Catching clams

noise. I heard my grandparents whispering over my head. It was a bright moonlit night, I remember, and I could see they were listening to something, so I listened too. Something was making a soft slapping sound against the side of the boat—and it wasn't the waves. There was a big cooking pot just beyond the head of our bed. The sound was coming from behind there. "What's that?" I asked, sitting up. "I don't know," said Grandpa. "We could turn over the pot and see, but might as well wait till morning."

So in the morning, right after breakfast, Grandma and Grandpa started poking around that pot. They had an idea it was a rat, so they hunted everywhere, in the pot and among all the cooking utensils. Finally they found what it was, lying under the firewood pile: a great big snake. It was an enormous blue-green snake, lying in a coil. It must have crawled aboard when we were anchored by the shore, and curled up for a snug winter's nap. Grandpa and Grandma looked at each other.

"Now what?" he said.

"If we throw him in this cold water, he'll die," she said. "We can't do that."

"No," said Grandpa. "Let's leave him be, then."

And they did. They decided to let that snake hibernate on the boat, and piled the wood back on top of it. I never thought anything of it either. In the spring we went to look for him again, and lo and behold he was gone. Must have sneaked ashore when nobody was looking.

Stores of rice and firewood had to be replenished on the boat, but not water—for cooking and drinking, lake water did the trick. It wasn't always clean, though. After a rain the water would be muddy. If I complained there was no water to drink, Grandpa would grin and say, "Don't worry. Coming right up." He had an iron teakettle he was proud of that whistled when the water came to a boil. He'd scoop up some muddy lake water into that teakettle and set it

over a flame. As soon as it boiled, he'd drop in two pieces of blazing charcoal. A few minutes later he'd say calmly, "All right, who wants tea?"

"Not me," I said the first time he did it. I'd seen that muddy water go in with my own eyes. But I was curious, so I peeked inside the kettle and what do you know—the water was pure and sweet. All fishermen cleaned their drinking water that way, Grandpa told me, and I never forgot it. After I got my own boat I did the same thing, so I never suffered from lack of water. Lately the idea is starting to catch on that charcoal absorbs dirt and odors from water, but fishermen knew it long ago.

The worst was when it rained in the day and you couldn't go fishing. We'd be moored in the reeds, with no place for me to play. Nothing to do but lie in bed under the straw roof. Fishermen in those days didn't wear raincoats, and there were no umbrellas on board. If a fish dealer happened to be nearby, you could go there to kill time; other fishing folk would be there too, so it was bound to be lively. No drinking ever went on, though, maybe because it cost too much.

Ordinarily, once the boat was moored in the rushes and the fishing net was set up in the water ready for action, it would be absolutely quiet. There'd be not a sound but the lapping of waves and the rustling of reeds. Grandma would go off to do the laundry. Grandpa would sit around mending his nets, and when he got tired of that, he'd find ways to amuse himself. He was really good at blow darts. First he'd take a three-foot length of slender bamboo and make a pipe by taking off the nodes. He was clever with his fingers that way. He made darts by whittling down five-inch pieces of bamboo to a point and gluing a paper cone to the end of each one with sticky rice. When he put one of those inside the blowpipe and blew, it would fly quite a distance. He could pierce a leaf on a tree twenty or twenty-five feet away, or aim at the trunk of a willow from inside the boat and hit it smack dab in the middle. Grandpa was so good he could keep going till he had a row of three or four darts in the same spot. He'd tell me to give it a try, and I would, but the blowpipe was nearly as big as I was so I never had much luck.

Sometimes he caught birds with his blow darts. Sparrows, especially. They wouldn't fall if you just hit them in the breast, but he was so good he could pin their wings together with one dart. That way they couldn't fly anymore, so they'd come tumbling into the water and Grandpa would pick them up. They were delicious. We ate them roasted with soy sauce, minus the wings. We even ate the bones.

When Grandpa saw I was bored, he'd tell me wonderful stories. One time he put together a year's worth of newspaper clippings of a serial novel about the exploits of a legendary hero and read to me from it every day. I'll never forget the scene where a weeping maiden was about to be sacrificed to an old rake, and the hero dressed up as a woman to rescue her, hiding in a basket that villagers carried into the villain's mountain lair. I listened with my heart in my mouth.

While school was in session I often couldn't go to the boat, and when it rained I'd look out the window and imagine how time must be dragging for my grandparents. When I went home, I cut out the story being serialized in the paper and fastened the clippings together for a present. Grandpa was thrilled.

His greatest pleasure was drinking saké at night. When they pulled up somewhere, Grandma would set off carrying a big, round container with a long neck, and fill it up with a couple of pints of saké. He'd polish that much off in two nights. I got sent out to buy him saké lots of times too. Once he put a string of old coins around my neck and sent me off. Grandma looked at the old money, shook her head, and said, "You can't use that stuff any more. It's worthless." But he sent me off just the same. I must have been four or five. There'd been a big flood, and the water came up to my belly button, I remember, but I pressed on. When I got to the store the man said, "Taka, this money's no good. But you're a good boy to come all this way for your grandpa, so this

one time I'll let you by." And he filled the bottle to the brim. I was beaming with pride. "Got it, Grandpa!" I yelled when I got back. "Did you now! There's a good boy," he said, all smiles. I can see his face even now.

Catfish Kyubei

There were some real characters in those days. When I was ten I met one I'll never forget—a fellow named Kyubei, who caught catfish in traps he made himself out of thin bamboo strips. They were cone-shaped, like loach traps, only bigger, a good four feet long. He baited them with earthworms. Kyubei made his living off catfish, especially in the winter. He was brilliant at it— everybody called him "Catfish Kyubei." Nobody could catch catfish in winter the way he could. Fish dealers loved him, and they were happy to pay top dollar for his catch.

He looked like an ancient Chinese sage, with long straggly white hair and a long white mustache and beard that hung down to his chest. He lived in a houseboat like ours. As a boy, I used to look at him and think he must be a hundred years old if he was a day, but probably he wasn't more than seventy. He and his wife spent all their time in that thatched-roof houseboat, and never cleaned house as far as I could see. The place was black with soot, not just the ceiling, but everywhere. They may have had children, but I never saw any. It was always just the two of them.

I'll tell you why he was so famous: in winter, he'd dive into the icy water and catch catfish in the buff. Went after them underwater, stark naked. Nobody else could pull a stunt like that—you'd freeze to death! Most of the time he dressed like any other fisherman, with a warm jacket in winter, but when he jumped into the water he stripped off all his clothes.

And I mean *all*. No loincloth either. His mind was made up that that was the only way to go after a catfish. He left his balls uncovered, but he did wrap a bit of straw around the end of his penis. I watched him do it: he'd stretch the foreskin down over the tip, and then tie it in place with the straw. "What do you do that for?" I asked.

He told me, "You know where a man feels the cold the worst? Right here at the end of his pole. Leave this exposed and your whole body suffers. Cover it up like this and you're all right."

I said, "I hear the water's so icy it burns, like jumping into a boiling cauldron. Don't you get cold under there?"

"Well, it's like this," he said. "For me to catch catfish, I have to make my body as cold as theirs. When I come near one under the water, as long as we're the same temperature it can't tell I'm there, but if I'm warmer, it's onto me in a flash and takes off. That's why I fish like this."

A sensible explanation, I always thought, but nobody I know ever followed his example. Come winter, Catfish Kyubei would be the only one out there catching catfish—with his bare hands, no less. There was one big rock where the catfish liked to gather in winter and huddle, not moving. Kyubei would come slowly up to one of them, head to head, and pop his thumb in its mouth. The catfish would clamp down on it in surprise. Catfish have a mouthful of teeth, but nothing long enough to bite a man's finger off. Once they get a grip, though, they won't let go. So up he'd come to the surface with that catfish hanging onto his thumb for dear life. The pain would be too much for most people, but that was Kyubei's way. Whether he ever wrapped anything around his thumb to protect it, I don't know.

Catfish Kyubei fished in the lake his whole life long. There was another big rock shaped like a turtle, and sometimes he'd swim under there to catch carp in the winter. Carp are another fish that lie still in the cold. He'd grab them from behind. He went on fishing this way all his life.

Two Deaths

Grandpa got sick soon after I got back from military service. I went to see them, and he'd collapsed. Grandma was worried sick. "He's paralyzed, you've got to send for help," she said, and I ran home and told my father, who went right over with a cart. They decided he should go back to Iwatsubo, where he was from. Father loaded him onto the cart and took him there, walking all the way. I remember how worried Grandma was.

I went to see him now and then, but for twenty-one days he wouldn't eat. He'd lost his spirit. "This is the end," he'd say. I couldn't stand seeing him that way, so I brought him some carp and saké. He sipped the saké from a spout cup, and I fed him slices of raw carp washed in cold water. He looked happy, and he chewed the food the best he could, but he just couldn't get it down. That made me think maybe he wasn't going to make it after all.

Then I noticed his body was all yellow. His face and arms were yellow, and strange as it sounds, even his bedding and covers were too. Yellow seemed to be oozing right out of him. "What's this?" I said. He said quietly, "It has to mean one thing: I'm dying." That shook me up, but when the doctor came, he took one look and said he had something called Weil's disease. Until then they'd had no idea what was wrong with him. The doctor sent off for blood serum, gave him an injection, and he perked right up. He stayed with us a couple of months after that, but pretty soon his hair fell out and he couldn't wear his precious topknot anymore. Little by little he weakened, until he couldn't go fishing anymore. He died around 1929. Not two months later, Grandma slipped away too, so we had two funerals in one year.

Fishing in Lake Kasumigaura

My father Gentaro was a born fisherman. He was almost never home, in any

Bitterling

season. He took his fishing boat around to Yogo Bay, Edosaki Inlet, places like that. It's all been reclaimed now, but back then there were all the fish you could want and more: carp, crucian carp, eel, *sai*, shrimp, bitterling … It was a fisherman's paradise. Nobody remembers what it was like anymore, so I'd better tell.

Edosaki Inlet was nice and sandy, with lots of duckweed. The oars used to get so tangled in it, you couldn't make much headway. In the fall, as the fish moved south they'd come to that place, take a shine to it, and stay. It had everything they needed. Two currents of water met there and formed a pool, so there was plenty of water, and it stayed warm even in winter, and of course there was all that duckweed. The fish would take one look and settle right in. Besides carp and crucian carp, there was all the catfish and eels you could want. The fish came in the spring to spawn, in the summer to feed, and in fall and winter to stay warm. So year-round, there was never any lack of fish. Some men fished nothing but that one inlet. There was a big fish wholesaler located there who ran the "Tonegawaya."

Farther in was a little place called Haga Marsh. It's all been reclaimed, and you won't find that name on any map now, but back then the water there was pure and clear. No duckweed grew there, so fish were scarce and most of the fishermen steered clear of it, but my father and I used to go there to fish for bitterling and another little fish called *yaki*. We'd spend months on end in the marsh, from December to February or March, catching bitterling in our nets and selling our catch to the Tonegawaya or some other dealer nearby. The dealers had to rush off to sell them in Tokyo, loading baskets of them onto bicycles and pedaling off like mad in the dark of night to make the first train. They had their share of difficulties too. Anyway, there were plenty of bitterling for the taking.

Local farmers couldn't have been nicer to us, inviting us to use their baths

at night. If we gave them fish in return, they'd insist we stay for a few drinks too. We always packed a month's worth of supplies when we left home—rice, soy sauce, miso, and other essentials—and the farmers kept us stocked with vegetables, pickles, and firewood, so we never lacked for a thing. None of those farmers did any fishing on the side, so my father and I had the marsh all to ourselves.

There was a peculiar bridge in that area, where the channel narrowed to just twenty-four feet across. They set up a series of boxes there as a kind of floating bridge. Four six-foot-square boxes were tied together in a row, and people would walk over those to cross from one shore to the other. When we went through with the boat, we had to loosen the rope at one end and line up all the boxes next to shore so we could get through, then put it back the way it was. That bridge was there at least till the 1930s.

Another place we went all the time was Yogo Bay. Hajiyama formed a barrier there against the north wind, so even when the wind was too fierce to go fishing anywhere else, it would be calm there. A perfect place for *watari* fishing. On Pigeon Point there was a big soy sauce manufacturing plant named "Jobishi," and *takase* boats carrying soy sauce to Tokyo were always going in and out of there. There were firewood dealers in Yogo too. I can see it in my mind's eye now—*takase* boats piled sky-high with bundles of firewood. And of course the tangerines there were famous—you could see them from a distance, glowing yellow on the trees. In those days it was hard to transport fruit very far, so even those tiny tangerines sold for a fair price in Sawara and Tsuchiura.

We always got up in the dark, and the first thing we did was make tea. When it was ready, my father would say, "Now let's give the gods their tea." First came the gods, then the humans. He'd set a cup of hot tea in the prow. Then pretty soon the eastern sky would turn light. That was the time of day that fishermen called *minatozuki*, "harbor moon." As we brought up the nets, the sky would get brighter and brighter until all at once the sun rose up out of the water in the east. There'd be nobody around but us two. The only other fishing boats would be way off in the distance. When the nets were up we'd take a break and have breakfast, and then a *takase* piled high with firewood, its white sail puffed out in the wind, would glide by. It was more beautiful than I can tell you. After the war that entire area was drained, and today it's all paddy fields.

When they started filling in the bay, the fishermen put up a hell of a fight. The drainage work dragged on, though, and we didn't quit protesting till it was all over. You'll never find fishing grounds as rich as those were, ever again.

I didn't go much to Takahama Bay. I might have when I was younger, but by the time I was fishing on my own, the lake bottom had been damaged and the fishing wasn't any good. The reclamation work in Yagi went on for ten years, starting in 1918. Every day they brought truckloads of dirt and dumped it in the water, and by the next morning that dirt would be entirely swept away. It was all for nothing. One time when I was seventeen my father and I saw something strange. We rowed out into the lake across from Yagi, and there were little hills sticking up out of the water—a whole lot too, as if a cluster of tiny islands had formed overnight. My father said to me, "Taka, that's funny. I never saw those before. What are islands doing in a place like this?" We rowed over for a closer look and what do you know—dirt from the reclamation work had washed all the way out to the middle of the lake and was piling up there. See, back then they didn't have the know-how to do the job right. They just dumped in dirt and more dirt and hoped for the best. But in the process they wrecked the lake bottom. No matter how much water there is in a lake, if the bottom's wrecked then plants can't grow, and if plants can't grow then fish won't come—and if fish won't come there's no point in going fishing.

Ukishima Island

It's connected to the mainland now, but in our day Ukishima was an island, shaped like a bird with its wings spread east and west. The center of the island rose to a peak, and on the southern shore was a good-sized village. Hardly anybody lived to the north. Let's see, I guess I went there with my father for the first time when I was about twelve. Twenty or thirty able fishermen used to work those waters. They were among the best there were. The space was so narrow, you *had* to be good—it was every man for himself, and if you didn't have the confidence and the ability to compete in those crowded waters and maneuver your boat just so, you could forget about it. Nobody who lived on the island was good enough to fish there.

Kashiro's place—that's the fish dealer there—was out on the point of Cape Wada, all by itself. There was a beach in front, and eulalia grass and a grove of pines out back. There was a great big parlor and a dirt-floor entryway, and next to that a kitchen area. Beside the kitchen was a smaller room where the family slept—Kashiro and his wife, and their son and his wife—while the fishermen slept in the parlor. There used to be so many fishermen in there, they lay wall to wall.

My father and I would stay with Kashiro for a week or ten days at a time. There was never any bedding, even in the middle of winter. We just slept in our clothes on the tatami mats. We'd light a fire in the fireplace and sit around talking, and when we got sleepy we'd go to bed. If you got cold in the night, you grabbed the next fellow's jacket or whatever and pulled it over yourself. We'd all wake up while it was still dark out, and check the wind first thing; if it looked good, we'd race to be first out on the water. We paid so much per day for our food, but as I recall there was never any charge for sleeping there. In exchange, we sold our catches to Kashiro, and he'd cook the fish and sell it wholesale.

Shirasu sardine

The first time I went there, I remember I sat down on the beach and got a terrible itch, head to toe. I couldn't figure out why. I was scratching myself like crazy and my father said, "You dummy. Don't you know if you sit down the fleas'll eat you alive? Gotta stay on your feet out here." Sure enough, the sand was crawling with skin-fleas. Skinny little things with hardly any insides, as if they'd been squeezed empty with just skin left. The second anyone came along, they'd be all over him. I went back the other day, but they were gone. They used to be everywhere, of course, at Kashiro's house. Summers you might expect it, but they were there in winter and spring too. Lord, how those bites itched! You'd lie in bed and scratch and scratch and scratch.

Around Ukishima, we did "sandbar fishing"—catching *shirasu* sardines in nets as they laid their eggs on the sand. It was a type of fishing you could do anywhere there were sandbars, but the ones around Ukishima went on for two miles, and they attracted lots of fish, so that was the best place for it.

As I said, we'd get up while it was still dark out and check the eastern sky. If there was an easterly wind blowing just as the sky started turning light—that moment of *minatozuki*—then the fishing would be good and the race would be on. Everybody wanted to be first to the best spots. Once you were awake, setting out was easy enough: nobody had spare clothes to change into—you just went the way you were. No shoes to bother with either; everybody just went barefoot all the time. Fisher folk never had anything on their feet, summer or winter. Before you went indoors you sat down and brushed the sand off.

Sandbar fishing took place between the shore and the *keta*, which is what we call the dividing line between sand and mud on the lake bottom. The shoals gradually deepen until suddenly the bottom falls away and the sand turns to mud. That is the *keta*. Sardines would gather between there and the shore, in the area known as the "middle offing."

The middle offing could be wide or narrow, but on average it extended about 330 feet. Fishing boats would line up in that space to drop their nets, but there wasn't room for even ten boats. Competition for a good spot was intense, I can tell you. If the weather looked promising, you'd race to your boat, push off into the water, and as soon as the sail was hoisted, let down your net. Whoever was first would fish closest in to shore. The next fellow would be out a ways, the next still farther out, and so on. Everybody wanted to be first, so we tore off quick as lightning. If you got there early the fish were all still in one place, so it was easy to scoop them up and fill your net in one go. The later you came, the more scattered they were—and the smaller your catch.

What complicated the business was trying to decide the best spot to fish. Sometimes the fishing was better close by the shore, and other times you wanted to be close to the *keta*. You had to be able to make the right call. The quality of your sail entered into it too. Newer sails took the wind better and gave more speed. By the time a sail was three or four years old, it slowed you down considerably, so to stay in the running everybody tried to keep their sail new.

Reading Underwater Rocks

The biggest reason why only the best fishermen could fish the sandbar around Ukishima Island was that huge rocks lay hidden underwater there. Each one was different. You had to know them like the back of your hand or you'd tear your net and ruin it. That meant knowing the exact position and shape of every single rock. They'd been there for tens of thousands of years; I went and had a look the other day, though, and couldn't find any of them. The water is dirty now for one thing, and they built a dike and changed the topography besides, so nothing is the way I remember it. In the old days you could look over the side of your boat and see the rocks below, as clear as day.

The best place to fish was a couple of miles west of Cape Wada, where Kashiro's place was. Fifty feet out from the cape was a huge group of underwater rocks that you had to get past in order to reach the fishing spot just beyond.

That rock group was named after a nearby shrine where four pine trees grew. This shrine was said to be a very scary place. My grandfather told me never to fall asleep there. Legend has it, he said, that if you did, three worms that inhabit the human body would escape while you were sleeping, fly up to heaven, and tell every bad thing you ever did. Once that happened, your days would be numbered. Whether there was anything to the story I couldn't say.

I do know that getting around those rocks to reach the good fishing on the other side was incredibly hard. The rocks were all sizes, from real monsters—the biggest in all the lake—to relatively small ones. The layout was complicated, and all it took was one miscalculation to rip your net in shreds. Only someone with a high opinion of his skills would go near the place. Incidentally, this is where Catfish Kyubei used to go swimming to catch his catfish and carp.

The first rock was a big flat one just six feet below the surface of the water. It was huge, 60 feet across by 600 long, and perfectly flat. It filled pretty near the entire space from shore to *keta*. Fortunately there were a couple of breaks in it just large enough for a boat to scrape through, one 180 feet from shore, the other 240. When I went back the other day I couldn't make them out, and again, the shape of the land has changed since my day, so it may not be exactly as I'm describing it anymore.

Three hundred feet west of that flat rock was another big one that extended north-northwest for a good 600 feet. The breaks in this rock were narrower than in the first one, just wide enough for your net to get through. If the wind changed right after you got past the first rock and you couldn't get past the second one, you had to hurry and take down your sail and pull up your net then and there. There'd be plenty of fish for the taking, from the shoreline to right there between the two rocks. Then you had to row like a demon back to Kashiro's, to get your catch back as quick as you could and sell it.

That long trip back always seemed like such a waste of time. We'd rather have emptied our nets on board and had another go right away, but then the sardines wouldn't be so fresh, and they couldn't be dried and sold. That's why Kashiro wanted us heading back as soon as we caught anything. Business was business, so that's what we did, like it or not. At Kashiro's they measured the size of the catch with a dry measure. As soon as you could, you'd tear back to the fishing grounds. The ones good enough to maneuver beyond those rocks could drag their nets farther and catch more fish at one time, and so they made more money.

The third rock in the group wasn't flat but round, kind of like a temple bell lying on its side, maybe 90 feet in diameter. It was off to the northwest some 180 feet from shore. Between rocks two and three, just a few feet below the surface was another one that we called Umbrella Rock. One time I wanted to look at it up close, so I got out of my boat and climbed down to stand on top of it. The water came just up to my chest. I'd say the thing was—oh, about 24 feet square, the size of two eight-mat rooms. It was an unusual color, bright orange. Being round on top and narrow at the other end, it looked just like a big orange mushroom or umbrella. You could see it clear as anything in the water, and next to it a bluish space, which was where you had to pull your net through. I looked for a reddish rock when I went there the other day, but there wasn't any. I guess the color doesn't show through anymore because the water is too dirty.

Anyway, getting your net hooked on that rock meant big trouble. The only thing to do then was take down your sail, untie one end of the net, and row around and around in a circle to untwist it and get it free. It worked best if you could get somebody to help you by pulling on the net from the other end, but not many were willing to take the time. The main thing was not to dawdle, but to get going and do what you could while there was time.

Mostly the rocks were down out of sight, so the only way to mark their location was to look for a pair of landmarks on shore and remember how they lined up. When you came back the next time you'd find your landmarks, check the position of your boat, and estimate the location of each rock. You had to make a series of split-second judgments, one after another. Anybody afraid of wrecking his nets wouldn't even try.

I'd say that for every thirty boats that tried to make it past the third rock, only three or four would succeed. The rest had to turn around and go back to Kashiro's. But if you did manage to outmaneuver your rivals, why then you had a clear field and could relax and catch all you wanted without worrying about the competition. That was the best fishing under the sun.

The first time my father took me to the rocks, I was mystified: I couldn't see anything in the water, but for some reason he kept swerving sharply. Of course, he was doing it to avoid the rocks. I remember how great I thought he was, being able to steer clear of invisible dangers—at least they were invisible to me. That's what all the fishermen did, though; you had to constantly keep in mind what was on the lake bottom, what direction the wind was blowing, how high the waves were, and so on. It took years of experience to be able to fish some of those places.

There were plenty of other rocks in the lake, of course. At the entrance to Takahama Cove was a particularly interesting one. It was huge, shaped like a turtle shell, with a hole that went all the way through. Catfish and carp would go in there by the hundreds to hibernate in winter. That was the place where Kyubei went swimming in the buff to catch them.

Passing the Time

As long as the wind stayed favorable, we'd keep on fishing the sandbank day after day, selling our catch at Kashiro's. A week or so of that and you'd go back home to spend some time doing chores or making yourself useful in the village, and then it was back to fishing. But when there was too much wind, there was absolutely nothing to do except wait it out. Sometimes it would stay windy for a whole week. Then I'd mostly go over to Kashiro's to pass the time, but some fellows would walk all the way to Inashiki to go drinking. The bars there had women, but there were no brothels. For that you had to go farther, all the way to Itako. I'm afraid I never went, so I can't tell you anything about it. I do know one story that happened before I was born, though. I heard it from my father.

This was just after the Russo-Japanese War, around the turn of the century. The villagers who'd fought in the war returned as conquering heroes, and one day four or five of them decided they'd go down to Itako to celebrate coming back alive. They went and whooped it up in a brothel. The next day a strong westerly wind came up, but for some reason they decided to head back. Well, the boat capsized and they all drowned. That caused quite a stir. After all, those were soldiers that had whipped Russia! Unlike World War II veterans, they got a hero's welcome wherever they went, and they acted like big shots too. Their families were bursting with pride. Nobody could believe those men had slipped into the water and drowned. My father said fishermen came from miles around to join in the search for the bodies.

There may not have been any brothels on Ukishima, but there were plenty up around Ushiwata. Shitozaki had an inn that catered to steamer passengers, and lots of drinking places too—usually with five or six women each. Fishermen with money in their pockets would crowd into those places, and no matter how much money they brought in, the women would wind up with it all. There's not a trace left of them now, but there used to be a steady stream of fishermen in and out of those places, and the whole neighborhood would echo with the sounds of shamisen and drums and women's voices singing and laughing. You'd never know it from the way Shitozaki looks today.

Boiling the Nets in Persimmon Juice

In the old days nets weren't made of nylon, but cotton. If you didn't keep them in good shape they'd rot, or shed fluff, which made them hard to work with. They'd slow you down in the water so you couldn't catch anything. A man had to take care of his nets, come what may.

Fishing villages would have a big vat for boiling nets that all the local fishermen could share. It was about two and a half or three feet in diameter. Every village had one, and it was in constant use. Whatever kind of nets you used, they had to be boiled once or twice a month in summer, and once every two months or so in fall, after the water temperature went down. We put something in the water called *katchi*. Sometimes we'd use persimmon pulp, but mostly it was *katchi*. I can't recall just what it was or where we got it, but it consisted of hard lumps that would melt in hot water. It was some sort of substitute for persimmon juice.

To boil your net, first you'd wring it out using a pair of ropes, then toss it in the vat and let it simmer for a while. Then you'd flip it over with the ropes and let it stew some more before taking it out. It didn't take too long—all in all about twenty minutes was enough. After that, you'd drag the net back

Mending nets

to your boat and spread it out to dry.

When the net was dry, you had to give it an application of persimmon juice—the astringent kind. That was a damn nuisance. If only we could have concentrated on fishing, and not had to mess around with the stupid nets! Persimmon juice wasn't something you could buy either. You had to make it yourself, and in huge quantities too. Just squeezing the persimmons from the tree in your yard, or your neighbor's yard, wasn't enough. I used to take off to neighboring towns with a cart or a wagon, on the lookout for persimmons to buy. You can imagine the competition, since fishermen were all in the same situation. Even now you'll notice that most of the houses in the Dejima area have persimmon trees. No doubt some produce sweet persimmons, for eating, but it was very common to make a little money on the side selling astringent persimmons to needy fishermen.

You could find the juiciest persimmons between about July 20 and August 10. You'd set off to buy them with a wagon, or maybe a packhorse, and as soon as you got back you'd set about crushing them to get the juice. By the time I got back with a load of fruit it would be evening, so I'd do my pounding after dark. I used a great big mortar and pestle—just like for pounding sticky rice. If I got carried away and pounded too hard the liquid would splash, I remember, so I had to watch myself. I'd work till late at night, getting eaten alive by mosquitoes while I pounded persimmons to a pulp by lamplight or the light of the moon.

When the fruit turned to pulp, you'd add water, pour the stuff out on a drainboard, and save the runoff in a barrel. You kept repeating the process till you were done. Any leftovers would be saved and dried, to use in the next boiling. At my house we used to keep twenty barrels of persimmon juice in storage.

To apply the juice, you'd pour it out into the hold of your boat, throw in the net, and then stomp with both feet so the tannin penetrated all the way through the cotton. One application wasn't enough either. You'd stomp on one section and then lay that out to dry while you worked on another section of the net. When you were finally done, and the net was thoroughly dry, you were back in business. One application only lasted ten days or so and then you had to start all over again, so the demand for persimmons was huge.

That reminds me of something that happened at the time of the Great Kanto Earthquake of 1923. My father and I had been out fishing the night before. We came home and slept a little bit, and then got up around noon because something seemed wrong. The ground was swelling up and shaking so hard you couldn't stand up straight. I looked outside and saw a river of persimmon juice in the garden. The barrels had all knocked together and fallen over, and the juice was pouring out of them. This was serious. It affected our livelihood. I was beside myself. "Look, there goes the persimmon juice!" I yelled to my father. "What are we going to do?" He said simply, "There's nothing we can do." It was a terrible shame. An inch-wide crack opened in the garden too.

Anyway, the old-style nets were such an aggravation. It was a revolutionary change when we switched to nylon and didn't have to boil our nets or apply persimmon juice to them anymore—that's for sure.

Disasters on the Lake

There was a pair of brothers from Namekata who were out fishing one fall day when the weather turned bad. The younger one struggled in the wind with the sail, got trapped in it, and drowned. When the older brother saw that other fishing boats were still out, he kept right on fishing, with his brother's corpse lashed on board. Those Namekata men were a tough breed. They were famous for going out fishing in stormy weather, when nobody else would dare. They'd lower the boom under the mast, fold up the sail as small as it would go, and carry right on. When a gale blew, you could tell it was bad from shore, as foam from the choppy waves blew back over the water in a fine white mist. Nobody in his right mind would go out fishing in weather like that—but sometimes we'd spot a boat on the waves, even so. It was always a Namekata man. They were somehow made differently from the rest of us.

One of the most skilled and fearless fishermen that ever lived was Toku-taro Ito from Namekata. But a terrible thing happened to him. One blustery December day I took the day off and was standing looking at the lake when I spotted a boat riding a huge wave. It was the only one out there. Somebody was inside, rowing for dear life across that oceanlike swell, heading for the far shore of the lake. The crazy fool, I thought—he's going to die! The waves were like small mountains, and he had to row up and down them, which was no mean feat. The guy must really have had a high opinion of himself, to think he could do that. "That'll be somebody from Namekata," we said to our-selves, standing around on the beach in the wind and watching the boat's progress. Then up went the sail, and we knew from the shape that it belonged to Tokutaro. We could tell the sail of every fisherman on Lake Kasumigaura at a glance, even from a distance. It had to be him. We figured not even Toku-taro Ito would let his nets down in that weather, though—he'd never be able to lift them back in. So we kept watching to see what he'd do. Eventually he rolled his sail back up, to keep it from taking in the wind, but even so his poor little boat was tossed like a leaf, totally at the mercy of the wind and waves. Then we lost sight of him. It seemed impossible that he could ever make it home alive, but we found out later that by some miracle he had—yet not entirely safely either.

Tokutaro told me later the wind was so icy that day, he could barely move.

He curled up in a quilted jacket and crouched in the hold, his body so stiff with cold that he couldn't stand up. He was literally frozen stiff. The wind carried his boat home, right to the banks by his village. His family couldn't figure out why he didn't get up and come ashore. They figured he must be alive, to have navigated his way home. The villagers went out and found him lying in the hold. He was breathing, but he couldn't move a muscle. They carried him home and made a nice fire of dried rice stalks to warm him up, and finally he came round.

I went to see him after that, and he held out his hands to show me. "Look at this, will you," he grumbled. "That's the end of me." He rubbed a fingernail, and it crumbled right off. All his nails went bad and came off. They never grew back either. That's how he got the nickname "Half-dead Toku."

One time a fisherman named Nao Harada from the village of Hatta, near Ushiwata, was trapped by a hurricane and died. It happened September 15, 1951. It rained hard that day till about three in the afternoon, and then the clouds broke up and the sky cleared in the west. I didn't like the look of things over Mount Tsukuba and Mount Fuji, but my sail needed drying, so I went out for a short run in the evening. A high wind came up and for the life of me I couldn't haul in my net. I knew I was in trouble so I made for shore, moored my boat in the rushes, and dropped anchor. Finally I got the net stowed away and pulled into a little inlet to rest in the moonlight. Then right before my eyes I saw another boat head out into the gale.

Who would be so crazy? The waves were so high I couldn't make out who it was. No matter—I figured he was a goner, since no one would be able to row back in that weather. In the meantime I managed to pole myself along the shore inch by inch and finally made it home. The whole family was out in the yard. My father yelled at me, "You damned fool! What the hell did you think you were doing, taking the boat out on a night like this!" I explained, and then I learned everybody else had abandoned their boats and walked home. I asked him if he'd seen that other boat head out, and he said yes, that it had made him heartsick, for fear it was me. "That was somebody from around here and no mistake," he said.

That night Nao's boat was reported missing. We waited till morning, but the storm never let up. The waves were wild. Fishing was out of the question, but a bunch of us made up a search party. Sure enough, we found his boat swamped, apparently deserted. No sign of Nao. We set to putting the boat to rights, bailing it out and then straightening the sail, but somehow the ropes were too heavy to lift. We all gave a pull together, and up to the surface came Nao, his corpse fastened in the ropes.

He must have known his chances were bad and tied himself that way just so that when a search party came after him, it wouldn't have far to look. We took his body home, and all the women broke down and sobbed because in the face of certain death, his last thoughts were for his neighbors.

There were other fatalities. One of the best and bravest fishermen around died when my father was a young man. People were in awe of him because he never let a high wind keep him from fishing, but that was his undoing. He went out one time in near-typhoon conditions. The wind started whipping the waves, and he must have rowed like the very devil to keep from going under—afterwards they found his oarlocks worn nearly clean away.

In the 1950s, boats started getting bigger, and everybody had their sailboat fitted with an engine, so there weren't as many accidents, but one time a couple out fishing on the lake froze to death. They must have thought the wind would let up that night, but it didn't, and they were swept away as far as Aso. They got soaking wet trying to bring in their net, and in the end they froze. By the time we found them their bodies were solid ice.

Reading the Weather

Not knowing how to predict the weather could be fatal. From the time I was little I was taught to read the wind. My grandfather and my father both used to say you could tell more from the way the wind was blowing than you could from any weather forecast. You wouldn't dare go night fishing without knowing which way the wind was blowing—you wouldn't catch anything without a feel for wind and temperature, anyway.

First you'd check the clouds over by Mount Tsukuba and Mount Oda, then over Mount Fuji, to the southwest. You'd look to see how fast they were moving, how ragged they were. When a summer storm was moving in, the clouds over Tsukuba and Fuji showed it. If they were black and fast-moving, that meant not just rain but high winds. Even if Lake Kasumigaura was peaceful and the sky overhead was blue, if you saw clouds like that over Tsukuba, you had to get a move on. There were no motorboats, so you had to get busy and row. There wasn't a minute to waste. By the time the clouds reached Mount Oda, it was too late. By then a wind would have sprung up on the lake; when that happened, you had to make for shore as fast as you could. You couldn't fix on going home or heading for any particular place. You just had to get your boat tied somewhere in the reeds so it wouldn't tip over, and hunker down. Summer storms would sweep in all of a sudden, but they never lasted more than three hours. If you sat tight, you could wait it out.

On a windy day you could tell by looking at Mount Fuji whether it was going to let up at night or keep on blowing till morning. On a clear, windy evening, if you looked just as the sun was about to go down and saw clouds go scudding by the mountain top, that meant the night would be windy too. If the clouds were bigger in back and came to a point in front, that meant serious trouble. But even when it was blustery in the daytime, if the clouds over Fuji were quiet, barely moving, you knew the night would be calm. Long, trailing clouds that held steady meant no wind at all.

The Night Terror

Scariest of all was the *yoru no odoshi* ["night terror"]. That was a fierce night wind in winter that would stir up waves two or three feet higher than normal. It was a terrifying sight. An *odoshi* always came after a quiet evening and a clear sky. It would come out of nowhere—just come roaring in all of a sudden. The water would be dead calm one minute, and the next it would swell up into enormous waves. Think about that. If you got caught napping, you were done for.

Before an *odoshi*, something like smoke would coil around the top of Mount Fuji in the evening. Snow and wind mixed with a cloud, I think it was, winding around the peak with its tail drawn out to the east. It never failed: if you saw that, there'd be a night terror that very night. Fishermen all knew it was coming, so they left off work and stayed indoors. That's why hardly anybody ever capsized because of an *odoshi*.

Once in my life I was out in one. I'd gone carp fishing with my son Kenji one night in December. I looked at the lay of the clouds beforehand and told him, "This looks bad. Let's not go tonight," but he outtalked me. He was only a kid of seventeen or eighteen, and so crazy about fishing he hated to miss a night. There's a time like that in every man's life. We were going to fish by Oyama, and it was a short hop from there to Yogo Bay, where we'd be safe, so I gave in. Just as we started to lower our nets, the wind came on. It happened so fast, I was stunned. There was no use going on, so we stowed the nets and headed for Ushigome. Then from the west we heard a big *whoosh* as the water rose up in a white foamy wave, bearing straight down on us. I let out a yell, and we rowed like maniacs for shore, and moored in the rushes around Magake.

I have no words to describe the ferocity of that blast. It snapped the dry reeds one after another, like toothpicks. The water swelled up, lifting us a good three feet straight into the air. Our boat rocked till I thought we were done for, but somehow we held on and stayed afloat. The wind came howling in from the northwest, icy cold. If we'd been out in the middle of the lake, it would have killed us and no mistake, because once your boat turns over in weather like that it's goodbye, no matter who you are.

The Sound of the Sea

We did our fishing after dark, but if there was no wind, we couldn't go out. That's just the way it was. That didn't mean we stayed home and went to bed; instead, we'd go hang out by the boats with friends and stay up talking till nine or ten. To stay warm, you'd wrap yourself up in your sail so just your face poked out. That's when we'd hear the sound of the sea. It came from different directions, and you could tell by the direction what the next day's weather would be. It had nothing to do with the direction of the wind—there *wasn't* any wind, otherwise we wouldn't have been there, we'd have been out fishing. Nowadays the noise of automobiles and other things blocks it out, but back then the evenings were perfectly still, and in the midst of the dark and the quiet, the sound of the sea would come echoing from miles away. We'd listen, and talk over what it meant, and gradually doze off.

See, we fishermen were always waiting for the least little wind so we could go to work. If it didn't come, then we just hung around the boats together, winter or summer, waiting. When the wind came up you'd be off like a shot, and if it died down while you were out on the lake, you'd drop anchor and sit talking with your friends about nothing. Awake or asleep, you were out on your boat, so you got to know the weather and the lake very, very well.

Rivalry

Sometimes you'd get mad at somebody and deliberately set out to capsize him. It was easy enough. All you had to do was take the wind out of his sail and over he'd go. If a sail suddenly went slack, you see, it upset the balance between the force of the wind and the weight of the net, so if you wanted to get back at somebody, you'd move upwind of him and block his sail. It was always a knock-down drag-out race to be first to the fishing grounds, and whoever was in the lead would deliberately block anybody who tried to overtake him, weaving left and right to bar the way. If someone did that to you it was maddening, so you'd go after his sail for revenge. Still, you knew if you succeeded, he was only going to do the same thing to you when he got the chance, so mostly you gritted your teeth and did nothing. It took a lot of aggravation to capsize somebody.

After the war, fishing was better than ever. With everybody gone soldiering all those years and nobody home fishing, the fish population zoomed. The lake was chock-full of every kind of fish when we got back. Even without bait, fish would surge into a trap and fill it so full you could hardly lift it out of the water. It wasn't all good news, though: catches were so big that the price of fish plunged. Prosper too much and you'll wind up poor.

One problem we had was getting a sufficient supply of salt. Dealers had to have a ready supply, to keep fish from spoiling so they could be sold on the market, but this didn't always work out. One time the situation was so desperate that one of the boats—the *Kyoei Maru*, I think it was—went from Lake Kasumigaura down the River Tone and out to sea, and brought back sea brine. They put that brine in a great vat in the yard of the wholesale market and boiled it to get the salt. The boat had to make any number of round trips to get enough brine, and twice it got caught on a bird-rope. That was something used for catching wild ducks. Hunters would make long ropes of twisted pampas grass, smear them with birdlime, and release them in the water upwind of the ducks. The fishing boat ran right over the bird-ropes, and that was the last time I ever saw them used.

A Fisherman and His Wife

Mr. Susumu Fujii (1911–1997)
Mrs. Ii Fujii (1911–2000)

Ii: My folks were farmers. When I was twenty-two, an acquaintance of ours brought a man over to the house. My mother said, "That's the go-between with a match for you, so go serve them tea." I served the tea, the man drank it, and that was that.[1] I never even thought of looking him full in the face, let alone talking to him.

Susumu: I walked five miles to her house with the go-between. We walked in and sat down, and a young woman brought us tea. The go-between told me to drink it, so I did. Things were different back then. About all I could see was her toes. Neither one of us had any idea what the other looked like.

Ii: No, we surely didn't. But I came to this very house as a bride, although the place looked quite a bit different in those days. His parents moved into a separate house on the same piece of land to make room for us. My family weren't fishers, so I didn't know the first thing about fishing till I was married. I learned—but oh my, it was hard. I remember his mother telling me they put her on a boat when she was young and made her fish, but she got deathly seasick. Said she'd sooner work her fingers to the bone in the fields than ever go fishing again.

Susumu: My wife was a tough one. She got sick at first, with the heaves and diarrhea, but she hung on and adapted. After we had kids, she'd take them right with her. We did *watari* fishing, roaming from one fishing ground to another in a little boat. We put up a makeshift roof and she slept on a straw bed with her babies.

Ii: But when we were first married, we had a farm. We grew rice on about four acres of land. My husband's two younger sisters still lived at home, and they were great workers—threshed ninety sheaves of rice a day, easily. I thought I could never do that, so I tried to bustle around and make myself useful in other ways. Then they were married off, and I had to take over the threshing. Before you know it I could finish off three hundred sheaves in less than

three days. My husband had to be out on the lake fishing, you see, so he couldn't lend a hand. I had to get the job done myself.

Susumu: Fall was the best season for fishing, so I never worked in the paddies at harvest time.

Ii: Once in a blue moon there'd be no wind, so he'd stay home and help set the sheaves out to dry, but the minute a breeze came up he'd be off again. Women did all the farming, because we had to.

Fishing As a Way of Life

Susumu: Fishing was second nature to me. I could row almost before I could walk, and fishing was my whole life. It was a different story for men who worked on farms or in town. Fishermen were almost a race apart from townspeople. Our faces were darker and more leathery from all the time we spent out in the elements. We spoke a different language; we talked differently, thought differently, had a different way of life. We were as different from other folk as night and day. Time was, you could tell fishers at a glance—not just men but women and children too.

Ii: That's true. Farmers and fishermen seemed like different species of people.

Susumu: I'm an old man now, but I'll never forget the day I was fifteen and rode in a fishing boat with a sail for the very first time. My father surprised me by telling me to take the oar in the stern. I was thrilled. There was a keen wind, but I was young and strong, and I felt ready to go on forever. I had arms like you never see these days—muscles like logs. My shoulders and neck were thick as a gorilla's. Never got tired for a minute, even with sweat pouring down my face. I just rowed for all I was worth, doing five miles at a stretch, easy, heading into a stiff wind. The waves would slap against the prow and lift the boat up, and I'd push with my oar so we came down smack

Planting rice

into the crest of the next wave, splitting it in two and making the spray fly. It splashed up where I was standing and hit me in the face, and that was a spur. I'd row harder than ever. I loved every minute of it.

It was a summer day, and I was wearing nothing but a loincloth. I stood dripping sweat, working the oar with all my might, till pretty soon I began to notice a strange sensation. I stopped rowing and looked down at myself, and saw to my amazement that my chest and stomach were white. I touched myself and realized it was salt. The sweat poured out of me as I worked and stuck to me as it dried, so I wound up caked in salt like a pickled herring. I licked the salt off my fingers and started rowing again. There was the sound of waves against the boat, and the feel of the spray on my face. I felt terrific.

My father looked back at me and grinned. "Not bad," he says. "Not bad at all." I grinned right back at him. "Nothing to it," I said.

Now and then other boats would come along from other villages, and then I screwed up my face and rowed like a demon because I hated to lose. I'd glare at the competition and row my heart out.

It may seem strange that we'd be out rowing in rough weather, but you have to understand that without wind the sailing boats were useless. We always rowed straight into the wind. If it ever died down and you were stuck on calm water under a clear sky, there was nothing to do but curl up and take a nap. It's strange, but the minute a breeze came along I'd know, even if I was fast asleep: my eyes would pop open. There was no time to waste so I'd leap up and set to work.

This was all at night, of course. A popular song of the day went like this:

Some things can't be taken in the day—
Other men's wives, and smelt.
For them it's the dark of night.

Threshing rice

Ii: Yes, I remember that song.

Susumu: We always fished at night. We'd set off from shore about the time the sun started going down, and by the time we reached the fishing grounds the sky would be crimson. Then we'd lower the net, hoist the sail, and get down to business. The best places to fish varied day to day, depending on things like wind and temperature. Every fisherman had to size up the day's weather conditions before setting out, figure for himself where the best fishing was going to be, and row as fast as he could in that direction. But after you'd all been doing it a while you tended to think alike, and usually it turned into an all-out race to be first to the same place. Nobody could stand to be beaten.

Ii: Even watching from shore, you could tell what a mad rush it was.

Susumu: The introduction of engines made our lives a lot easier, but in those days a fisherman prided himself on the strength of his arms. A strong-armed fisherman could row farther faster, and drag his nets that much longer a distance, so naturally he caught more fish.

When you got to the fishing ground and hoisted your sail, the wind would catch it in the middle, bellying it out so that it seemed to fill the whole sky. Looking up at it from below, it really looked like the sky had turned to sail. That was a lovely sight—never failed to make my heart swell. No motor-powered boat could ever give you such a thrill. There was something special about the old sailing boats. Handling them was tricky, though. In a heavy wind the boat would rock while you threw the net overboard. Without net and tackle the boat was lighter, and that only made the rocking worse. Not only that, having the net in the water shifted the boat's center of gravity, pulling the boat lower on one side. You had to raise the mast quickly, letting out just enough sail so the force of the wind balanced the pull of the net. That would stabilize the boat. If you didn't know what you were doing, just standing up could be a challenge, and if you were too hasty the boat would lose balance and capsize, which was a real catastrophe. Even if you managed by some miracle to set the boat upright again, the mast would be slippery, the sail would be waterlogged, and you might as well pack it in. You had to go through some hard lessons before you got the hang of it. I know this from experience—I capsized all the time when I was young. The tackle was awkward and heavy, and time and again I'd fumble and tip myself right over. Then I'd have to crawl up on the hull and spend the night there, just waiting for dawn. It was mortifying. I can't tell you how miserable it was.

To anyone not a fisherman it may seem that once you'd gotten the hang of things, you had it made—that all you needed to do then was toss your net into the water, sit quietly, and catnap while the wind filled the sail and sent your boat drifting backward, dragging the net through the water. Well, they're wrong: that's when the fighting began.

There'd have been no problem if the boats all drifted back at the same rate and stayed out of each other's way, but that rarely happened. There was a constant danger of collision because the boats traveled at different speeds. It all hinged on a fisherman's strength and skill. The better rower got to the grounds first and caught more fish, so he made more money. With the extra income, he could take better care of his boat and buy bigger sails and finer-quality oars. The average mast was about twenty feet high and the average sail fifty feet across, but this varied depending on the skill of the owner. So you can see a bigger boat would quickly bear down on its smaller rivals. Instead of altering course to keep from crashing, the fisherman would yell bloody murder for everyone to get out of his way.

Despite all the rivalry, fishermen looked out for each other too. Once somebody stole my net and my catch. Another fisherman was robbed too,

Portrait of Mr. Fujii fishing

and he went to the police. The culprit turned out to be somebody I knew. The other guy, Kihara, took him to court, and I was called to testify. I told Kihara, "Let me handle this." I went in front of the judge and told him I wanted the man freed. I said I'd die rather than testify against one of my own kind, that the man had expressed remorse and I wanted him released. I had tears in my eyes. How could I let a man get a criminal record over a matter of a few fish? And so he got clemency. Kihara hadn't suffered as great a loss as me, so my words carried weight.

Ii: You used to go fishing even in the dead of winter.

Susumu: Yes, starting off at two in the morning and rowing all the way to Tsuchiura. You have no idea how cold it could get. Winters are much milder nowadays than they used to be. One time the lake froze all the way from Ushiwata to Tsuchiura. Generally in winter there'd be a thin layer of ice that crunched every time the prow hit it. You wouldn't hear the noise of waves against the boat as you plowed along through the darkness, just that steady *crunch, crunch.* Thicker ice could cause serious damage; excursion boats used to have a wooden triangle attached to the prow, making them into a kind of primitive icebreaker. Of course if the ice was too solid, you took the night off. Solid ice meant there was no way to gauge the strength of the wind. In the morning the lake would lie flat and shining, in a kind of spooky way. That's a sight you never see anymore, so I suppose the climate and the water have changed somehow.

She'd make my breakfast in the dark and then pack a tubful of rice for me to take along. It was pitch-dark, so I did my work by feel. Instead of warm pants, we wore *monpiki*, the same close-fitting cotton trousers that rice farmers wore. Gloves were unheard-of. When I rowed, I pulled the sleeves of my jacket down and wrapped them around my bare fingers to keep them from freezing.

Sunset and sunrise—they're both called *mazumi* in the local dialect—are the best times for fishing, because that's when fish move in large numbers. That's why I put out from shore so early in the morning, so I could arrive at the fishing ground and slip my net in the water just as the sun was coming up, right at *mazumi*. On a good day you could see huge schools of smelt sweep through the lake water in giant arcs, making it shine silver. That always meant a bumper catch, the net filled to bursting. Sometimes there'd be more fish than you could ever possibly catch. It was unpredictable, though; another day you might go to the exact same place at the exact same time and come up dry. In late November and December the catches finally got so small we gave up and went after freshwater mussels instead.

Ii: They're gone now, but you used to bring home mountains of them. Some were twelve inches long, remember those?

Susumu: Yes, huge ones, there for the taking. The water used to be so clear, I could see them burrowed in the sand six or seven feet below the boat, just their mouths showing, wide open. I'd lower a pole and stick it into an open mouth, and the mussel would grab hold in surprise. Then all I had to do was lift the pole and the mussel came right up with it. In deeper water I hunted by feel, using a pole with a hoop and a net at one end and dragging it over the sandy bottom till I could feel the half-inch or so of mouth poking above the sand. The second I made contact, I'd dig down and scoop the mussel into my net. Some people could catch as many as six hundred a day that way. Average was more like two to four hundred.

After a week or so of mussel fishing around the lake, the men would row home with their catch. The wives took over then, slicing the mussels open with a small knife to prepare them for market. Mostly people sold their catch, but on a cold winter's day lots of us liked a hot dish of mussels and dried radish cooked in soy sauce. For some reason, those mussels turned your

Getting ready to fish

stool black. One time an enterprising fellow from our village took a load of mussels to Tokyo and claimed they had magical properties that would ensure a long and healthy life. "If you don't believe me, try one," he'd say. "If it works, your stool will turn black. That's the proof." I hear he made a killing.

Mussel shells we took to the Miyoshi Button Factory in Tsuchiura. The young ones had blue shells, which didn't sell. The shells were too soft to use. They had to be black. In the 1930s, as I recall, we made two or three yen per sack.

We fished for bitterling too, wandering around the lake from place to place and fishing with fixed shore nets. This was known locally as *watari*, itinerant fishing. Dozens of men did it. We were like migrant birds, away from home sometimes two or three months at a time.

I'd put up poles on my boat and fashion a makeshift roof to keep off the rain, then live and cook there on the boat, all by myself. During the day I'd go around and set up my nets, and when I was finished I'd moor my boat in the rushes for the night. Come morning I'd check my nets, and if the catch was fair I'd sell it to the nearest dealer for cash. I used the money I earned to buy rice, miso, soy sauce, firewood and whatever else I might need. Then I'd pull up my nets, move to some other likely-looking spot, and start all over. All in all I managed pretty well for myself—I can't recall a single time I stayed in an inn or ate in a restaurant. I saved on oil by going without my lamp, so once the sun went down, I had only the light of the moon to stave off darkness. Since I was all alone, there wasn't a hell of a lot to do anyway. I used to go to bed as soon as it got dark. It was plenty warm sleeping in the boat. I'd put a layer of loose straw on the deck, cover that with straw matting, and lay my mattress and bedding on top. You'd be surprised how snug I was. I never felt the cold. Anybody who did wouldn't have lasted long in that life, that's for sure.

Would people back then rather have lived a soft life? You bet we would. If it was up to us, none of us would have chosen to spend the winter out fishing all alone in a little boat. Who wouldn't like to sit and warm himself by the fire? Sure, we'd rather have stayed home like anybody else, but money was scarce and you had to eat. That came first, and creature comforts came last. My family did some small-scale rice farming to supplement our income, but it was hardly worth the trouble. We produced five bags of rice, of which half went to the landowner in payment of rent. The rest had to be invested in fertilizer and this and that, so two months after the harvest it would all be gone. There was never a grain to eat. A man named Kaemon Yakushiji was a big landowner in our area, and he'd gladly loan you a couple of bags of rice to tide you through the winter, but when the interest came due the following year, you'd only slide into worse debt.

You can see that until the Agricultural Land Act came into effect, there was a world of difference between landowners and ordinary folks. Tenant farmers didn't own enough dirt to throw at a crow, I'll tell you that.

Ii: No, we didn't. We didn't have a fistful of soil to call our own.

Itinerant Fishing

Susumu: When you think how far we've come, we've really got to be thankful. Back then farmers took to fishing to keep from starving. I'd go anywhere to catch fish—sometimes the most remote places. The fishing season was strictly enforced in Lake Kasumigaura, and offenders were caught and punished, but over in Chiba you could bend the rules. There weren't many fishermen there either, so you could move around as you pleased. It used to take me three days to travel down to the Chiba marshland called Imanuma. It's changed now, I hear, but back then it was a huge expanse of reeds and rushes, with not a house or living soul in sight. Nothing but fish and water-fowl. I used to spend long stretches there, like a hermit. Day after day of total silence. Sometimes there'd be a sudden whir of wings and a flock of birds would take to the air, turning the sky black. When the sun went down at the edge of the marsh, I'd curl up and go to sleep. I'd wake up while it was still dark out, with the moon reflected in the water, and start a fire to make rice for breakfast. Little by little the moon would fade and the stars would go out; the winter sky would first turn pale, then slowly change to crimson. It was beautiful, I tell you. Nobody else fished there, so mine would be the only fire trailing smoke.

Watari was a damned hard life, though, with more troubles than I could begin to tell you. I'll never forget the time I went to Sawara to catch bitter-ling and set glass fishing globes in the River Ono. The idea was to bait the globes so the bitterling would swim in and be trapped inside. The traps weren't available locally, so I sold a bag of rice to raise the money and ordered several dozen through a dealer in Tsuchiura. Then I set off for Sawara, where the bitterling were. There were no real fishermen there so I reckoned no one would mind, but I was wrong. Farmers and townspeople all came out in force and threw stones at my traps from the riverbanks. Smashed every last one. It burned me up, but I was an outsider from Ushi-wata and if they didn't want me setting traps in "their" river, what could I do? The river did have a lot of traffic from nearby villages, and maybe my traps got in the way, I don't know. If the same thing happened today we could talk it over, but back then they ganged up on me, threw stones, and smashed all my precious globes to bits. When it happened I just broke down and cried.

Another place I often fished was a large area of marshland this side of Sawara called Yodaura. It was an eerie, godforsaken place with nothing but rushes for miles on end. No sign of human life or even a single bird. It was the kind of place you expected to see a ghost in broad daylight.

When I went off to an out-of-the-way place like that, I used to make a deal with the owner of "Tenjinya," a fish shop in Tsuchiura, to come where I was and buy my catch. He had a steam passenger launch, and he was always out on the lake. When I ran into him I'd tell him where I planned to go next time and for how long, and he'd show up on the appointed day for my catch. After he weighed it and paid me on the spot, I would be off someplace new.

One time I got into real trouble. A huge area of the lake in front of the naval air force base was off-limits to fishermen. That was where the navy practiced seaplane landings and takeoffs, so no fishing was allowed. But the fish were no fools—they knew damn well that that was a safety zone, so that's where they hung out. The water there was swarming with fish. We knew it because every so often somebody would sneak in and catch so many he could hardly lift the net out of the water.

I was determined to see for myself, so one night I rowed in. No sooner did I set to work than a patrol boat caught me red-handed. They locked me up overnight and interrogated me. "What the hell were you doing there?" "I didn't know it was off-limits." "Ha. All you fishermen know that much." "I didn't know where the boundary line was." "You seriously expect us to believe that?" And so on.

In the morning a soldier came into my cell and made me swear I'd never go back there. After that a noncommissioned officer ordered me released, and I was finally free to go. I couldn't beat the navy.

Women's Work

Susumu: By the way, I want you to know what a hard-working woman I'm married to. My fortunes looked up the day we were married. She used to stay up all hours weaving straw into mats and bags. Everything today is cardboard or plastic, but in the old days straw bags called *kamasu* were a necessity for shipping. You could pack anything in them: dried sardines, fertilizer, potatoes, charcoal, grain, whatever you wanted. City folks would come and buy them up, so village women earned good hard cash making and selling them.

Ii: I had a foot-powered loom that I could use to make four or five mats a night. They were used for drying food on, or in place of tatami.

Susumu: In the winter when there was no farming to do, she'd make fifteen in the daytime too.

Ii: That's right. Fifteen in the daytime and another five at night. When they were done I'd leave them out to dry in the sun for a couple of days. Often I'd sew them back to back to make bags.

Susumu: She worked her heart out. She had no leggings or warm clothes then either, just a thin kimono. Night after night she worked barefoot in an unheated shed. No wonder it affected her health.

Ii: Sitting in that cold room working the loom all day and on into the night gave me neuralgia and a bad heart. I also had a constant cough from breathing in particles of straw.

Susumu: In our village, once a wife sat down to the loom, she wasn't supposed to get up unless she had to pee. That's the way it was. There was no room for lallygagging. Competition was fierce.

Ii: It was. The mothers-in-law would get together and compare notes about how many *kamasu* their daughters-in-law made each day. "Ours made twenty." "Oh? Well, ours made twenty-one." They liked to brag—and if the son's wife next door was making more, look out! The only thing to do was get up earlier and work harder. The wives were all trying to outdo each other.

Susumu: She'd go in the shed and shut the door so no one could see in or hear. You couldn't have the clatter of the loom giving the neighbor's wife ideas, getting her to work all night to get ahead, so you had to make as little sound as possible. Next morning she'd be up before the neighbor's wife and sit right back down at the loom, without even attending to her face or hair. To help out, I'd sit down next to her and hand her straw. Wives didn't even want to take the time out to eat. They were barefoot all year, even in winter, so their feet were like lumps of ice, but they couldn't stop to warm themselves at the fire. The mother-in-law kept strict watch. So they just plugged away from morning till night.

Ii: We surely did. After the war the agricultural cooperative assigned inspectors to rate your work, so the competition heated up even more. If the neighbor's wife brought 200 or 250 mats into the office for inspection, and you showed up with only 100 or 150, it was humiliating.

Susumu: She and my younger sister together could weave four or five hundred bags a week.

Ii: Black-market traders liked them and came to buy them, so we made good money.

Susumu: In between weaving she helped with the fishing too.

Ii: Oh, I did everything, even rowing and hauling nets. He couldn't fish for gobies alone, so I had to help.

Susumu: It wasn't only goby fishing. We did *watari* fishing together too, roaming all over the lake for weeks at a time, crammed into a tiny boat. Looking back, I don't know how she stood it.

Ii: I went even when I was expecting. I remember we were near Tsuchiura one time and we passed a covered boat with geisha on board; you could hear the shamisen music and the women's laughter. I just watched it go by. There I was, pregnant and operating a winch, which was hard labor.

Susumu: Back then, if a woman said she wasn't going to help with the fishing

because she was pregnant, she'd have gotten knocked across the room. A fisherman's wife had to start work before dawn and keep going till she was ready to collapse at night. Townspeople couldn't have imagined what a tough life it was.

Ii: I went for firewood to Nakadai. That was four miles either way. I don't know how many times I made that trip when I was pregnant, carrying back a huge load of firewood on my back.

Susumu: Nobody ever worked as hard as my wife did. I mean that. She's what kept this family going. Of course, our son helped out on the boat from the time he was little. I taught him the ropes myself—gave him a good knuckling if he didn't do as he was told. Everybody had to work, kids too. He'd go to school in the day and come fishing with me at night.

Father and Son

Susumu: I'll never forget one thing that happened. He and I rowed out to Shitozaki to do some fishing one night. We hoisted the sail and lowered the net, but the boy fumbled and got a corner of the sail wet. I was so steamed I cracked him over the head with a broom handle. We went on with the night's work, and pretty soon the sky grew lighter. It was a beautiful morning. The eastern sky was red, with mist trailing over the water. I started to get sleepy, so I rubbed my eyes and checked the sail again. Then I saw my son sitting under it, his head and his whole face bright crimson. Turned out when I whacked him with the broom handle, I'd cracked his head wide open—and we'd gone on fishing all night like nothing was wrong. Now in the morning light I saw he was drenched in blood.

One look had me terrified. I rowed home as fast as I could and brought him in the house. Then I got down on my hands and knees in front of my wife and my mother, put my forehead to the floor, and apologized. That was the first and only time in my life I ever bowed down to my wife. I told her what I'd done and begged her to forgive me. She told me to get off the floor and take the boy to a doctor. I was ready to, when he spoke up. "I'm not goin' to any doctor," he said, glaring at me. That threw me. I tried to convince him, but he wouldn't listen.

We had to do something, so we decided we'd at least give him first aid. The two women went to town and bought some disinfectant, got him cleaned up, and wrapped a white bandage around his head. They fixed him right up. Little by little the gash closed up, and finally it mended.

The boy's like me, stubborn and tough as they come. You see, I wasn't just being mean. For him to make it as a fisherman, I knew he had to have guts. I wanted him to be strong, a survivor. On cold winter nights a fisherman's got nothing to keep him going but know-how and sheer grit. It's no life for a sissy. I wanted the best for my son—I wanted him to be a man, and that's why I used to be hard on him, but that one time I went too far.

Ii: My husband is a tough-minded man, but he was shedding tears as he mopped up our son's blood. "Forgive me, forgive me," he said over and over. He was truly alarmed. He's got a soft side, you see.

Angling for Eels
Side by Side

Mr. Midori Nemoto (1932–)
Mrs. Toshiko Nemoto (1938–)

Midori: Eel season runs from the end of March through June. We used to catch them by trolling with a long line we call a *naado* that was about 330 feet long. Before the war it was made of cotton and afterwards of nylon. We'd bait it at intervals of a fathom or two, so there'd be forty or fifty hooks on a line. In spring we used earthworms, in summer shrimp or smelt, and in the fall earthworms again.

Toshiko: I liked trolling for eels. It was great fun. There's nothing better than reeling in your line and finding an eel on every hook.

Midori: That line was so long, you had to be careful or it would get in a hopeless snarl. I'd take the oar and control the movement of the boat while she reeled in the line and coiled it in a bamboo basket lined with straw. When she came to an eel, she'd slip it off the hook and then go to the next one.

The straw rope lay coiled inside a flat basket that was about a foot and a half across; the rope was about the thickness of a man's forefinger. The fishhooks would fasten into the straw as she reeled in the line. You had to lay in thirty or forty of those ropes, and some people had as many as a hundred.

Toshiko: What made it hard was we weren't the only ones trolling. There'd be a crowd of fishermen, each with dozens of lines in the water that were forever getting tangled.

Midori: Yes, it was maddening. You'd mark your lines with a special color at the base of the hooks, but they'd get mixed up anyway.

Toshiko: Suppose somebody else got up early, went out fishing before us and got his line tangled with ours. What would he do? He'd reel in, cut the lines, and help himself to our catch. You had to get up early and scoot out to the fishing grounds as fast as you could to keep that from happening.

Midori: We had our troubles, but by and large we did all right. I'd say we never got less than a hundred eels.

Toshiko: You could feel them tugging on the line. It was a wonderful sensation. Only someone who's ever done it would know what I'm talking about.

Midori: To fishing folk, that sensation is what makes life worth living. It makes you feel so good, it's addicting. But she had a tough time at first, when she was still new to the life.

Toshiko: I know I did. Sometimes I had no idea where my line was going. The eels would thrash and jerk the line all around, and I'd be sitting down in the boat so I couldn't see much of anything. He'd be standing in the stern with the oar, rowing, so he had a good view of which way the line was going, but I didn't—and with other people's lines all around, it didn't take long before there was a snarl.

Midori: When that happened, usually you'd separate the lines carefully, but sometimes you couldn't. Then you'd cut your line free, tie the two ends back together, and put the other line back in the water. Sometimes five or six would get mixed up at one time. That was a nightmare. Someone with no conscience would separate only his own line—cut all the others, tie them in a knot, and throw them back in the water. Then there was no way to tell which one was yours. You had to reel them all in, look for any fish-hooks with your color, and work your line free. It was a terrible headache.

Toshiko: Yes, but tying the loose ends together was at least some help. What was worse was the people who'd leave only their own line in one piece, cut off all the rest and just throw them away. You'd reel in your line and come up short, with no way to tell where the rest of it had gone. When that happened we used a little anchor called an *uzu*: you'd throw that into the water, and if the missing line was there, you could snag it and raise it to the surface. You couldn't see a thing in the deep water, but my husband knew where to throw the *uzu* every time. The line was invisible, but when we pulled in the *uzu* there it would be, like magic. It never failed to impress me.

Midori: I had an instinct, I guess. Had to, to keep going.

Toshiko: Getting your line cut happened fairly often—maybe once every five or six trips. People often have an impression that fishermen lead easy lives, but that's a big mistake. To most people the lake appears calm and peaceful, but to anyone trolling for a living, it's full of hooks. There were lines everywhere—by Tsuchiura, off Ushiwata, in Yogo Bay, up by Takahama— everywhere you went the water was full of hooks and lines. If every fisherman had 30 lines, and each one was 330 feet long, that's half a mile. Make it a hundred fishermen, and you're talking 50 miles of line.

Midori: The more lines you were operating at once, the harder it was, and the more skill it took.

Learning to Fish

Toshiko: Early in the morning, before dawn, we'd set off to find the lines we'd put out the night before. I'd put a float in the water to mark the spot, and then start reeling in.

My folks weren't fishers, so it was all new to me in the beginning. I used to get yelled at for every little thing I did. And I got seasick too. My job had me sitting down all the time, looking at the water. But the water was always changing, always catching the sun, never the same for two minutes. Staring at it, I would forget where I was and what I was doing, and start to feel dizzy. Next thing you know, I'd be sick to my stomach. Before I'd gotten the line half reeled in, I'd have to go back to shore. I don't know how many times that happened.

Midori: At first you didn't have the stomach for it. You'd be shaky on your feet when we got home.

Toshiko: I can smile about it, remembering it now. Your mother, by the way, was one of the best eel fishers around. Baiting hooks was woman's work. It needed skill, not strength, so even older women could do it.

A good worker could wrap up the morning's work and be back for breakfast, but a slow person might take till after ten a.m. As soon as you got back it was time to take the eels to market, then go reel your lines for the next day. That meant neatly rewinding all those miles of barbed fishing line. Dozens of lines had to be gotten ready. That was a painstaking job, and it took time. Everybody in the house had to pitch in and help, old and young, or the lines wouldn't be ready in time. It took a lot of hands to get the work done, so people with small families used to hire workers to help them.

Midori: When the lines were ready you'd take them straight to the boat, load them on, and go off to set them in the water. By then it was late at night. It didn't matter if it was raining or stormy, you still went. It pretty much took a typhoon to keep us home.

Willow-Worms

Midori: One thing I remember is using willow-worms for bait. Usually we used earthworms or shrimp, but before I was married we often used willow-worms, which were a kind of insect that nested in willow trees. They were reddish in color, an inch long and a little thicker than an earthworm. Eels loved them, and when we used them for bait we always had a big catch. Willow-worms were in great demand among eel fishermen; people would go out looking for willow trees along the banks to chop off their branches. You could tell the branches that had the worms because they'd be covered with holes, with wood shavings or droppings nearby. When you found a branch like that, you'd cut it off and chop it into lengths of two feet or so. There'd be any-where from fifty to a hundred of the worms inside each one. We'd make a

Canal lined with willows

bundle of willow branches, take them home, and use the worms for bait.

The eels liked them, but they had a terrible smell. They really stunk to high heaven. You could tell which houses used those worms for bait just by passing the front door and getting a whiff. An ordinary person could never even drink a cup of tea in a house like that. Fishermen got used to it, though, and never even noticed any smell. They'd handle those worms and then eat rice-balls without washing their hands, and never think anything of it.

I used them too, but eventually all the willow trees got stripped and there weren't any more. A bunch of us would go off to the River Tone or the River Kokai in Chiba to look for willow branches. We went to the Iruma in Saitama too. If anybody caught us chopping off branches we'd have been in trouble, so we used to go in the daytime and innocently look around, then sneak back after dark to get the branches with worms. It was harder than you might think because the riverbeds were pitch-black at night, and you could easily get turned around and lose your bearings. We used to tie towels to trees in the daytime as a signal to help us find them again at night. The trees didn't belong to anybody so we weren't really stealing, but since we weren't from around there we had to be careful.

Little by little we'd go farther and farther from home on these jaunts; finally we went all the way to the Shinano and the Agano rivers in Niigata Prefecture. That was June 1959. Four or five of us took the noon local train from Ueno Station. We were all carrying saws and hatchets and gunnysacks. We got off at a likely-looking station in Niigata and then took a bus. We had no map or anything, we were just following our noses. We asked the bus driver if he knew of any riverbanks with willow trees growing on them, and he made a suggestion of where to look. We thanked him, got off the bus, and walked off to see what we could find.

The biggest problem we had was communication. We talked the country dialect of Ibaraki, and those people spoke Niigata dialect. Neither of us could understand a word the other said. We could manage with the bus driver fairly well, but if we ever talked to people walking down the road, we couldn't tell what the hell they were saying. You can travel all over Japan now and make yourself understood with no trouble, but back then people from Ibaraki and people from Niigata might as well have been from different worlds.

Our other big problem was finding a place to sleep. After dark we came on a cheap lodging house and went in, lugging our hatchets and all, but the master took one look and refused to let us stay. We must have looked pretty suspicious. He was terrified. We did our best to explain, but then he couldn't understand a word we said. We didn't do much better trying to understand him either. It was a real dilemma. We had to use gestures and charades to get our meaning across, and finally he relented and let us stay. A bunch of other fishermen traveling separately from us had the same sorts of problems.

We fastened together the branches we'd cut, crated them up, took them to the station and shipped them home. We spent days tramping around like that. One time, near the River Agano, the bus driver warned us to stay away from the river because some terrible disease was going around. He didn't know the name of it, but he said it was bad. We were scared, but not enough to stay away. Fortunately nothing happened to us, but it wasn't long after that that the scandal broke about *itai-itai* disease.[2] The bus driver must have known something.

Nobody used willow-worms after about 1960. It was too expensive and too much trouble to go after them anymore. Then the eel population gradually fell off too, so that ended that.

Fishing for Shrimp

Mrs. Ryu Kaito (1899–1987)

I was born in a lakeside village called Sekigawa, where there weren't any fishermen. Before I was married I never set foot on a boat, but once I was married to a fisherman I had no choice: I got to know boats, and I learned to fish.

I specialized in shrimp fishing. We had rice paddies to look after, and shrimp fishing fitted in best with rice farming, so that's all I did. I had a thousand traps in all. That seems like a lot, but you weren't be taken seriously as a fisher unless you worked that many.

We used to row all the way across the lake and back, which was very demanding. In the beginning I had no idea what I was doing; I used to make the boat go round and round in circles. It was the same with all the girls from out of town who married into local fishing families: their husbands would always yell, "What's the matter with you? Can't you row in a straight line?" Keeping at it every day, though, it wasn't long before you picked up the knack.

But as I was saying, rowing across Lake Kasumigaura was a huge undertaking. There were waves as big as a house out there. And when the wind was up, look out! Unless you were a big, strong man rowing as if your life depended on it, you'd never get anywhere. There was a saying: "Enough wind on shore to ruffle three strands of a woman's hair means you'd better stay away from the center of the lake."

Why did we go so far? Because the fishing was so much better over there. There were too many others fishing our side of the lake. One time our luck was so terrible that we decided on the spur of the moment to try the other side, and that's when we realized there weren't many shrimp trappers over there. The shrimp we caught were big, and there were lots of them. They were lovely. From then on we went back again and again.

Of course, you couldn't go and come back the same day. It took hours just to get there, so we'd sleep in the boat under a makeshift roof, on bedding laid over straw. In the daytime we caught shrimp and cooked meals over a fire. If

you kept all your cooking things right on board, you could live on the boat for a week or ten days at a time.

We sold our catches to a dealer on the island of Ukishima. They took good care of us there.

When we went shrimp fishing by Ukishima, we'd take our bait with us. At home, by Tsuchiura, we used fish bones and guts, but when we crossed the lake we took dried pond smelt. We'd make stock with that, mix in rice, cook the mixture down till it was soft as a *mochi* rice cake, then stuff it in tubes made of straw. When we brought up the shrimp traps, we'd take out the empty bait tubes and put in new ones. It wasn't easy. The tubes had to be dry, so one set wasn't enough; after one use, they had to be left out to dry for a day or two. We would need extras if it rained, so we took along three or four sets. That's three or four thousand in all!

Not many fishers around Ukishima used traps. Mostly they fished by sailing trawlnet. When their boats came drifting toward us in the wind, it was terrifying. The fishermen would row into the wind as far as Ushiwata or Shitozaki, put up their sails, and then let the wind blow them right back toward us. It scared me to death. The boats were huge; one of those sails alone was many times bigger than a house. Imagine having ten or twenty of those coming right at you! I used to be sure we were going to crash, but we never did.

We fished even in the rain. Oh, yes. We'd just throw on our straw raincoats and hats and carry right on. The raincoats kept the rain out, and so as long as there was no wind, you were snug and dry.

Making Traps

The best season for shrimp fishing is summer, July and August. By the end of October it's over. The shrimp get too cold to move and they won't go into the traps anymore, so we'd spend the winter months making traps instead. They had to be made of just the right bamboo. We bought up bamboo in large quantities, and we were very particular about it too.

Common *madake* bamboo was best. None of your fancy varieties. The bamboo needed to be as straight as possible, with long joints. There was a bamboo seller in Tsuchiura who knew what we liked and used to save it for us. We'd go over by boat to pick it up—two boats joined together usually, because if you piled it too high in one, you'd go under. We'd lash two boats side by side and bring them both back piled high with bamboo.

Then we would measure the bamboo off. Before we could cut it we needed to cool it and then dampen it. It had to be flexible and moist to whittle properly. When the traps were done, they were set out to dry, and then we women would sit and weave hemp-palm ropes. We couldn't just help ourselves to hemp palm growing in the mountains, mind you—we bought it from landowners with hemp palms on their property and paid a man to deliver it. Making the ropes was another hard chore.

Hemp-palm stalks are hard and leathery. We'd crush them and knead them, over and over, to loosen and separate the fibers. Then the individual fibers would be finely combed and processed in something like a thresher. After that, you were ready to start weaving your twine or rope.

If you had a thousand traps, about a third needed replacing every year. Whatever else you did, you had to make enough hemp rope for three hundred or more traps a year, which was a tall order. Also you had to make *michinawa*, the ropes that ran between the traps; the traps were laid out at twelve-foot intervals, so that's twelve thousand feet of rope. Plus you needed a thousand *chinawa*, thinner ropes that were attached to a cable; those were each three and a half feet long. The thicker ropes would last five or six years, but eventually they'd wear out too, little by little. A woman had to work on the ropes

Shrimp trap

every second she could find. There was such a lot of work to do! Clean the house, cook the meals, mind the children. On top of all that, mend the ropes. It was enough to make your head spin. The closer we got to shrimp season, the wilder things got. Making traps with nobody at home to help out meant no end of work.

Inside the Target Area

My parents-in-law died early, leaving just my husband Renji and me. We did all the work ourselves. What choice was there? Even after being out on the lake all day, you still had to get ready for the next day's work. That meant working late into the night, so that's what we did. There was hardly time to eat or sleep. There was nobody to bring us so much as a cup of hot tea. We had a thousand shrimp traps to see to between the two of us. We'd lay them out on the boat in order, in sets of one thousand, and when we came to the fishing grounds, I'd toss them in the water at regular intervals. I had to be careful or I'd get them out of order and destroy the pile. When it was time to bring them up again, Renji would haul them out of the water one at a time; I'd tap each one on the bottom to shake the shrimp out into a big basket. The basket had to be good and deep—the shrimp were so lively, they'd flip right back out otherwise. We used to catch such gorgeous shrimp that it was all worthwhile.

Back before the war, a naval air squadron was based near us, with a target practice area in the water between Kihara and Oyama. Bombers used to fly over it and drop dummy bombs for practice. The practice area was huge, and off-limits to fishermen. We had to lay our traps on the far side of it, and since we couldn't cut through we had to make a big detour around.

Once our friends the Yamanakas went over there by themselves, and Renji was just itching to follow them. The wind was coming from the northeast,

Lifting a basket full of shrimp

which wasn't right, so I tried to talk him out of it, but he wouldn't listen. In the end I gave up and went along. The wind got worse and worse, until we couldn't make any headway at all. I said, "Come on, let's turn back," but he kept right on rowing. Before we knew it we'd drifted inside the target area and couldn't get out. The boat was rocking violently and the traps were going every which way.

Renji said, "Look here, we'll have to dump them overboard for now and come back later." I knew he was right, so I agreed. Besides, if we were caught messing around in those forbidden waters there was no telling what might happen to us, so there was no time to argue. We went ahead and unloaded two hundred traps to lighten the boat, and headed for home. We figured on going back to retrieve them as soon as the wind died down, but it kept up for days, still from the northeast. Still, we couldn't abandon them there, so finally we went back despite the gale. We were really taking our lives in our hands, the wind was that fierce.

Conditions were so rough when we got there that Renji had to man the oar while I emptied the traps all by myself. The waves splashed right into the boat while I struggled, but what a surprise—every single trap was stuffed full of the most gigantic shrimps I ever saw in my life. I emptied the first set of traps into a big basket, and that was enough to fill it to overflowing. The shrimp started leaping out like crazy, swimming in the water that had washed on board. I've never seen anything like it, before or after. We lifted just half the traps that day and made our escape. When we went back later for the rest, they were just the same. That was a once-in-a-lifetime experience.

A Farming–Fishing Village

Mr. Yoshio Okubo (1899–1983)
Mrs. Ko Okubo (1903–)

Ko: We were married in 1922. There were only about twenty-five houses in the village of Ishida then, and today it's twenty-eight. In sixty years, the village has grown by all of three houses!

Yoshio: This never was an easy place to live. The land is so low, you can't really build more houses. It all used to be underwater—there's sand everywhere. Folks here have always been rice farmers who earned extra money fishing on the side. Pretty good money too. They'd go out and fish before breakfast, mostly. My grandfather liked to set traps for carp and crucian carp in the early spring, when they came to lay their eggs in the rushes.

Ko: Most people caught shrimp in bamboo cages.

Yoshio: That's right. You'd put the bait in the front part of the trap. A shrimp would go inside and eat it. Then other shrimp would come along and push the first ones deeper and deeper inside, till finally they couldn't get out. For bait we took fish heads and innards and left them in a barrel to spoil, then mixed that with rice powder and boiled it up. The smellier the better. That's the way the shrimp like it.

Ko: People whose main work was shrimp fishing made their own traps, but since we were rice farmers first and foremost, we had a man come up and make traps for us, to save time. He was from Kihara.

Yoshio: Yes, that's right.

Ko: We had a wooden storehouse by the gate where he lived while he worked for us. He liked it there so much he slept there even when he was working for other families in the village. We knew him for years.

Yoshio: Making traps wasn't easy, not even for a specialist like him. It took enormous time and trouble: first he'd split the bamboo, pare it down and dry it, then prepare the hemp fibers and weave them into cordage. Then he'd tie the bamboo pieces together and fashion a cage fitted with inserts. Even on his best days he couldn't have made more than twenty. He'd stay with us for two or three months at a stretch.

Ko: Whoever was hiring him at the time paid for his meals. He ate with us and used our bath too. He was like one of the family.

Yoshio: My grandfather was always the one who got up early and went after shrimp. When he died, my mother asked me if I'd keep his fishing equipment since she hated to throw it out. That's how I got started—I tried setting out the traps once just for the hell of it and caught so many I was hooked. I'd leave early in the morning and be back by seven or eight, so it never got in the way of the farming. There was a lot of rivalry, but I have to say we made good money off shrimp. I can remember in the 1930s taking my catch to the dealer and getting paid five yen. A small fortune.

Ko: But there was a saying: "A fisherman is half thief." So many times you'd go to bring in your catch—carp, especially, in the cold weather—and find that somebody else had gotten there first and sneaked off with all of it. It happened over and over. Some people were shameless.

Farming

Yoshio: We had a courier boat. A man named Sekozawa provided the service, and I don't know what we'd have done without it. We used it even for little errands that you'd hop on a bicycle to take care of now, but back then the roads were lousy. It took forever to go overland from Kidamari to Manabe, but the water route was much more direct. You could send freight too. That courier service was a godsend.

Ko: I remember the freight rate was five sen. You could ask him to do your shopping for you or help get the rice polished. We used to have that done in Tsuchiura; the boat would carry the rice to the mill for us and then bring it back when it was done.

Yoshio: Two houses in Ishida faced directly on the lake. One belonged to a dealer named Kichibei Hanari, and the other to Jirobei Takasaki. Hanari was a firewood dealer. He'd bring down a great big wagonload of wood from the mountains and dump it in a pile in front of his house, and women would bundle it up to be taken to Tokyo on a *takase* riverboat. When I was a kid, I'd climb up on the woodpiles, and old man Hanari would light into me. Besides selling firewood, he sold fertilizer. Around here they used "oil cakes" [the residue of soybeans after the oil is extracted]. He had them sent up from Choshi and put in his warehouse for storage. When farmers were ready to spread them in their fields, they'd come and load them in horse-drawn wagons.

Ko: Water caused us a lot of headaches. There never was a dry year. A little rain and the water would be up to our hips, or our waist. We had to bend down and grope underwater to harvest the rice. I did it every year, year in and year out, even when I was pregnant. Sometimes when people bent over to work all you could see was the crisscross of the cords tying back their long sleeves. As soon as the silkworms were finished in late fall, the rains would start up. The road by our house would be a sheet of water.

Yoshio: That's why families all had two boats, one for farming and the other for fishing.

Ko: People who weren't used to it would take sick. There were women from Kashima who came up to do seasonal work, and all sorts of men and women from around here too who used to come around begging for work. Those people would take sick with something called Weil's disease and die young.

It wasn't only the water that made life hard. Everything had to be done by hand. To get mulberry leaves for silkworms, you had to go off and pick them by hand, cram them into huge shoulder baskets, and spend half a day lugging them home. The basket would dig into your shoulders. You never went out walking without carrying some sort of load. If it rained, men used straw raincoats, and women wore *goza* [straw mats]. Think of that! After a while we got oxcarts, and that made life easier. That was around 1925. Until then, if you went anywhere, you walked. If I wanted to go back and visit my parents after I was married, I had to walk the eight miles, carrying one child piggyback and holding the others by the hand. On top of that we'd all be barefoot. Nobody thought anything of it, no matter how far you were going.

I have to say that Ishida folk were certainly hard workers. In May, when we were setting out the rice seedlings, we ate four meals a day: first at three a.m., when we got up, and again at ten a.m., after working all that time. Then we'd have something at three in the afternoon, and supper in the evening. We'd go to bed around ten or eleven at night. It was exhausting, but somehow we held up.

For the Love of Fishing

Mr. Kenji Sakurai (1939–)
(Son of Mr. Takamasa Sakurai)

I was crazy about fishing even before I started school. When I was four or five, I used to catch fish in flooded rice paddies for fun. Fishing was in my blood, and it still is. I make my living the same way I used to play, and you can't beat that. Of course I'm not saying a fisherman's life is all fun and games, but whatever happens, as long as you have Lake Kasumigaura you can keep on going, so you forget the bad times.

I couldn't really pin down in a few words what I loved about it so much, but I know this—as long as there was fishing to do, I had no time for schoolwork. From about second grade I was nuts about a kind of fishing we called *tsukushi*. The older boys would let me tag along. You'd get a four- or five-foot length of flexible bamboo and add a couple of feet of string with a curved hook at the end. When you were ready, you'd go out among the reeds and cut down an area about a yard square. When a fish was hooked, it put up a fight, and if you didn't cut down the reeds, your line would get tangled and the fish would get away. About five or six of us would go together and help each other out. If this was my spot, the other boys would pitch in and help me clear the reeds, and then we'd all go and do the same for whoever was next. We might clear ten or twenty places. Then you'd catch a live frog, impale it on your hook, and let it go. It would hop around all night with that hook stuck in its behind, and sooner or later a catfish or a *raigyo* [snakehead] would come along and snap it up. If you used a *raigyo* instead of a frog, you'd catch an eel. Just the thought of what might be on the line was so exciting I couldn't stay in bed in the morning. I'd be wild with curiosity. I'd close my eyes and see a catfish lunge for the frog and then swim off, pulling on the line. That was enough to lure me out of my bed before sunup. I'd sneak off and take a peek, and if there really was a big fish on the line, I'd jump for joy.

We did *tsukushi* from about June, when the reeds came up thick, till late fall. I'd keep it up till the water got so cold my feet turned bright red and lost all feeling. At school, I'd dream about fish and never pay attention. Back then, when it rained hard, fish would go right into the paddies and swim around on their sides, splashing, and it was a treat to catch them. The minute school was out I'd tear off to catch myself some.

Fishing at Night

We'd go fishing at night too, with homemade torches on sticks to light the way. We dug up pine roots for the torches. The roots were lumps like petrified wood, with their own distinctive color, and we'd go off with harrows and hoes to dig them up. There was no petroleum back then, so we set great store by those lumps of resin. They were in such demand that even when I was a boy it was hard to find any. When you finally did find one, you'd bring it home, cut it into strips, fasten it with wire, and light it. When you carried your torch down the paths between the rice paddies, the light would flicker on the water and you could see right to the bottom, clear as a bell. If there was a carp sleeping there, you'd see it and spear it, or catch it in a pail. All the kids did it. They'd come from all over with fish baskets on their backs, swinging their lanterns in the dusk.

There used to be heavy rains every fall that flooded the paddies, and carp would go after the rice. They'd peck at the unhulled rice, nibble at it. My grandfather would see traces of pecking, and that told him where to set his nets.

I never lacked for spending money as a boy. I'd catch birds and sell them. I begged Grandpa to buy a net for me, and finally he did. I'd set it up at night and capture a lot of different kinds of birds. People came up from Tsuchiura to buy them. They went around on bicycles with baskets attached, buying rabbits and chickens from farmers, and they'd buy birds from me too. A sparrow was worth eight yen, a greenfinch, six. A thrush was fifteen yen, and a gray starling, ten. Mostly I caught sparrows and siskins, sometimes dozens at once.

I never got hundreds of yen, but sometimes I might earn an even hundred. So my pockets were always lined.

One thing I'll never forget is going off to catch elvers, or young eels. The littlest ones are called *shiroko*, and those an inch long or bigger are called *kuroko*. There was a short time, from 1958 to 1961, when they flourished in Lake Sotonakasaura—that's between Kasumigaura and Kitaura. It's a shallow lake, so Kasumigaura fishermen generally didn't go there. My father and I were about the only ones, and we got started by sheer chance.

In the winter of 1954, when I was a schoolboy of fourteen, I took some carp to Sawara to sell to a shopkeeper named Tomura. Motor-powered boats were still a novelty, but my father rigged one up, borrowing the motor from a farming vehicle, and it worked well. I got assigned to take the carp he and my grandfather had caught and sell them to the dealer in Sawara. Even with a motor, crossing the full length of the lake in midwinter was a tough job for a fourteen-year-old. My grandfather was against it, but I knew I could handle it, and my father never doubted I could, so Grandpa gave in. And off I went.

I'll never forget all the wild ducks I saw on that trip. The surface of the lake was black with them, and when they took off, the beating of their wings sounded like a big waterfall. There are still water birds on Lake Kasumigaura today, but there were hundreds of times more back then; nobody hunted them with guns, and they had a plentiful food supply. On my way back, I remember seeing Mount Tsukuba outlined against the sky, with the sunset staining the lake crimson, and hundreds upon hundreds of wild ducks swimming on the red water.

Anyway, from then on it was my job to cross the lake in my school uniform and sell the catch. One morning in Sawara a fisherman about twenty-five years old came up and asked where I was from. Ushiwata, I said. "Yeah? On

Dejima?" he said in a surprised kind of way. I said that's right, and he went on staring at me in disbelief. It stumped him that a kid like me would have come all that way by myself. His name was Hagiwara, it turned out, and he was a master fisher. Hagiwara and I got to be friends, and he told me a lot of things. He even told me how to catch elvers, which he had learned from a friend of his. He must have taken quite a shine to me.

To catch little eels you used a technique called *taguriami* ["draw-net"]. After what we were used to, it sounded like child's play. The net was a dozen yards long. You'd stretch it out straight and attach twenty-gallon barrels to it as floats, with the belly of the net in the center. You'd attach ropes to either end of the net and pull. The boat is at anchor, so pulling on the ropes draws the net in. In some places where the water was shallow it would be like scooping the eels up from the lake bed. I told my father about it, and he was game, so one spring day we packed a few days' worth of food and some equipment, and set off to catch elvers. We'd sleep right on the boat, of course.

We did everything by the book, but the net came up empty. We did it again, with no better luck. And again—still nothing. What could be wrong? Maybe there just weren't any left, I thought, but my father said that didn't stand to reason. Fishermen wouldn't come all the way from Hasaki if that was true. "I'm not giving up," he said. "I'll figure it out if it's the last thing I do. We'll keep watch together."

"For what?" I asked.

"For Hasaki fishermen."

"What'll I do if I see them?"

"Never mind, just keep your eyes peeled."

I did, but nobody came. I started losing interest as the sun went down and night came on. It was a glorious starry sky. In the old days there weren't so many lights at night, and it really got pitch-dark. Finally I couldn't see where

the land left off and the lake began. It seemed pointless to hang around anymore, but my father never budged, so I stayed put—and little by little my eyes
got used to the dark. I guess the human eye is a little like a cat's. After a while
I could see starlight reflected off the waves; the land was ink-black, the water
grayish, with silver glints coming off the waves. The dancing motion of the
waves started making me sleepy. Then my father whispered, "They're here."

"Where?"

"Over there."

I couldn't see anything.

"Are you blind?" he said. "Open your eyes. They're skulking by the edge of
the water."

I still couldn't see anything, but I wasn't going to admit it. I kept staring
and sure enough, after a minute I could see a flat-prowed boat hugging the
shore, inching our way. Boats on Lake Kasumigaura had a high prow because
of the big waves, but boats on the River Tone were flatter.

They stopped and let down a net. We moved in for a better look, and
apparently they saw us, because they pulled up their net and hightailed it out
of there. For some reason they didn't want us watching. Maybe they mistook
us for local fishermen protecting our territory. That didn't figure, though.
They were so hush-hush that we guessed it must be something else. My father
had a hunch it was money—they were raking in a bundle and didn't want anyone else finding out about their cash cow. In that case, they'd never tell us
their tricks. We'd just have to steal them.

One thing we'd figured out already: you couldn't catch elvers even in the
moonlight, let alone in the daytime. Second, the tide had to be moving out,
since that was when the *iba* would come crawling out of the sand. The *iba* was
a water bug the elvers liked for dinner, that looked just like a centipede. As
soon as the *iba* appeared, elvers gathered to eat them. There were freshwater

mussels galore in the water there, but they were dying off in large numbers because of the higher salt content of the water, and the elvers fed on their remains too. The salt content had gone way down for a while, due to a buildup of sand at the estuary of the River Tone, but around 1960 they started to remove the sand, so at high tide the briny seawater could come in, and the salt content of the lake suddenly went back up. That was too much for the freshwater mussels, and they started to die off. I can remember how salty the water got; you couldn't drink it or cook rice in it. I'm no marine biologist so I can't explain it in detail, but the upshot was that the bottom of Lake Sotonasakaura was thick with mussels, and when they all died, the elvers gorged themselves.

After seeing the Hasaki fishermen in the dark that night, my father figured out what to do. The next night that there was no moon, he put out his net. The result was staggering. The net sagged with the weight of the catch. We caught enough that one night to fill a round basket two feet across. We were ecstatic, I tell you. My father was beaming. I'll never forget the weight of that catch. In the morning we sold it for a fantastic price—ten thousand yen for every eight pounds. In all we made forty thousand yen. That's more than a hundred thousand yen in three days! It was mind-boggling. The average monthly salary for a new employee of the municipal government at the time was probably around eight thousand. That explained why the Hasaki fishermen had been so hush-hush.

Well, after that we hardly did anything else. Our catch wasn't always so enormous, but it was still miles ahead of what we would have landed in Lake Kasumigaura. The other fishermen caught on eventually too, heating up the competition. One fellow earned three million yen in a month and built himself a new home. He should have called it Eel Palace.

There are no more *kuroko*, but you can get a good price for the littler ones, the *shiroko*. This year [1995] I heard two pounds fetched a million yen. That's a bit unusual, but ordinarily you can get three hundred to four hundred thousand. That's because the only way to raise eels is to catch natural elvers and nurture them—they can't be bred in captivity. So even today eels are worth their weight in gold. If we'd been able to go on catching *kuroko* at the same rate in Lake Sotonakasaura, it would have been fantastic, but after three years the eel population there dropped way down.

Underwater Gear and Gambling

After the eels, we caught carp. Put on diving gear and went after them underwater in the winter. The rest of the time my grandfather Gentaro and my father Takamasa caught carp in nets, but in winter you can't do that. We used to catch them in corrals; we'd sink a pine frame into the water, and when the water got cold they'd go in there to hibernate. We would set a net around the corral and stir it up with a stick to make them jump out in surprise, and catch them that way. But I always had a sneaking suspicion that they might be hibernating in other places too.

Then one day I read in the newspaper about a fellow named Tadashi Osawa who caught carp with his bare hands at a weir in Suikaido. What a character he must be, I thought, and I decided to get on my motorbike and go talk to him. The roads were horrible, bumpy and full of dust, but finally I found his place—a tiny little shack by the River Kokai.

I yelled a hello, and he came out to meet me—a small man with fair skin. You'd never know from the look of him that he was a professional gambler as well as a carp fisherman. He was as nice as could be to me, even though I showed up without any notice like that. I was maybe eighteen, and he must have been about thirty.

There were two young women in the house with him—one was his wife and the other his mistress, I heard later. They all lived together under the same roof. He had two cute little kids, a girl and a boy; I remember being surprised to see them gambling to see which of them would get what school supplies.

After I visited Tadashi a man came up to me and wanted to know what my business had been with him, where I was from, and so on. I had nothing to hide, so I told him everything. I asked Tadashi about it later and he said, "That's a detective." He liked getting the villagers together to gamble now and then, so the cops kept an eye on him. When I told Tadashi I'd come all the way from Lake Kasumigaura to find out how he caught carp with his bare hands, and to see him do it if possible, he was flabbergasted. He quickly agreed to show me. He put on diving gear and went underwater. While he was diving, his wife and his mistress together worked the pump to send him oxygen.

They improved the river there later, and now it's a famous spot for cherry blossoms, but at the time the weir was supported with a pine lattice and the carp would go in there to hibernate. Tadashi just reached in with his hands and grabbed a big one. He brought it up to show me and I thought, "Well, I'll be damned. He really does it!"

I couldn't wait to have a go myself. I borrowed his diving gear, which he was nice enough to let me do, took it home and tried it out. Nobody had ever done such a thing in Lake Kasumigaura before, so about ten fishermen came along to watch. I decided to dive around the big rock where Catfish Kyubei used to go.

I carefully climbed down a ladder into the water, listening to the rush of the oxygen in my helmet and sending up bubbles with every breath. The water was so clear, I could see dozens of feet ahead. There were the rocks—I go up close and what do I find? The spaces between them were crammed with hibernating carp. Not just hundreds—thousands! They looked nothing like carp usually did. They were pressed together in every conceivable position, including upside down and sideways. I never saw anything like it. I only wish I could have taken a photograph.

The water was freezing cold, so I put on work gloves. I held the net in my left hand and grabbed carp with my right hand and put them in the net one after another. I could fit in about ten at a time. They put up no fight whatsoever. I pressed them carefully into the net and when it was full I took it up to the boat and emptied it, then went back down for more. I caught more carp than I had ever seen in one place before. It was like a dream.

Tadashi had warned me that once I started catching them, I had to keep going or they'd get away. I kept on as long as I could, but after a while my hands were so numb with cold I could barely move them. I decided to take a break and warm myself up on the boat. Instant ramen had just come out, and I heated some up and ate it. It was delicious, and the hot broth revived me. After that I was ready for another go-round, but when I went back down, sure enough, every single fish was gone. There'd been thousands, maybe tens of thousands, and not one was left. It was as if someone had come along with a giant broom and swept them out. Tadashi had certainly been right.

I suspect the fish could sense the difference in temperature. When I came back warmed up, they knew it, and headed for the hills. I was impressed with what I'd seen, though, and decided to buy my own set of equipment. Tadashi helped me go to Yokohama and get everything I needed. After that, I went diving in lots of other likely spots, but I never had the same luck. I did find pockets of carp, but nothing to compare with that first time.

That was one reason I gave it up—the results weren't all I'd hoped for. Another reason was that I got symptoms of the bends. Even though I never dived very deep, afterwards when I got on my bike my sense of direction would be haywire. I'd think I was going in a straight line and veer off into a rice paddy instead. That happened many times. Also I felt tired and listless,

Pearl oysters

not myself. At one point I realized I was damaging my health, so I quit.

There was another reason too—pearl oysters. Around 1962 their price went sky-high, sparking a kind of gold rush. Fortune-hunters scraped the lake bottom with heavy nets and stirred it up, catching so many pearl oysters the boats rode low in the water. That was the end of the old ways of fishing. The breeding grounds of carp and other fish were forever destroyed. The fish wouldn't even go near the rocks anymore, since those were raked over too. That marked the end of an era.

Generations of Fishermen

My boy is going to follow in my footsteps, so that's five generations of fishers in one family. It makes me happy to think we've been able to stay here so long, making our living from Lake Kasumigaura, getting along with nature. It's a great life. I ship carp from here all over Japan now. As long as this lake goes on, it'll support the lives of fishermen like us.

My father died last year at age eighty-eight, after a lifetime on the lake. He was a hero to me. They were all heroes, the old-time fishermen. They fished this lake up and down with sailing trawlnets and no motors. The only one left now who actually remembers what fishing was like back then is my neighbor, Susumu Fujii. He's a superman. A true champion.

Trawling wasn't the only kind of fishing done on the lake, of course. People used an endless array of fishing styles. The sailing trawlnets became the most famous because the sails on the water were so beautiful, but it was one hell of a tough job. I tried it, and my hands nearly froze. You had to row into the wind, which is extremely difficult to do, and you had to go all night without any sleep. When you finished work at dawn, your arms ached so much you could hardly pull on the ropes. Your body felt swollen from lack of sleep and heavy labor. Men like my father and Mr. Fujii had iron constitutions—they did that work for dozens of years, hardening their bodies. That's why my father was able to die sitting up. His life was different from other people's, and so was his death.

That morning, he got up the same as usual. At noon when my wife called him there was no answer, so she went to check on him and found him leaning back in his chair with his hands folded in his lap, his head a little to one side, his eyes closed. His body was still warm, but he had stopped breathing. He was sitting straight up. It still seems amazing. What a way for a man to meet his death.

3

VILLAGE LIFE

When There Were Tangerines in Hajiyama

Mrs. Kaoru Yokote (1890–1980)

I was born in a little town called Hajiyama, on the Tsuchiura side of the lake, by Yogo Bay. That area's been reclaimed—it's all rice paddies now, they say—but it used to be a quiet, lovely inlet. We lived up on a mountain that stuck up like a fist over the bay, so the view was wonderful. On a misty day the world would be white below you, as the mountain rose above the clouds. I used to imagine I lived in the legendary Dragon Palace under the sea.

The morning sun would shine on the blue water and make it sparkle, and that was beautiful too. By the end of the bay was a sandbar covered with reeds. The sunlight would hit there first and gradually work its way up. You could see all the boats on the water, going to and from Tokyo or swinging into the bay. Their shadows would be ink-black, the water around them a sheet of silver with rippling waves. It looked just like an angel's robe fluttering in the wind.

Sunsets were spectacular, the colors reflected in layer after layer on the water. Silhouetted against the sky there'd be the smokestack of the soy sauce factory on Pigeon Point and a scattering of houses with thatched roofs. It was so quiet you could almost hear the voices of fishermen on the far shore. Little by little, the sun would drop lower in the sky. As a girl, I used to feel so sorry to see it go that I'd sneak out when nobody was looking, climb up on a stack of firewood, and sing to the sun while I watched it go down.

There were always huge piles of firewood sitting waiting to be shipped out. Dealers would bargain with landowners until they agreed on a price, and then woodcutters would go out in the hills and spend all day chopping wood. Younger sons of farming families generally did that for a living, because they had no land of their own.

Anyway, they'd leave bundles of chopped wood here and there in the mountains, and packhorse-men would go around and load those on horseback and bring them to the dealer's. Then a clerk would come out and count them off in a ringing voice. I can hear it now: "*Hito hito hito, futa futa futa ...*"

And so on, all the way to ten, which he'd call out even louder: "*TO-YO!*" Then an apprentice beside him would hold up a card, and the clerk would start over again. Every time he came to "*TO-YO,*" the boy would hold up another card. The sound carried to every corner of the village, and we children would imitate it as we played: "*Hito hito hito, futa futa futa ... TO-YO!*" The clerk had to keep an eagle eye on things to keep his boss from getting cheated, you see. He had to keep a strict tally and write it all down in the books.

After that, women workers would retie all the bundles and pile them up in great big stacks higher than the shed. When a *takase* boat came in, the women would load the firewood on board, and off it went to Tokyo.

The captains and the boatmen all wore towels tied around their heads, and loincloths under bright padded *dotera* jackets. They talked in loud voices and kind of swaggered around. We children went to gape at them when they came in. None of us had ever been anywhere, and since they went back and forth to Tokyo all the time, they seemed awfully big and important.

There were only seventeen houses in Hajiyama, but in the mountains nearby we had two shrines and a temple. When the boatmen finished their work, they'd go there to pay their respects. It always gave me the strangest sensation to see those rough men in their loud *dotera* praying with deep devotion.

I came to Tsuchiura as a bride of twenty-one, and that was the first time I ever set foot out of my hometown. Not that I minded much—it was the same for everyone, after all. Life in Hajiyama was slow and relaxed, and the scenery was beautiful. I'm eighty years old now. Looking back, I'd say my years in Hajiyama were the happiest of my life.

Tangerine Orchards

What I remember best are the tangerine orchards. They've vanished now, like

the smoke in the tale of Urashima Taro, but back then there were orchards on all the hills around Hajiyama. Fruit was hard to come by at that time, and our tangerines were popular. People came from all over to buy them. The mountains blocked the cold north wind, and to the south was the bay, so tangerines did well in the mild, moist climate. They were big and juicy, and the trees grew very tall. From below you could see their branches spread out against the sky, all over the mountain. In fall the fruit shone bright yellow. From a distance it looked like gold coins hanging on the branches. The boat captains used to say that when they entered the bay, they could look up and see the trees covered in gold coins.

At harvesttime we needed all the hands we could get. Young men from the greengrocers in Tsuchiura would come and stay for a week or so to help out. Instead of climbing up the trees to pick the fruit, they'd lean a ladder against the trunk and cut the branches off with shears. *Snip snip snip*, and down they crashed, each one with five or six tangerines attached. What fun that was! I remember running around the bottom of the trees till whoever was on the ladder yelled at me.

Tangerine branches piled up on the ground till there were so many you could hardly walk. The women would gather them up, spread them out on matting, and carefully remove the tangerines, one by one. Then they measured the fruit, packed it in sturdy bags made of straw matting, and shipped it off to the dealer in Tsuchiura by boat.

Below my house was the firewood dealer, Jizaemon Asano, and in front of his place was a big channel where a *takase* riverboat could come in. Big straw bags filled with tangerines would be loaded on deck by the hundreds, and then the captain would lift the plank and slip the moorings. All hands stood on deck and pushed off with poles, leaning into them from their shoulders with their full weight. The boat would move slowly away from the shore, as if it didn't want to go. The sight always made me somehow sad. I would stand alone on the bank and watch as the boat put up its white sail and went off, getting smaller and smaller until it disappeared.

Tsuchiura wasn't the only market for tangerines. Brokers transported them to Takahama by boat, then by wagon to other towns. So times were good. I was just a little girl and I didn't know the first thing about business, but I do remember hearing once that we'd made a hundred yen. That was a small fortune—enough to build a new house. My father's purse was always heavy, filled to bursting. Once I remember wheedling him for some pocket money. He grinned and said, "All right, kitten, here you go," and handed me his entire purse. I opened it up, looked inside, and there was more money than I could even count. I was floored. I certainly didn't have nerve enough to take it!

Playing in the Lake

We had great fun playing in the lake on summer days, naked as jaybirds and burned black by the sun. Our parents never worried about us, because they must have played the same way when they were little. One thing we always did was steal eggs from waterfowl. We'd wander out waist-deep in the reeds and find grebe nests everywhere, with darling little eggs inside. We never took them all; that would've been mean. I'd take half home, and Mother would boil them for me. Oh, they were so good.

There were moorhens too, pretty birds with black wings and a red beak. Their eggs were bigger, like chicken eggs, and delicious. Moorhens would play together in enormous flocks—not a few dozen birds, mind you, but hundreds, well over a thousand. When we kids came near they'd move off, and we'd chase them till they took to the air with a great whirring and beating of wings,

Sappabune among the duckweed

skimming low over the water like hydroplanes, hundreds and hundreds of them at a time.

In winter the water turned dark with wild geese and ducks. They flew straight in one line, like a piece of string pulled taut in the sky, or in a V shape or a double line. They always came, but I never did collect any of their eggs.

Believe it or not, there was a restaurant nearby, and people came from far and wide just to eat there. When he had a houseful of guests, the master would give us children money to gather mud-snails for him in the little streams nearby. We'd tuck up our kimonos and go out wading, and bring him back a big basketful. He was always pleased as punch. He'd give us each a sen and cook up mud-snails for his guests as a special treat.

"Bamboo-Leaf" Boats

All the rice farmers by Yogo Bay had little boats so small they were called *sappabune*, or "bamboo-leaf" boats. We used them to gather duckweed. The bottom of the bay was sandy, and fine duckweed grew there. Fishermen wanted the prawns and carp that hung about in the duckweed, but farmers used the plant as fertilizer. Nearly every morning we'd get up early and go out for some, using a long-handled tool with a blade like a big scythe at one end. The duckweed would wrap around the blade in a tangle. We loaded it onto the boat and took it back to shore, heaped it in wagons, and carted it to the fields, where we spread it out evenly. We did this nearly every day from June till September, when it was time to harvest the rice.

It was so nice being out on the lake in the early morning mist, with other boats drifting in and out of sight, and no sound but the splash of poles in the water. The duckweed clung together just like devoted couples. There's a well-known, ancient love poem:

Waterwheel

Even the seaweed
in Lake Nasaka in Hitachi
can be pulled apart
but nothing in this world
could separate you and me.

Waterwheels

Hajiyama was a very good place to live except for one thing: the rice paddies were awfully far away. They were across the mountains far to the west, and the only way to get there was to walk. It was hard getting water to the fields too, because they were up so high. Once—this was before my time—there was a terrible drought and the paddies were bone-dry. The rice crop was heading for disaster. The villagers got together and made a series of foot-powered waterwheels to transport water uphill, but it was an enormous job and the men were soon exhausted.

Then one of the wealthiest men in town, a firewood dealer, took a huge roll of money over to where the men were working, waved it at them, and told them he'd see they were all well paid if they saw the job through. "That's not all," he said. "I've got lots of bean-jam buns and white rice back at my place, so whenever you get hungry, come on over and help yourself!" That cheered the men up, and they set up twenty or thirty waterwheels in all and the rice was saved.

Here's how it worked: the first waterwheel was out in the channel in Lake Kasumigaura. When you pedaled it, it lifted water up about three feet. The next one would lift that same water three feet higher, and so on. Thirty, of course, raised it very high indeed. But people's legs wore out. They'd get tired, and the flow of water would slow to a trickle and stop. That's when the shop-

Tending silkworms

keeper walked around with his bagful of money, perking up everybody's spirits so they could keep on working till the paddies were flooded and everybody's crop was saved. He didn't do it just for his own selfish interest, you see. Nobody ever forgot what he did for the village. Anyway, that gives you some idea of how much money the firewood dealers had at their disposal.

Preparing for Marriage

Girls would begin preparing a marriage trousseau at age twelve or thirteen. It was the custom then for unmarried girls from reasonably well-off farming families to make all the kimonos they would need for the rest of their lives, whether cotton or silk. Suppose she wanted to get married at twenty. That didn't leave much time—there were so many kimonos to weave and sew before then!

You couldn't buy things easily then, either, the way you can today. You couldn't even buy ready-made thread. You had to make your own the hard way, breeding silkworms, gathering the cocoons and boiling them, and then reeling the silk by hand. There was a Mrs. Naganuma in Tsuchiura who gave lessons to young girls from miles around. Some of us walked hours to get to her house, carrying a lunch. I went when I was fourteen. There were five or six of us in her class, all of us farmers' daughters, taking the first steps in getting ready for marriage.

To make silk thread, first you'd set a cooking pot over a fire and boil the cocoons. Every girl had her own portable clay cooking stove and pot, and we'd each set our cocoons to boil. Then we'd extract the threads. It never went right at first. The cocoons would stick together, bobbing around in the boiling water, and you had to find the end of the thread in each one and lift it out with chopsticks. You'd try to retrieve five or six filaments at once and twist

Weaving

them together. At first you'd botch it, bunching them up so the thread came out uneven, some of it too thick and some too thin, instead of a nice even size. After a while you got the hang of it, though. I learned how to get just as many filaments as I wanted to stick together—six or eight or whatever—to make thread of just the right thickness. It took about a month to get the knack. After that, we each went back home and kept on reeling. Once you had enough silk thread, you sent it to be dyed, and when it came back, then you'd weave it on a loom.

The rattle of looms was everywhere. I can still hear it: *karakara patan, karakara patan.* People would listen and comment on how skillful so-and-so had gotten. All winter long you could hear that sound coming from houses where young girls lived.

A skillful weaver could finish one roll of cloth [about twelve yards] a day, although it took longer if you added a design. Generally, a girl with a practiced hand could start in the morning and be done by sundown. Then a *hiroiko* ["gatherer"] would come by. That was a person who walked from house to house, collecting orders for cloth to be dyed. She—usually it was an old woman—carried a basket on her back with samples in it, and the girl or her parents would look those over and pick one out they liked. Then the *hiroiko* would take the cloth back with her to be custom-dyed. Fine-quality silk was treated differently—it had to be sent off to Kyoto to be dyed properly. In all, a girl prepared three chests full of kimonos before she was married.

When I came to Tsuchiura as a bride, I stepped into a boat in front of my house that was loaded with three chests containing dress kimonos, a wedding kimono of soft, smooth, white habutae silk, everyday cotton kimonos, plain kimonos for my old age—basically everything I would need for a lifetime. I had dozens of undergarments and accessories too, of course.

On the boat I wore traveling clothes, and after reaching Tsuchiura I had my hair done up in the traditional *takashimada* style at the go-between's house. Then I put on a cotton headdress and changed into my pure white wedding kimono. You weren't supposed to take off the wedding headdress until you'd finished the ceremonial sips of saké with your new husband. You couldn't let him see you before then, either. That's the way folks did it in the old days, in the country anyway.

Soon after the wedding, the bride had to pay calls on all her new relatives. A couple of attendants carried a big lacquered box attached to a pole. You and your parents-in-law went on foot from door to door, and everywhere you stopped, you'd open up the box and take out a kimono and try it on, to show it off. When everyone was done admiring one, you'd take it off and put on another one. Then on to the next relative's house and start all over. Nobody has to do that anymore, which is a good thing. It used to be such a lot of trouble. It wasn't easy on the relatives, either, since they had to prepare special food and wait around for you to arrive.

I paid calls way off in the country too. It must have been five miles to Nakanuki. I walked all the way there and back, with my hair done up in a fancy style and the skirt of my kimono tucked up to keep it clean. I went to Oda as well, but that time I rode in a horse-drawn cart with its horn blaring. That's sixty, no, seventy years ago now. The landscape's all changed. Yogo Bay is no more, they tell me, though I've never set foot on the reclaimed land. When I close my eyes, all I see is clear, bright water.

A Family of Weavers and Dyers

Mr. Yoshimitsu Naruse (1903–1995)

My family lived originally in the town of Namegawa along the River Tone. We were weavers and dyers by trade, and had been for generations. River commerce flourished unbelievably in past centuries, and all sorts of cities and towns sprang up along the river, from Choshi in the east to Sawara, then Toride, all the way to Sekiyado. Namegawa was another such town, and apparently it was a thriving place full of fine homes and storehouses. But the opening of railroads [at the very end of the nineteenth century] dealt a fatal blow to water trade. Goods were all transported by rail after that, and shopkeepers along the river—dyers, rice merchants, innkeepers, what have you—couldn't make a go of it anymore. They virtually disappeared. Naturally, the towns fell into ruin. My father racked his brains over what to do and finally made up his mind to move to Shitozaki. He used to travel all over Ibaraki taking orders, so he had connections everywhere; he'd married a woman from the village of Anju in Inashiki County, so they knew the area extremely well—and at the time there were no weaving and dyeing factories along the shores of Lake Kasumigaura, so he figured the future looked bright. He made the move right at the turn of the century.

Dyeing and Weaving

Luckily for him, the area turned out to be one of the few regions in the country where sericulture was practiced. From the mid-nineteenth century farming families had raised mulberry leaves and fed them to silkworms that they bred at home for the sake of the cocoons. The best cocoons were sold to dealers, but when there was a great quantity, some would be inferior. These were called "waste-cocoons." They couldn't be sold, but many families would keep them and boil them to make their own silk thread. Dyers would dye the thread whatever color was wanted, but some of the bigger families would

Hiroiko

keep a vat of indigo in the dirt-floor entryway of their house and dye it themselves. They couldn't manage other, more complicated colors, though—for
those they turned to specialists like my father. Of course, rice farmers were
too busy to take time off to make their orders in person, so we employed a
number of women called *hiroiko* whose job it was to collect orders. We had five
working in Namegata alone, another two in Inashiki, and countless more in
Dejima, which was close to home.

Most of them were women past middle age. Often they did it to earn a little
extra spending money after their son took a wife, since they had less to do at
home then. They'd carry samples in a basket and go around from house to
house looking for business. We would dye whatever they brought back, according to the customer's specifications, and then the *hiroiko* would deliver the finished product and collect the payment for us. We always had a mountain of
thread waiting to be dyed. You could also have someone make thread for you;
one factory employed five or six girls to smoke waste-cocoons dry (till the silk-
worm larvae died, which took all day and all night), then boil them and reel the
silk.

The customers would use the thread to weave cloth. Today you have to go
pretty far to find a loom, but back then every house had one. When the fall
harvest was in, everywhere you went, you'd see young women sitting out on
the veranda working the loom. Again, for complicated patterns, or for special
occasions such as a wedding, when no one wanted to take a chance on damaging fine material, people would turn to a professional weaver. Most people
wove their own everyday clothes and had everything else made special. That's
where my family came in.

We handled fine silk fabrics like crepe, damask, and habutae silk. No one
else for miles around did that. We hired three factory girls and even put in a
jacquard machine, which back then was the last word in technology. We were

pretty famous. Five girls or so became live-in apprentices, and plenty of young men came by too, wanting to learn how to dye special patterns or colors. Men slept in the factory, women in the house. Just feeding everybody was a job. We always had two women as full-time cooks.

Itinerant Artisans

Artisans then were of a different stripe from those today. A cook could wrap one knife in a piece of bleached cotton, tie it around his middle, and wander up and down the country wherever his fancy took him. Dyers were the same. Many of them traveled all over, from one dyer's shop to another. "Mind if I come in?" they'd say, and then they'd tell you their name and ask if they could stay and work for you for a while. If you agreed, they might stay a couple of weeks and then disappear as suddenly as they came. Most of them never showed up again, but every so often one would find his way back a year or so later. No one had references. They came with the clothes on their back and nothing else. You had to be a quick judge of character. If you didn't like someone's looks, you'd hand him a bit of money for travel expenses and send him on his way.

Artisans were men of few wants. They certainly weren't out to make a fortune and buy themselves a house, for example. There's a saying that the true man of Edo won't hang onto his earnings overnight, and I can vouch that it's literally true. They were perfectly content living from day to day.

They had a strong sense of responsibility, though. If they botched a job they didn't need telling off—they'd quietly move on without waiting to be fired. They'd fire themselves, you might say, just up and disappear. Where they went or what they did after that we never knew, but I suppose they found work with some other dyer. Their names were outlandish. Somebody from Tochigi whose real name was Kumakichi, say, would be known as Tochikuma.

One fellow carried an *anpera* [rush-mat bed] to lie on when he slept outdoors, and he called himself Anpera Kin-chan. Mostly we didn't know their real names or where they were from.

One fellow I'll never forget was an artisan named Ide from Kagoshima. He went off to be a soldier in the Russo-Japanese War, leaving his wife and children behind, and while he was gone his entire family was wiped out in a volcanic eruption. He was the only one to survive. After that he lost the will to live and became a vagabond. Once, while he happened to be up in Tango, he saw someone weaving and decided to learn the trade. He settled down there for a while, but as soon as he'd mastered the skill he went back to being a drifter. One day, as he was walking along the shore of Lake Kasumigaura, he came to our shop, and he ended up staying on with us. Ide was even less money-minded than most. If you tried to pay him a salary, he'd turn it down flat. "All I need's tobacco money, that's plenty for me," he'd say. He was taciturn, and a hard worker. He always carried a photo of his dead wife and children, and every so often he'd take it out and look at it.

One day he vanished. We thought he was gone for good, but a year later he was back. To our astonishment, he told us he'd walked all the way to Kagoshima and back. When we marveled that he could travel so far without a penny to his name, he scoffed. "Who needs money?" he said. "If you get hungry enough, someone'll always give you something to eat—and besides, I had this."

In his basket was a complete barber's kit, with clippers, razor, and mirror. All he had to do was squat down in a village square with his barber tools on display, he said, and sooner or later a farmer would come along and pay to get a shave and a haircut. So he never starved. He said he had one close call, when he was eating in a bamboo grove and a bear came after his lunch. He set his rice ball down and told the bear casually, "Go on, help yourself. You want it? It's yours." But in the end the animal backed off without taking anything.

A man like that is close to God. He died of old age, during the Pacific War when all the men were off fighting and only four women were left in the factory. His last words were of his wife and children—he wanted their picture enshrined in the local temple. The power was out when he died, I remember; we washed his body with alcohol, groping in the dark, and held his wake by candlelight.

After the war the weaving and dyeing business dried up. It was probably at its height around 1920. We depended on business from farmers, so when they stopped raising silkworms, that was that. My mother's generation was the last generation of women who all weaved at home—that would be women who were born in the middle of the nineteenth century. Anyone born in the twentieth century has hardly laid a hand on a loom. By the mid-1920s the dyeing business fell off, and then so did weaving.

Visiting Customers

By the time I was born, in 1903, the number of village households had swelled from a dozen to about a hundred. The place was never very well suited to farming, being located right on the lakeshore with steep cliffs behind. Most people supplemented their income with fishing. Towards the end of the nineteenth century, bigger boats were being made and fishing flourished. Especially after Ryohei Orimoto developed the technique of catching smelt with sailing trawlnets, smelt hauls went way up; as people began to realize there was good money in fishing, more and more moved down closer to shore. A few years before I was born Shitozaki had become a regular stop for the steamer *Tsuun Maru*, which brought lots of different kinds of people to town.

Shops catering to steamer passengers sprang up. The steamer made it possible to sell all sorts of items in Tokyo, not just firewood and rice, so merchants of all kinds set up shop too. The village even got its own inn for travelers.

The steamer always anchored far offshore, in the deeper part of the lake, and a lighter transported people and goods to and fro. I rode on the steamer many a time, starting when I was a little boy, so I have lots of memories. As I said, my family were weavers and dyers, so I would go to Tsuchiura for dyestuffs and chemicals. And when a kimono was finished, it was my job to take it to have the family crest put on. When I was in fifth grade, the fare from Shitozaki to Tsuchiura was ten sen. It doubled in no time, and by the mid-1920s it was up to fifty sen.

The first time I went, my father came with me and took me around to the different craftsmen and shops to introduce me. "From now on my boy will be coming in to take care of business," he'd say, "so take a good look at him." We went to the local inn too, the "Hidakaya," and he explained to the innkeeper that I'd be staying there by myself from then on, when I came to town on business. After that, I was on my own.

School let out at four. I'd tear home, grab the rolls of cloth from my mother and carry them slantwise on my back. If I hurried, I could just catch the steamer. It was a two-hour ride to Tsuchiura.

The *Tsuun Maru* was a slow-going boat, and how I loved her. There were straw mats on the floor of the passenger area, and you could sit wherever you liked. Old people would stretch out comfortably and chat. The big wheels turned round and round like waterwheels on either side of the boat, and the sound they made penetrated through the floor directly into your body, in a comforting kind of way.

The boat took a crisscross path. First we'd stop at Ushiwata, then at Kihara on the far shore. After that came Shimazu, east of the naval airforce base, then back across the lake to Okijuku, and finally up to Tsuchiura. As soon as we landed, I'd be off like a shot to run my errands. By the time I got back to the Hidakaya it would be nighttime—too late to go home. I ate at the inn, had my bath, and went upstairs to bed, leaving word for someone to wake me up at five a.m.

If I didn't catch the first steamer in the morning, I'd be late for school. I was so scared of oversleeping that I always asked for a wake-up call, but nine times out of ten I'd wake up by myself first. That's because the railroad tracks were nearby, and just before dawn a train would rush past. The Hidakaya was an old wooden building, and it shook so hard that the vibrations woke me out of a sound sleep. I'd leap out of bed, get ready to go, and run off with no breakfast. I'd be back in Shitozaki by seven, so there was just time to slip home and eat the hot breakfast my mother had waiting for me, then sprint to school and be in my seat when the bell rang at eight.

The Excursion Boats

The excursion boat of the Watabiki Express Agency got its start when I was thirteen, which would make it around 1916. The agency was a partnership financed by wealthy backers along the shores of Lake Kasumigaura. Each member built a wharf, and together they supported the transportation of people and goods using a steam passenger launch with a hot-bulb engine. It held up to forty people—a bit smaller than the *Tsuun Maru*. It left at six every morning from the dock at Tamatsukuri, then went on to Tega, then across the lake to Kashiwazaki, Tabuse, and Shitozaki, getting to Shitozaki at eight in the morning. After that it made stops at Ushiwata, Sakibama, Kawajiri, and Okijuku, before reaching Tsuchiura.

Shitozaki had two inns: the "Magakeya" for the *Tsuun Maru*, and another one run by Mr. Watabiki that catered to passengers of the excursion boat. The two inns were in constant competition, and they both did good business. Anyway, the boats made getting to Tsuchiura a heck of a lot easier than it had been. Before, you had to walk or ride in a wagon, which took half a day, one way. The

The *Tsuun Maru* (at lower left)

roads were terrible too—after a hard rain, it was like slogging through deep mud in a rice paddy. You can't imagine how miserable it was. But when the steamboats came along, why, as long as you could pay the fare, you could be in Tsuchiura in two hours, and sleep all the way if you wanted. Now that was convenient.

One other boat was in business after the turn of the century. It was called the *Kaizuka Maru*, and it made regular trips between Kashima and Tsuchiura. It went out of business around 1915, though, after losing to the *Tsuun Maru* in a price war.

Watabiki also ran a rice-polishing mill; he was the first to mechanize on Dejima. The machinery was motor-powered, and it fascinated the local foreigner, a Mr. Hirsch. He was always dropping by to look at it.

The Neighborhood

Watabiki's neighbor to the west was a fellow named Yageta, who made and repaired fishing nets for a living. There was another net-maker between the Watabiki house and the inn, as I recall, who came up from Choshi around 1900. Across the street to the west was another net-maker who learned the trade from Yageta; he's probably the only one around who still repairs nets for a living today.

On that same street was a confectioner whose store was called "Ainoya." He made and sold all sorts of sweets and also ran a public bath. Most people didn't have their own bath at home, so when I was a teenager his place was very popular. A soak then cost two sen.

East of the confectionery was one of the oldest houses in Shitozaki, and the only soy sauce manufacturer. The maker, Tokizo Kaizuka, loaded soy sauce in horse-drawn wagons and sold it in all the surrounding villages. He used to employ a number of apprentices as well. But after a while business fell off. He went bankrupt and left in about 1920 to settle in Hokkaido.

East of him was Kikuchi, the fish dealer. Fishermen would bring their catches straight to him in the middle of the night. I can remember lying in bed as a boy and hearing old lady Kikuchi measure out the volume of the smelt catch in a rhythmical sort of chant. She had a fine, clear voice. When she'd finished counting, she'd always give the running total for the night. She sounded so satisfied, it made me happy to listen to her. Old man Kikuchi became a grain dealer later, and then he went to Tokyo for a while, but after the war he came back to Shitozaki and started up a movie theater. It might surprise you to hear we ever had a movie theater here, but we did. I remember when *Kimi no Na Wa* [What's Your Name?] played, the theater would fill to overflowing. Back in the days before television that movie was all the rage. Besides operating the theater, Kikuchi was also a fisherman.

The next house down belonged to another Kikuchi, a farmer and rice cracker–maker who also worked as a fisherman, and next to him was my house. We of course ran a weaving and dyeing factory and kept unbelievably long hours, I have to say—but then everybody did. It was how we lived. The looms made a godawful racket too.

There were lots more shops and craftsmen in Shitozaki besides those I've already mentioned. Near my house was the tofu shop, run by an old man and woman who made the tofu together, but they didn't sell it by walking around town carrying it suspended from a shoulder pole; instead, people would bring their cooking pots directly to the shop and buy the tofu there. Next door to them was a rice farmer who also ran a cheap sweet shop and made fine lacquerware besides. Down the lane from him lived several more fishermen and farmers, and Shitozaki's lone tatami-maker, a rice farmer by the name of Oshio.

There was a shop called "Aiya" where they dyed thread in big indigo dye vats, using balls of indigo leaves. We had a saké brewer too, named Eguchi—he

A courier boat

was also a landowner. Across from Eguchi was a ship carpenter named Sugasawa who specialized in making fishing boats, and a Nakaizumi who farmed and
fished besides making boats. That was all the houses on the east side of town.

On the west side, besides the net-makers and the bath operator I mentioned before, there was a big fish processing plant. Fishermen could boil
their own catch in salted water, then lay it out on straw matting to dry before
selling it. Towards the mountains, away from the lake, there used to be a cotton
manufacturer. There was also a man known as the "courier": if you wanted
something from Tsuchiura, all you had to do was tell him and he'd row over
and do your shopping for you. People loved it because they could get him to
buy kimono material, dishes, handsaws, or anything else. Next to him was
Yaguchi's dried fish shop.

Matsutaro Kaizuka, the man whose steamer lost out to the *Tsuun Maru*,
eventually gave up and rented out his land out to the Nakamura Silk Mill.
That place did particularly well. At its peak as many as seventy local girls must
have worked there. They used to say Nakamura's profits came to ten yen a day.
Unfortunately Hatsutaro Nakamura, the owner, squandered all his money living it up in Tokyo and Yokohama. The mill stayed in operation till about 1930.
It collapsed in the depression, when silk mills went under one after another.

There was also a Shingon temple in town called Jiganji, and in front of that
lived a doctor named Ishijima. He was the only doctor around, and he'd been
practicing since before I was born. He made local house calls on foot, but
everywhere else he went by rickshaw. The only rickshaw man in the area lived
in our town too. We also had a basket-weaver, a sawyer, and a fellow who
would make or repair hoe handles and wagon wheels.

I'm eighty now. The old-time fishermen are gone, the steamers are gone,
and the movie theater's gone. Things are a lot quieter than they were, that's
for sure. I can tell I've lived a long life by all the change there's been.

The Foreigner's House in Ayumizaki

Mrs. Ko Gunji (1906–1993)
(Sister of Mr. Yoshimitsu Naruse)

There used to be a foreigner's house on the hill where the temple of Kannon is, in Ayumizaki. The house was there as early as I can remember; it must have been built around the turn of the century, or just after. The owner was a German man named Mr. Hirsch—a chief mechanical engineer who came to Japan by special invitation of the government. He oversaw construction of the first railroad line in the country, between Shinbashi and Yokohama. Most of the time he stayed in Yokohama, but on his vacations he'd come up to Ayumizaki. It's a little hard to figure why a foreigner from Yokohama would build a second home out on the tip of Dejima—it certainly wasn't a fashionable place to live. But according to my father, Mr. Hirsch used to come up to Tsuchiura every so often and ride around Lake Kasumigaura in a motorboat, and apparently he lost his heart to Ayumizaki. Back then the hill was covered with pines that had been there for centuries—yes, the woodlands were gorgeous—and the water was pure and clear. The lake would have been dotted with hundreds of fishing boats, their square white sails puffed out in the wind. I can imagine the German climbing the hill, looking out on that vista, and making up his mind to build a summer house there.

That area used to belong to Eguchi the saké brewer, so the German went to him to negotiate a deal. The trouble was, he couldn't buy property since he was a foreigner. So instead he rented it on a ninety-nine-year lease. Once the contract was signed, he hired local people to cut down trees, level the ground, and build a mansion. It had a gallery on the second floor where you could look out on the lake. A magnificent house with a magnificent view.

The Iron Gate

He was a cautious fellow, that German. Kept pretty much to himself. He surrounded the property with a tall fence of red pine, and then topped that with barbed wire. The gate was a big heavy thing made of iron, and it was always locked. If you wanted to see him about anything, you had to ring a little bell to one side of the gate. A servant would come and ask you what your business was, and then unlock the gate.

I remember the German as an old man, about seventy. His wife was a much younger Japanese woman, about forty—for some reason the servants all called her "Miss." They had six children: a boy, four girls, and a little baby. I was best friends with the oldest girl, Isha, and so I was allowed inside their house to play. My father ran a textile factory filled with jacquard looms, which at that time were the height of modern technology. Mr. Hirsch was very interested in them and often came over to observe. That's how he got to know me, and how I received special permission to go inside his mansion.

I still remember the noon meal there. At twelve o'clock a maid in a white apron would come upstairs and ring a bell—the same sort of bell that hangs in the steeple of a Christian church. It had a string hanging down, and when she pulled it, the bell would sway back and forth with a loud *clang clang*. There wasn't a bell like that anywhere else around, so everybody in the village knew when it was mealtime in the foreigner's house.

On the first floor was a huge dining room with a great big table made of a reddish wood—mahogany, I think it's called—and over that a chandelier. The master sat in the center in a high-backed chair, with his wife beside him and the children seated all around the table. Apparently the children were very strictly brought up—none of them ever made any noise. They ate perfectly quietly. One time only I sat down with the family for lunch, next to Isha; I'd never laid eyes on a knife or fork before, and I had no idea what to do with them. I could hardly eat a thing.

In another room was a refined old woman who lived in seclusion. The maid carried in her meals, and she ate in there by herself. The rumor was that this was his real wife, and the Japanese woman was a former servant. Of course I was only a little girl with no way of knowing if the rumor was true or not. Still, anyone could see that the German did dote on his young wife. The two of them were always going off in the motorboat for long outings together on the lake, but he never, ever allowed his children in the boat.

At Christmastime Mr. Hirsch would invite important local men over for dinner—men like Mr. Eguchi the saké brewer, my father, and Mr. Watabiki, who ran the local rice-polishing mill (he had a large machine that Mr. Hirsch was always dropping in to look at). After dinner they'd go upstairs. More than a hundred children from the village would gather below the balcony. Mr. Hirsch would toss out little bags of cake to us, and we'd scramble over each other like mad to catch them. It was bedlam. If you lived in the country back then, there were no fancy sweets or confections to be had, so those cakes were a real prize.

Something else that we all admired were the turkeys roaming free in the German's front yard. Birds like that were unheard-of in those days, and he had a small flock. We kids loved to chase them and see them spread their wings and then beat them against the ground in anger. It was fun to squeal and run around after them. In the middle of the yard was a big wire enclosure where all sorts of birds flew around—red ones, purple ones, ones with tail-feathers that were a foot long and contained every color in the rainbow. I used to marvel that there could be so many beautiful birds in this world. He must have spared no expense to collect them and bring them back alive from the south seas.

A little distance from the house was a grove of pine trees with an octagonal hall built about the same time as the house. It was big—the size of twenty mats, I guess. Every now and then Mr. Hirsch and his wife would have tea there, but mostly it was closed off. Near it was an enormous pine tree, with

Ayumizaki

two carved stone lions at its foot. They were big—taller than me. What was amazing about them were the eyes: they were made of real gold. They were about the size of a baby's fist. Solid gold, if you can believe it, with jade in the middle. They took your breath away. Everybody who came on the grounds would stand and stare—not just kids but grownups too.

We couldn't stay and play forever. At four in the afternoon the bell would ring; then all the children would be led out the front, and the iron gate would slam shut. After that a watchman went around and inspected every corner of the grounds with a dog in tow.

Besides Christmas, the other time that people could enter the grounds freely was during the Kannon Festival. That's July 16 by the old calendar. People used to come by boat from every village around Lake Kasumigaura, so the hill would be packed solid with them. They came waving banners and beating drums. All the boats, big and little—*takase* riverboats too, not just fishing boats—were decorated with banners, and the crews would be playing music and dancing, wearing fox masks or masks with funny faces. The sound of drums and flutes echoed off the water. Watching from up on the hill, I'd feel like dancing too. My father was good on the transverse flute, and he used to go down to the jetty playing his flute in welcome. Boats came by the dozens, one after another, so the shore was a madhouse of people coming and going. This was the height of summer, so everybody was dripping sweat.

Down at the landing there was a boat shed built by the German that was big enough to hold four or five motorboats. The roof tapered to a point and was decorated with a bird. You couldn't see inside, but everybody would go round and round the building, gawking at it. Then they'd set off for the temple to pay respects to the Kannon deity. There'd be such a crowd you could hardly set one foot in front of the other. The road would be lined with stalls, and in the evening the lanterns would be lit. This was the one night of the

Buying sweets

year when young girls all put on makeup and dressed up, and the air was full of excitement. The Tsuchiura police sent twenty men over to keep an eye on things in case the mood turned wild. They patrolled the grounds around Mr. Hirsch's house too, to keep troublemakers away. I remember seeing the officers on duty being served tea in the octagonal hall.

But no matter what precautions you take, if a thief really wants something he'll find a way to get it. I don't remember exactly when it was, but one year someone stole the golden eyes out of one of the stone lions. Whoever it was climbed over the tall fence, barbed wire and all, and made off with two of the gold balls. It made Mr. Hirsch so mad that he took the other eyes out himself for safekeeping.

He died in 1917. There was an epidemic of Spanish influenza that year, and he came down with it and died just a few days later. Everything in the house was put up for sale afterwards, and the building was torn down. Even the big birdcage was sold. The one thing the young wife kept was the octagonal hall, which I heard she shipped to Yokohama and had rebuilt on the family's estate there.

By Rushlight

Mr. Buemon Sugaya (1889–1984)

When I was small, our house was lit by rush lamps. We ate all our meals by rushlight, and Mother sat up nights and sewed by rushlight. You'd pour oil in a little dish and soak a rush in it, and that provided a slow, steady light. It gave off a small glow, just enough to see a needle and thread in your hands if you sat close up to it. At even a little distance, you could hardly see well enough to tell who someone was. We used rapeseed oil. To keep from using it up too fast, there were only one or two rush lamps in the whole house.

We also used *andon*, paper-covered lamp stands, but those didn't give off much light, either. You'd set a rush lamp inside a box frame covered with old paper, and if you put your face right up close to it, then just your face would be lit up—but everything around you would be black. You couldn't use them for reading or working. So nights were really very dark. When the sun went down, the village would be pitch-black, with just the paper doors of stores glowing a faint white. You couldn't walk the streets at night without a paper lantern on a pole. Someone could have come up and tweaked your nose and you wouldn't have known who it was—that's how dark it was. Except on moonlit nights, which were very bright.

There are probably a good 150 households in Kashiwazaki today, but in the old days there were only half that many. The village was divided into four sections: Kamijuku, Shimojuku, Sakibama, and Yokomachi. There used to be a lantern-maker in Kamijuku when I was a boy. He'd sit out in front of his store in a kimono with the sleeves tied up out of his way, bending bamboo staves into a spiral shape, then covering the frame with paper. When it was dry, he'd write something on it with a calligraphy brush. We kids loved to watch him work, and we'd squat there for hours just watching. We had no kerosene lamps till I was eight or nine. Until then the nights were very long.

Kashiwazaki is a lonely little place now, but it used to be quite lively. They say it was even livelier two hundred years ago, when *takase* boats would stop

Cleaning kerosene lamps

here to wait for a favorable wind and spend money in the meantime. Boats carrying rice payments to the shogun would cross the center of the lake, you see, heading for the River Tone, but if the waves were too high it was risky, so they'd stop off here to wait it out. There were inns and bathhouses and brothels, and sometimes boat captains would stay on for days. I remember a place in Kamijuku called the "Inariya" that had several prostitutes; later it went bankrupt, but around the turn of the century it did a rip-roaring business.

The Ferry Across the Lake

The *koshiban* was the captain of a ferry across the lake. Kashiwazaki is on the easternmost tip of Dejima, and ferries used to run regularly between here and Tamatsukuri, which isn't far. There was a little shack by the water's edge, on both the Kashiwazaki and Tamatsukuri sides, where the *koshiban* would wait for fares. Inside was a tiny one-mat room where he could spend the night, and next to that was a candy stand run by a fellow who'd watch the place while he was away. The ferry left as soon as anyone wanted to go. It could seat five or six, but it would leave if there was even one. When the two ferries met anywhere along the way, they would exchange passengers and go back—they could only pick up passengers on their own side, you see. In the old days, the fare was five sen.

They used to auction off the position of *koshiban*. The highest bidder in the village got to be *koshiban* for a year. The ferry was the easiest way to get across that neck of the lake, so there was a lot of business and the money was pretty good.

I remember seeing off soldiers for the Sino-Japanese War of 1894–1895. Five men left for the front from our village. They hadn't been issued uniforms yet, so they were all still in kimono with towels at the waist and wooden *geta* clogs on their feet. The whole village gave them a big send-off. Everybody got on little dinghies and rowed alongside the ferry partway.

When the Russo-Japanese War started ten years later, I was fifteen. That time, eight villagers went off to war. The soldiers were on farm horses, and the whole village turned out on foot, everyone waving flags and yelling "*Banzai! Banzai!*" from the local shrine in a big procession down to the waterfront. They went off on the steamer. Sannosuke Kuriyama's father fought in the Sino-Japanese War, and then he and his brothers fought in the Russo-Japanese War, and every one of them came back safely.

Hand to Mouth

I was a fisherman and a farmer and always had to scrape to get by. We hardly had anything to wear or to eat. Nobody had a store of rice in the house. You'd sell your day's catch and use the money to buy that day's rice. Some of the rice dealers sold saké too, but fishermen never drank saké. Around 1910, a bottle of saké was thirty sen, and a measure of smelt was five. If you fished all night and caught a hundred measures' worth of smelt, that was a great haul. That made five yen, which was a great sum. But you couldn't do that well every night. Most smelt fishermen made three hundred yen a year, I'd say. Very few made as much as five hundred yen. The upshot of it was, nobody drank saké, young or old. It was out of the question.

There were certain times of year you could drink all you wanted, though. Six times a year, three each for smelt and whitebait, the fishers and the dealers got together to negotiate a price. They had to get us in a good mood, so they gave us all the saké we wanted, and all the cakes too. Other than that, we couldn't touch it.

New Year's didn't amount to very much. There wasn't any fishing or any

other kind of work, and it got bitterly cold, so you'd just stay scrunched up in bed without doing anything. Or you'd go to the pawnshop. There wasn't one in Kashiwazaki, so we'd go to Tamatsukuri. All the fishermen did. When the fishing season ended, we'd pile our sails and nets in a boat and go put them in hock. The next summer, when it was time to get them back, nobody'd have any money, so we'd troop over to the dealer for a cash loan. He'd groan and say, "Not again!" but if he didn't lend us the money we couldn't fish, and then he'd be out of work, so what choice did he have? We paid him back little by little out of what we caught. It was a hardscrabble life.

Compare that with now. I get a pension for no reason except I'm old. My medical expenses cost me next to nothing. I drink half a pint of saké every night and a glass of milk a day, and I read the whole newspaper. On a night when the moon is out over the lake, I go out on the veranda and look up at it while I sip my drink. That's what's changed the most in my life these ninety years—that a fisherman like me can sit and do nothing and enjoy himself.

The Village Candy Store

Mrs. Sato Numajiri (1905–1993)

Even now, along country lanes in Dejima you can see big stone markers carved with the words "Gathering of the Twenty-third Night." In my childhood, people used to get together on the twenty-third of every month by the lunar calendar to wait for the moon to rise. They'd gather at a different villager's house every month. The most important gatherings were in November and December. Even us children would stay awake as late as we could, knowing there'd be special treats to eat. The moon didn't come out till one or two in the morning, so we'd go to bed early, and someone would come shake us awake when the moment arrived: "Hurry, hurry, it's coming, get up!" We'd go out on the veranda, rubbing our eyes, and there would be the lovely round moon, shining down on the water. The moonlight on the waves was like a dream. We'd all put our palms together and pray for freedom from sickness and calamity, and for the well-being of our families, and then we'd enjoy the food.

I'll never forget the time my family was in charge, and we served pork. There weren't any butcher shops in the country in those days. Two or three men caught somebody's pig, drowned it in a bucket of water, cooked the skin and chopped up the meat, and set it all to simmer with onions and things. My father was a candy-maker, so we had plenty of sugar and other seasonings too. I remember how excited he was, presiding over the cooking with a towel tied around his head, saying, "All right now, just leave everything to me!" And when I tasted it—oh, it was out of this world. That's what it means to have something melt in your mouth. Everyone eats pork all the time now without thinking anything of it, but that was my first experience, and I remember being astonished that there could be anything so good.

The Seasons

Winters were dreadful then, much colder than they are now. You wouldn't

The lake

believe it. Lake Kasumigaura would be covered in ice along the shore, extending out for quite a distance. It sparkled and shone like a mirror in the morning sun, but ice or no ice the fishing boats had to go out. Off they would row, getting smaller and smaller, leaving a wake behind them. By the time the wake was gone, they'd be far away.

A great deal of snow fell too. Our family ran the local candy shop, so we did a good business, but when there was a morning snowfall, people would stay home for "snow-viewing." You'd throw open the paper doors, sit back and drink tea, eat sweets, and chat while you watched the snow come down. It was a great pleasure to watch snow pile up silently on bamboo leaves and stones.

By and by one of the men would set out grains of rice under a basket propped up on a stick. Sparrows were hungry, so when they saw the rice they flew down and went inside the basket. Then all you had to do was pull on a string attached to the stick and they were trapped. Somebody was always putting a sparrow in a birdcage for me. People had time on their hands in the cold weather, you see, because often as not it was too cold to fish.

When the weather turned warm, the fishermen went back to work, catching their prawns and eels and so on, and we children caught loaches. The rice paddies were terraced, and we would set our basket right at the bottom of the hill, where the clear, fresh springwater flowed. If you waited a little, you could catch loaches one after another, little ones about an inch and a half long, black on top. They'd flop and jump inside the basket, flashing their white bellies. It was so much fun that as soon as school let out we'd race for the stream and have a full basket to take home in no time. Mother would be as pleased as punch. She'd make loach soup for dinner, with egg in it, that was just delicious.

We used to pick tender dropwort in the streams too. She served that mixed with sesame. What a wonderful smell it had!

In summer, after playing naked in the lake, we'd dig for clams and mussels. They were good chopped up in dumplings, or whole in soup, or fried in tempura. Or we would cut them up fine and cook them in soy sauce.

When the fishermen came back they'd rap the sides of the boat as a signal. Then everyone came flying out with a basket. The fresh-caught smelt would still be jumping, and the whitebait were so transparent that you could see every one of their little bones, thinner than threads. We'd dump the fresh fish in a bowl, mix them with equal parts vinegar, soy sauce, and saké, then add a little miso, and wolf them down. I'll never taste anything so good again.

The Candy Business

The town was a lively place in those days, with people of all different occupations, not just fishing. There were dealers in grains and fertilizer, indigo dyers, tatami-makers, carpenters, barbers, and handymen, all living side by side. My family's business was booming then too. We were the only wholesale confectionery in all of Dejima. We made all sorts of sweets. About five or six people worked in the kitchen full-time. We made everything right on the premises, but the ingredients came from Tsuchiura. Once a month a local captain would transport mountains of sugar, agar, flour, adzuki beans, and whatever else we needed. My father often took me along on those shopping expeditions. Once I can remember staring in amazement at a young woman who was supposedly one of the three greatest beauties in the city. She was so different from anyone I'd ever seen. Her clothes were gay and smart, her hair was done up in a fancy way, and above all her skin was pure white. Everybody I knew was burned black by the sun. She really seemed like a creature from a different world.

The kitchen was always so busy it was like a great battleground. To make

Tsuchiura's main street

bull's-eye candies, we used a work area about two feet wide and twenty-five or thirty feet long. First the candy would be boiled, then stretched out, then cut into little pieces using a hemp string. The worker would hold one end of the string in his mouth and the other in his right hand, and use the string to cut off the pieces smartly. The string was rubbed with sesame oil to keep it from sticking. The next worker would roll each piece on a floury board, making it into a ball. They made thousands every day.

They boiled adzuki bean jam too. There were three brick cooking stoves. They'd set a huge cooking pot three feet in diameter on the fire and simmer the beans slowly. The wooden pestle they used to stir the beans was very long, so the stirring could be done from a distance. As the stuff simmered, it would jump out at you every now and then, and if hot paste landed on bare skin, it'd burn. That's why there had to be such a long handle on the pestle.

The way of cooking the jam depended on how it would be used. To make filling for the wafers called *monaka*, you had to stir the pot hard and boil it down till you could see the bottom of the pot as you stirred, keeping an eye on the flame all the time. I never got tired of watching the workers.

Sweets weren't common in the country in those days, so all kinds of people would come by hoping to get a free sample. A wooden hearth was cut into the floor of the kitchen, and over the fire hung an iron kettle, always filled with boiling water for tea. Somebody would invite himself in and say casually, "Mind if I sit here a spell and rest?" Then whoever was nearby would make tea and say, "You're just in time. We've cooked up a nice batch of bean jam. Have some before you go." They'd hand the visitor a plate of sweet bean jam, and since that was why he'd come in the first place, he'd lick his chops and gobble it up. Lots and lots of people did that.

When you make so much candy, not all of it comes out just right, and anything that couldn't be sold we gave away to local farmers and fishermen, or to

Candy seller

visitors. It was a welcome gift too. In return, fishermen would share part of their catch with us, and farmers would bring by vegetables. So everyone was happy.

We made *karinto* [fried finger-shaped cakes], *okoshi* [millet-and-rice cakes], *mamedama no shibori* [a type of hard candy], *ankodama* [bean-paste balls], *yokan* [sweet bean jelly], things like that. They all had to be arranged neatly in boxes that were three feet high, two feet wide, and two and a half feet deep. Each box had three drawers, and they were lined up ten deep. Every day, itinerant candy vendors came by to lay in stock, each pushing a cart. They had no fixed store, so that cart was where they did business. They had five or six square boxes with glass lids so customers could see inside. They walked around from village to village ringing a little bell and swelling sweets to children. In three or four days their stock would be gone and they'd be back for more. The store was always bustling with people like that.

Now our old place is gone, and so are the other neighborhood shops. People nowadays must have no idea what it was like.

The "No Cooking" Festival

Mr. Minoru Fujii (1901–1983)

There are twenty-four households here in Tajuku now. In the old days there were a couple more, but it's never gotten any bigger. I heard that long ago, down in the paddies below—halfway between two post towns—there used to be a lodging house where travelers could stay, and a village surrounding it. That's how the name "Tajuku" [literally, "paddy-field lodging"] came about. But a flood wiped everything out, so the villagers relocated up here, to higher ground.

Just east of here is a village called Akatsuka, but people there are completely different from us in personality. It's funny, but we've never had anything to do with one another. For water rights and fire prevention we've dealt mostly with the village of Sakibama instead. But there are no stores there, or here, so for daily necessities we have to shop in Akatsuka. Even so, there's precious little mixing between the two villages.

There are no true fishermen in Tajuku. Folks here are mostly rice farmers, with one or two who do *sasabitashi*, or longline fishing. Until the war it was all tenant farming, mostly for Unpei Kawashima, the biggest and richest landowner in Dejima.

There's nothing remarkable about this village, but on January 25 by the old lunar calendar we have a festival at Tenma Shrine. It's called the Nabekakezu Festival, the "No Cooking" Festival, because nobody cooks at home that day—the whole village gets together at the house of the village head to eat, drink, and live it up.

The way up to the shrine is long and steep, so young folk go out on patrol the day before to inspect the path, clear it off, level it, and shore it up as may be needed so people can walk on it with no trouble. On the day of the festival villagers gather at the house of whichever family's in charge and weave *shime-nawa* [sacred ropes hung at shrines]. There are a lot to make: one for the *torii* gate outside the shrine, one for the inner shrine, and one each for the stone

Planning for a festival

buddhas, Dainichi Buddha, the water god, and all the other gods. Each one has to have its own *shimenawa*. It takes all morning to make them. When they're ready, we take them over to the shrine and take down the old ones and put up the new. Then we pay our respects.

First in line are the oldest members of the head family, and then comes everybody else. Finally last year's head and this year's head perform a ceremony before the gods to mark the transfer of authority. When that's over, everyone comes back to the village and gathers at the house of the new head family. Every family brings along two measures of rice. Part of that goes to make *amazake* [sweet saké], and the rest of it is steamed. When the rice is ready, the whole village sits down for a meal. That's quite a production. We may be a tiny hamlet, but for everybody to sit down and eat together, including all the old people and women and children too, the main rooms of the house aren't nearly enough. Every nook and cranny is opened up, including the dirt-floor entryway, and even then there's not an inch to spare. Male elders and female elders aren't supposed to eat in the same room either; they have to have separate dining places. It's so crowded that children have no place to sit down, so they eat walking around.

There's one other thing I can tell you about Tajuku. In the old days, down in the lower paddies there used to be a brothel. They did serve food, but the place was only half-restaurant. I tell you, that place nearly sent us all to the poorhouse. Back then, farmers did nothing but work outside, men and women both, and get burned black by the sun. Then suddenly we had women sashaying around in pretty kimonos, their faces and necks coated with white powder; in the evening you could hear shamisen music starting up. Well, the young fellows couldn't concentrate on their work. They'd be out carousing till all hours, not getting in till morning. It nearly tore the village apart. Word traveled around that folks in Tajuku were lie-abeds.

Let me see, the place went up when I was sixteen, so that'd be 1917. It was a fancy two-story building called the "Kozantei," and a man called Kichino-suke Koyama ran it. It was quite big. Must have been five or six rooms on the first floor alone, if not more. His wife went scouting for young women all over. Some came not knowing what they were getting into, others were sold by their families. Before you know it, folks from other villages were rowing over to Tajuku to get in on the fun. For a while people couldn't get enough of that flashy living, but finally, when they saw the village was going to rack and ruin, they lost interest. Ten years after it opened, the brothel went out of business.

The Community of Akatsuka

Mr. Yoshiaki Ishikawa (1895–1985)

In Akatsuka, every five households formed a unit, and those five would help each other out. If one man had financial troubles, the others would muster what money they could, or anything else that was needed to keep his family together. So nobody here ever got to be a millionaire, but nobody ever had to run away in the middle of the night because he couldn't pay his debts either.

We had two shrines. To the east was Kamo Shrine, where we had our own festival just like the one in Tajuku. Ours was December 14–16. Festival eve was December 14, the next day was the actual festival, and the day after that was cleanup. For all three days, no one cooked at home—they ate and drank at the chief family's house instead.

People had "shares" in the festival. Residents were all entitled to a share, and newcomers couldn't participate in the festival until they acquired one. The shares came from fields and forests that were shrine property. That land belonged to the shrine and its parishioners—people whose names were carved on a stone monument in the shrine grounds. There was a rice paddy of about half an acre, and a field the same size. The harvest would be sold and the proceeds saved. People didn't work the land together; it was left in charge of whoever requested tenancy. A small farmer having trouble making ends meet, for example, might put in a request to the association, and if they thought he was a good worker, they'd okay it. Then half of what he produced went to the shrine, and the other half was his to keep. That way the shrine managed to stockpile a lot of rice. There were also a lot of trees that were centuries old on the shrine property. If one of those was struck by lightning or fell over during a storm, they'd ask permission from the shrine council to cut it up for lumber. Someone from the council would come over to check it out, and if they approved then the tree would be cut up and sold, or else the wood might be saved and used for repairs. All this money was used to sponsor the festival too. That's how villages with shrines used to manage their affairs.

A village festival

The rule was that two sacks of rice went for saké on festival day. We didn't make the drink ourselves; we'd sell the rice and use the money to buy unrefined saké. It bought a hell of a lot.

We also had a summer festival at Yasaka Shrine, which was inside the grounds of Kamo Shrine. On July 31, the young fellows would carry the portable shrine around the village. It wasn't a very colorful festival, but we held it every year. Only shareholders—local people—could participate in village festivals. Other folks could come and watch, but they could never go into the village elder's house or have any saké.

One thing Tajuku had that we didn't was a brothel. A lot of folks from here used to go over there to have fun. There were four or five women at the inn. Their hair was done up in fancy hairdos with hairpins and tortoiseshell combs, and their skin was painted white with makeup, from the neck on up. Some of them were very pretty too. When that place was in its prime, we heard everyone was upset because young folk stopped attending to their work.

Things are more convenient now, with better transportation, but nothing's the same. The good old days are gone without a trace.

The Ferryman of Tabuse

Mr. Shichiro Sakamoto (1907–1990)

The district of Tabuse is made up of nine smaller areas: Ishida, Kita-Maebara, Yamada, Okinouchi, Nemoto-Maebara, Yokosuka, Kamine, Ushiroji, and Nakadai. When I was a boy there were about a hundred households in all, and now there must be three times that many. I'm from Ishida, where lots of fisher folk lived. My ancestors were all fishers, and I myself used to fish for a living, but starting in 1943 I became a ferryman.

There used to be dozens of big willow trees planted along the shore of the lake. They're all gone now, but in the old days they went on for miles. They served a great purpose. During the rainy season the water level would rise by as much as a foot or two, and all sorts of stuff would come floating down— driftwood, junk, you name it—and lodge in the rice paddies, which weren't far from the lake. To keep that from happening, people planted willow trees long ago as a kind of fence. Still, after the fall rains, the paddies would get so flooded there'd be no choice but to harvest the rice underwater. You'd wade out into chest-deep water, bend over, and harvest the rice by feel. That's why the rice crop hereabouts never amounted to much. Life was hard, and most people chose fishing instead of farming.

There was always a ferry in Tabuse, from way back—though how far back it goes, I couldn't say. The ferry ran between Ishida and the towns of Tama-tsukuri and Takasu. There was another one between Kashiwazaki and Tama-tsukuri. Everybody used the ferries.

I didn't start ferrying till 1943, but there was always someone doing it; people's livelihoods depended on it. I was thirty-six when I started. You had to have a permit. If too many people applied for a permit, the job went to the highest bidder. For example, if Yahei put in a bid of fifty yen a year, and Kichibei put in a bid of eighty, Kichibei got the job. Suppose he earned two hundred yen in fares over that year—eighty of it he owed to the prefecture and the rest was his to keep. In my day, a successful ferryman averaged around seventy yen a year.

I was always a fisherman and never had the slightest inclination to be anything else. But when the war came, the young men all went off to be soldiers. With them all gone, the old men had all the work they could handle and nobody had time for the ferry. Well, that left the village high and dry. They'd had that ferry for over a century, and they needed it and weren't about to give it up without a fight. A village elder came to me on his hands and knees and begged me to take it on for the sake of the village. I said yes. What else could I do?

The fare was originally five sen, and it went up to ten sen around 1920. When I started in 1943 it was thirty-five sen, and by 1960 it was a hundred, or one yen. In the old days it was a rowboat, seating five or six passengers at most. When the wind was right, I'd put up a tiny sail. It was small, but it helped. There was no roof, because the wind resistance would have made it almost impossible to row. If it rained, I put on a straw raincoat, and so did my fares.

While I was waiting for fares, I would go in my little hut and weave straw sandals or some such thing; as soon as someone came along, I was ready to go. I never kept anyone waiting. There was no schedule to stick to, no minimum number of passengers. It often happened that after setting off, I'd row a little way and then hear someone shouting "Hey! Wait for me!" When that happened, I'd turn right around, row back, and pick them up.

Lots of times I would run into the other ferry coming the other way, from Tamatsukuri. When that happened we'd swap passengers, turn around, and go back. That way we each only had to row half as far, which meant we could get back faster and the next people didn't have to wait so long. That was a lucky break, since we could each only pick up fares on our own sides of the lake. Of course, the passengers riding with us had to change boats in midstream, but nobody ever seemed to mind. If the wind was high and the boats were shaking, it wasn't always easy to step out of one and into the other, but in all my years I never saw anyone take a tumble.

That neck of the lake was narrow, so we often came close to bumping into fishing boats. You had to watch out for their nets underwater, and gauge where the belly of the net was, since it changed all the time depending on the wind. I had to row with one eye on the wind and another on the boats around me.

The Boat-Builder

Mr. Ikunosuke Kojima (1901–1988)

I started training to build boats when I was fourteen. Back then the materials for boats came from the mountains around here. There used to be huge cryptomerias, all you could want, and dense forests everywhere you looked. Those trees have all been cut down now, and you've got to travel a long ways to find good lumber anymore, but back then it was a dime a dozen. Farmers were only too happy to sell you wood from their property. If you made a purchase somewhere, people would crowd around and beg you to buy from them too. You could have your pick of the best wood there ever was. You'd never get offers like that these days. The mountains have been stripped bare. The scenery around Lake Kasumigaura will never be the same.

The biggest reason for the trees' disappearance was the war. When your trees are commandeered by the military, you can't say no. Didn't matter if was was a sacred tree in the village shrine, or a towering tree that had belonged to the same family for generations—once the army requisitioned it, it was chopped down before you knew it. One after another, trees were made into boats or burned for fuel. In the old days most farmhouses were flanked by several huge zelkovas, but they were all requisitioned and chopped down. There are hardly any left. War doesn't only take people away to be soldiers; it takes everything a village has—its financial resources and even its natural environment too. All we have left now is the grove in the shrine precincts.

After the war, it was hard work scraping up materials to build a boat. Never used to be that way before! The only hard part used to be the competition, since that drove the cost up. There were about thirty boat-builders in the Kasumigaura area, and everybody was competing to buy the best materials. The seller was after the highest price he could get too, of course, so prices were never as cheap as you'd like. But farmers were always ready to talk cash, and if you made them a fair offer, they were willing to do business.

To get the cryptomeria from the owner, we used a woodcutter called a *negiri* ["root-cutter"]. That's a lumberjack who cuts so close to the roots that none of the tree is wasted. There used to be a lot of them around, but no more; I have to hire a man now who comes all the way from Fukushima. But it was different back then. The *negiri* would live in a little hut next to the trees till the job was done. If there was somebody local who could do the job, you'd ask him, and if not, you had to take a man there, build him a little hut, and see that he had everything he needed. Once the trees were felled, a sawyer would strip off the bark and cut the logs into boards one or two inches thick. When that was done, a group of men would load the lumber onto *takase* boats or carts and transport it to the shipyard. From Inashiki, which is miles away on the other side of the lake, it was a long haul with five or six wagonloads of lumber. Sometimes we used the big *daitoku* boats, which by law could only be used for fishing between July 15 and December 15. The rest of the year they sat idle and could be used for other purposes. That raised your expenses, of course, since you had to pay the boat owner as well as the farmer who'd sold you the trees, so it wasn't easy.

Filling Orders

I could make about three fishing boats a month. Orders gradually fell off, though. That's because there was a fixed number of fishermen, so there was a natural limit to the number of orders for fishing boats. To make ends meet I had to do something else, so I started making boats for rice farmers. A lot of them fished on the side. Some places had more flooding than others, and over by Jurokushima there were so many channels that you needed a boat just to get around. You won't believe this, but there were hardly any roads. Farmers had to get to their paddies by boat. You needed one boat for every two and a half acres of land, it was said. There was actually more demand for boats

from farmers than there was from fishers. I would negotiate with farmers in the area and make around eighty boats a year for them. That's over a hundred a year in all. I had five men working for me, from early in the morning till late into the night, with a constant ringing of hammers and sparks flying out across the water. Now that I think of it, we worked like fury.

I got paid straight off in cash sometimes, but mostly I'd wait till harvesttime and then get paid in either cash or rice. If someone took two years to pay me, I charged interest. That made it easy for people to do business with me, so I had no end of orders to fill. I'd finish a dozen boats, then string them together and tow them all down to Jurokushima. Then I'd go around from house to house, making my deliveries. The village of Kessa has about 160 households, and I sold boats to 130 of them. Since I didn't demand instant payment, people felt free to place orders with me. I'd wait till September 18, harvesttime, to go around collecting the money.

During the war, I worked in the Kasumigaura Shipyard by Tsuchiura, making ships for the navy. There was another shipyard in the Arakawa Racecourse. Parts made there were loaded on trains and shipped south, where they were assembled and used for transport. Naval cutters were made there too, using boards fourteen feet by eight inches and two inches thick, all of it good solid wood. About seventy men worked in the Kasumigaura Shipyard, which was a privately owned outfit. So many men had gone off to war that they hired anybody—not only shipbuilders, but bucket-makers, house carpenters, anybody who knew how to work with his hands. We all slept right there, and worked like the dickens from morning till night.

In Kasumigaura, we made a hundred-ton ship. A lot of cryptomeria and zelkova from around here was sacrificed for the prow. Some men specialized in buying wood; they'd go out in their straw sandals, scouring the countryside for likely-looking trees. Anyway, when it was finished, it rode too high in the water to make it under the bridge at Ushibori. We brought two or three hundred kids from the local primary schools and put them on board to weigh the ship down and deepen the draft, and that's how the ship made it under the bridge and out to sea. There weren't any other bridges after that. The kids loved it. That was an engine-powered boat, but it had sails too.

During the war the lake was bombed. Rumor had it that Tsuchiura was destroyed. We heard an ominous roar in the sky, and everybody dived into a bomb shelter. The planes went right past without anything happening, so we thought it was safe and poked our heads back out. But the bastards turned right around, came back, and started bombing the Kasumigaura airfield. The haze was so dense you could hardly see. They dropped those bombs in the wrong places, from Kakeuma to Omuro. Bombs rained down on the lake too, bringing up huge sprays of water—it was some sight! The impact of the blast stunned the fish, and the surface was covered with them. Us old fishermen who were left went out to pick them up, but there were more than we could handle. Before we could get to them all, they started coming back to life and most of them got away.

The shrine at Takahisa took a hit that day, and dozens of huge cryptomerias were felled. When I heard about that, I made up my mind to buy them. I meant to use that wood to build me some fishing boats when the war was over. I lined up some men to help, and I bought six trees. There were sawyers and lumberjacks who'd been drafted to serve in the shipyard at Kasumigaura, and I got them to help me cut the wood into boards. I set those aside. Then a fellow from Tokyo came along with copper for sale, and I bought two tons. That set me back forty thousand yen. It was the finest quality, though, and I was damn lucky to get it. Soon after that the war ended. Fishermen came pouring home from the battlefields, but they had no boats. Bingo! So many orders came in that I had to work round the clock to fill them. Without a doubt, that was the busiest and most rewarding time of my life.

The Ship Carpenter and
the Grudge-Bird

Mr. Kakuji Sakurai (1905–1988)

When I was twelve, I finished primary school and was apprenticed to Tatsuzo Sugasawa, who lived down below the Ayumizaki Kannon. Back then there were dozens of shipbuilders along the shore of Lake Kasumigaura. Even today sixty-five houses belong to either ship builders or net-makers, but it was many times that number in the old days. That's how essential fishing boats were to the life of the region. And not only fishing boats either. Every village had one or two courier boats that would go on shopping expeditions to Tsuchiura or Sawara, and a lot of farmers used boats too. Especially around Jurokushima, you needed a boat in daily life, whether it was for shopping, getting to your paddies, going to a meeting, or going to a wedding. You couldn't do a thing without a boat, so many families owned three or four. Sometimes we couldn't keep up with the demand, and we had to work like crazy, morning, noon, and night. Being in such demand, you might think we carpenters were making money hand over fist. Far from it. Times were hard.

When I became an apprentice, I took with me only the cotton kimono I was wearing and nothing else. My master didn't fit me out with any clothes or supplies, so for a while I had to make do. We were paid no wages either, so I couldn't buy myself anything.

Apprentices worked until they were nineteen, when they had to have their army physical. You had to clean, wash, and cook for yourself and the master's family, and in between you would do whatever you could to help out with the master's work. If he thought you showed promise, he'd give you the materials to make *akakumi*. These were devices used to scoop water out of a boat.

My master told me, "Take this and make yourself some *akakumi*. Then go sell them, save your money, and buy yourself some work clothes." An *akakumi* was as essential to a boat as a broom to a house, and every boat had at least one on board. When they wore out they had to be replaced, so they were sold at hardware stores everywhere. I took mine to a store and the owner paid me

Mr. Sakurai (at far right)

eighteen sen for it. Then he'd turn around and sell it for twenty-five, you see. I spent one whole year making *akakumi* and nothing else; every time I finished one, I'd walk two and a half miles to the shop and back again till I'd saved enough money to buy myself a short *hanten* coat printed with the shop name, and a pair of close-fitting trousers called *momohiki*. That's the way it was with everyone. A man with a family often couldn't make a go of it; with his tools on his shoulder, he'd take his wife and children from town to town, working six months for someone here, three for someone else there, never settling down and working on his own. An awful lot of folks lived that way. People today wouldn't dream of such a life.

I buckled down and learned the trade till I turned nineteen and then had my army physical. I stayed on for one more year of free service, which was the custom, and only then was I a ship carpenter in my own right. I still didn't set up my own place, though. I went around on foot from one shipyard to another, getting more training. You had to study with more than one master or you'd be limited in what you could do and how much you knew. Most young artisans would spend time in a variety of places to get all the experience they could.

You'd go up and introduce yourself. "Hello, I was apprenticed to so-and-so for such-and-such a time. I'd like to stay here and work a while if I may." The boat-builders all knew each other, so he'd ask me various questions and then invite me to stay and work for him as long as I wanted. And he'd give me a place to live. Wherever you went, there'd be a mix of full-time workers and itinerants. You'd sit and talk with them, and that way gradually figure out what the world was all about.

Finding Work

Around 1928, I apprenticed myself to the Ajiro Shipyard in Tsuchiura. They

Tsuchiura fish dealers' shops

manufactured motor-powered boats called *chaka*—three and a half horse-power with electric ignition—that could carry up to thirty-five sacks of rice. *Chaka* were so handy I was sure the old-style boats would be driven out of the market in no time, but it didn't work out that way. The reason was that neither farmers nor fishermen ever had the ready cash to buy one. Times were terrible, and for most people just going on breathing in and out was challenge enough. Much as they might have wanted a motor-driven boat, they couldn't afford it. Of course, there were bound to be a few well-heeled fishermen who would gladly buy one, but it was thought unfair to have two classes of men, the one relying on muscle power and the other on motor power, to do the same work—and so attaching motors to fishing vessels was outlawed. I think another reason was that they were afraid power-driven boats would make fishing too easy and wind up depleting the resources in the lake. That ban wasn't lifted until 1967.

Chaka ended up being used mostly by fish dealers in town. They used them to go around from boat to boat collecting each fisherman's catch, without waiting for it to be brought in early in the morning, the old way. Itinerant *watari* fishermen, who roamed from place to place on the lake, would arrange to meet the dealer on a certain date at a certain time in a certain place. The dealer would go there, weigh the catch, and pay cash on the spot. The fisherman would use the money to buy provisions on shore, and then go out fishing again. Courier boats in villages also switched over to motor power; by 1940 they'd probably all made the conversion.

I'll never forget that in 1929, just when I was finishing up a *chaka* for some shopkeeper, a German Zeppelin flew over to Japan. I set out in the *chaka* with a bunch of my friends, partly as a trial run and partly to get a look at the Zeppelin. The sheer size of the thing was amazing. There I am, so proud of my little three-and-a-half–horsepower *chaka*, and flying in the sky right over my head is something tens of thousands of times bigger, that has come to Japan all the way from Germany. It really shook me up. I could see how far the world had come, but at the same time it scared the living daylights out of me.

Building Boats

Besides Ajiro Shipyard, I also hired myself out to the Hida Shipyard in Namegata. At the Hashimoto Shipyard in Tamari I made little boats about twenty-two feet long, commonly known as *sappabune*, or "bamboo-leaf" boats. Takahama Bay was muddy because so much fertilizer flowed into it from the River Koise, and lots of fine waterweeds grew there. Local farmers went out in those little boats every morning to gather duckweed for fertilizer. Oil cakes—what's left of beans or fish after the oil's been squeezed out—also made good fertilizer, but duckweed was free, so that's what they used.

What was worst about my job was not getting paid for the work I did. I had to pay cash for the wood I used in making fishing boats, and for the nails and rust-resistant copper and so on too. Yet I myself got paid on delivery only about a third of the time. The rest of the time it was, "I'll catch up with you soon as I catch some fish." I'd agree, figuring they'd pay when they were able—but when they did have a great catch, they'd blow the proceeds in one night on a wild spree and then go back to their usual down-and-out way of life. Meanwhile, I couldn't start my next boat till I got paid for the last one. I'd tell my wife, "So-and-so owes me two rice bags' worth of money, so go collect it for me." She'd come back empty-handed. "It's no good," she'd say. "They haven't got a penny to their name." Now that was hard to take. It was bad enough not having money to make another boat, but sometimes there was no money for food. For a while we managed by planting barley around the house and eating that, but the ground there was too wet to grow much of anything

on. There were no dikes, so it would flood regularly and the barley crop would be ruined. It was enough to make a grown man weep.

I decided to build boats originally because my father built houses in Akatsuka, and he never had two coins to rub together. I decided I'd build boats instead and make a lot of money to buy rice with, so I'd never starve. Well, that didn't work out. We were headed straight for starvation. In desperation, I got a friend of mine to lend me a patch of land in Tabuse, and I farmed it for all I was worth. That way we finally had enough rice to live on. That helped.

Then I got to thinking. Buying wood from a lumber dealer was what put me in the hole, so why not go out and find the wood myself? From then on, when somebody asked me to build him a boat, I'd go round from village to village looking for what I needed, and when I found a good tree, I'd deal directly with the owner. After we settled on a price, I'd go find a woodcutter to cut it down for me. They used to be everywhere. When he'd chopped the tree down, we'd load it on a cart and haul it to the shore. The fisherman who'd asked me to make him a boat would come with all his friends, and together we'd work at full tilt, tying the trees together to make a raft, then towing the raft by boat to my place. After that a sawyer spent days cutting up the trees into planks the right size, and when they were ready I'd set them to dry a few months before getting down to work. You can see that after all that time and trouble just getting the wood, if I didn't get paid when I delivered the finished product, it was a disaster.

There's no denying that fishermen led very hard lives. Nomads—fishermen who lived in their small boats and roamed all over the lake with no proper home—sometimes went decades without looking after the boats properly. The craft would be literally falling apart, the wood soft and rotting all over. They'd bring me a mess like that and beg me to fix it up, but what could I do? You can't repair rotting wood. The best I could do was nail bits of pinewood over the leaks, and stuff newspaper around the edges. That didn't last long, but it staved off the worst leaks. Boats like that had to be bailed out constantly.

A lot of those nomads were skilled fishermen, but the older they got, the harder it was. Some that I knew ran out of food and only kept themselves alive by eating boiled water oats with a little salt.

The biggest difference between a house carpenter and a ship carpenter is in the way you hit your nails. If you don't do it with a good rhythm, your work won't last long. The best way to pound nails is in time with the song of the *yoshikiri* [reed warbler], which goes like this:

> *Chonchiki chonchiki chaka chaka*
> *Chakka chaka chonchiki chonchiki chakka chakachaka*

If you keep to a rhythm like that, the nail slides into the wood easy, with no strain, and the wood grips it tight with no leaking. It's in there to stay. The first time I heard my master doing it, I thought he was goofing around. I thought all you needed to do was hit a nail straight on, *bam bam bam*, so what the hell was he doing? But when I tried it for myself, I realized getting the right rhythm is vital.

Chonchiki chonchiki means you hit the nail good and hard, but when you come to *chaka chaka* you ease up and turn your hands just so, kind of pressing the nail into the wood. You feel with the tips of your fingers how the nail and the wood are taking to each other. And then you go *chakka chakachaka*, just like the busiest part of the reed warbler's song, striking the nail with swift little taps. Getting the right balance is the hard part. You can sit outside the house of a ship carpenter and listen to the sound of his hammer and tell straight off how good he is.

There used to be reed warblers all around the shipyard where I worked. There used to be another name for them—the stableman's grudge-bird. Long ago there was a man who took care of a feudal lord's horse, and one day he lost one of his master's riding boots. The lord was furious and cut off his head. Then the stableman's head opened its mouth and sang this song:

Kutsukata kutsukata kutsukatakata, nan no sono, sa kire, sa kire,
Sa sa kire kire, kutsukata kutsukata katakatakata.
[One boot, one boot, one boot boot, why what's that, come kill me, come kill me,
Come come kill me kill me, one boot, one boot, boot boot boot.]

And then the head turned into a reed warbler and flew away.

I heard this story from one of the masters I signed on as apprentice to. He told me, "See, that's why the reed warbler is called the grudge-bird. He's singing in the face of certain death, as if his life depended on it. If you listen to his song and absorb its rhythm, you can pound nails as if your life depended on it." Then I realized it was true. There's nothing relaxed about the way that bird sings. He's always desperate. So I learned to listen to the reed warbler and pound nails for dear life.

Two Excursions on the *Tsuun Maru*

Mr. Washichi Takimoto (1902–1984)

In 1912 I took a sightseeing trip to Tokyo by paddle-wheel steamboat. Near Iwai is Sugao Marsh, which used to be so big that even a big *takase* riverboat could enter it with no trouble. The village of Nakazato had a steamer inn with a waiting room. Nowadays the village is farther back from the marsh, not on the water's edge anymore, but back then the inn was right on the water, looking directly out on the jetty. Passengers could stay overnight at the inn, which doubled as a restaurant. A number of women worked there as waitresses and maids. If you were coming from far away, you'd spend the night there and take the steamer next morning. The scenery around there was relaxing, with lots of water birds out playing on the water.

The day of the excursion I left home early with my dad and my sister. When we got on the *takase*, there were a dozen passengers there ahead of us. The captain and the crew numbered about five, and as they each took a pole and pushed off, the boat began to glide slowly along in the stream. It was a warm April morning, I remember, with mist floating over the water, a beautiful morning, really. When we left the marsh, we came out on the big River Tone. I'd never seen anything but small streams before in my life, so my eyes just popped. We floated slowly on down the river till we came to the juncture of the Tone and the Kinu, where the *Tsuun Maru* was waiting. Passengers came down on the Kinu too, but that river was so shallow that neither the steamer nor the *takase* riverboats could navigate it. Those people had to ride smaller flat-bottomed boats called *beka* down to the river junction.

I'd never seen anything but privately owned boats before in my life, so the sight of that steel ship with smoke puffing out of its funnel bowled me over. When the great paddle wheels began to turn and we set off, I was happier than a clam, running all over the ship and gawking at everything. My dad got peeved and warned me to quit rushing around or I'd fall overboard, but I couldn't sit still.

The *Tsuun Maru*

When I went to use the bathroom, I could see river water moving along right beneath me. It terrified me so much that I couldn't make water. There was a little chink in the floorboards, and through it you could see the blue water flowing past at a good clip. I felt as if I was going to be sucked down into the river. It took quite a while before I could pee normally again.

I went on another steamer excursion with my classmates in second grade. We left school very early in the morning and walked to the River Tone. Usually you'd take a ferryboat across, but there were more than fifty in our group, which was too much for the regular small ferry. We crossed over instead in a "horse ferry," which was designed to carry several horses and carts. It was a great big flat boat, ugly but solidly built, so it had no trouble accommodating fifty excited kids and their teacher. When we reached the other side, we got off and walked as far as Noda. That's seven and a half miles. We never stopped to look around; we just kept going straight through till we came to the ferry across the River Edo, on the edge of town. Noda was in Chiba Prefecture, and across the river was Saitama Prefecture. We got off in Kanasugi and plodded on again, past Matsubushi, on and on till we reached Koshigaya. The train there took us the rest of the way to Tokyo. Until we got on the train, we never stopped to rest, except for lunch. That was a good seventeen or eighteen miles.

By the time we got to our inn in Asakusa, it was dark. Well past seven, I'd say. My feet were burning. That night we saw a movie in a theater in Asakusa.

Next morning we went out to see the sights, but as we walked along in two lines, the Tokyo kids came up to us and jeered, "*Inakappe, inakappe!* [Country bumpkins!]" We went to Ueno Park and saw the museum, which was so huge it amazed me. I lay down flat on the floor to stare up at the ceiling, and a guard came rushing over. What did I think I was doing, lolling about in the imperial museum, he said. After that we went to Kudan to see Yasukuni Shrine.[1] There were trophies from the Russo-Japanese War. Then we walked over to the Imperial Palace, bowed down at the bridge leading to it, and had a picnic lunch in Hibiya Park—just rice and pickled plum, wrapped in bamboo, but we were so famished it tasted like heaven. Then we went to Ginza to look all around, and then back to Ryogoku in Tokyo, near Chiba.

The teacher who took us was a young fellow in a black suit, with a beard. He was a wonderful teacher. He told us, "Don't worry if people here stare at you. Hold yourselves tall, keep in straight lines, and walk proudly."

In Ryogoku we saw the chrysanthemum dolls,[2] and then we got back on the *Tsuun Maru*. It was only about eight p.m., but everybody collapsed and slept like the dead till morning. When we got up we were surprised to find we still had a long ways to go—we didn't get in to Noda till after three in the afternoon. It took longer going back because the ship was towing two *takase* boats that were loaded down with cargo. The whistle sounded over and over, but we made very little headway. We kids got bored and started climbing up on the roof, rolling around and roughhousing, just having fun. Past Noda I remember we could see farmers out gathering ginger. Then off in the distance we could see Mount Tsukuba, outlined clearly against the sky. I saw that and got a lump in my throat. "We're really back," I thought.

The Captain of the *Tsuun Maru*

Mr. Tomekichi Kuroda (1889–1987)

I was born in Ushibori, near the southern end of Lake Kasumigaura. At seventeen I became an apprentice to a maker of *tabi* socks [fitted, split-toe socks] at a shop in Nihonbashi, Tokyo, called the "Naraya." There were rivers everywhere in that part of the city, with boats tied up along the banks and at bridges. Whole families lived on board. You could look down from the railing of a bridge and see little children running around on the boats below and hear their mothers yelling at them. On rainy days they'd all crowd in under the roof, huddled together, and look up at the shore. Hundreds and hundreds of people lived like that.

When I was eighteen, I quit that business and spent the next six years on freighters. At twenty-seven I passed the test to be a captain and transferred to the *Tsuun Maru*. Being captain of a passenger ship was easy after freighters. I'd been on them so long that I knew the course of every river by heart; I could have navigated them with my eyes shut. That's no lie. I could be in bed asleep, and the sound of the engine would penetrate my body. That's all I needed to know exactly where we were. If it changed even a little, I'd think, "Aha. The river bottom here is different now; it's gotten to be such-and-such." There's a navigation device now called an echo sounder that can gauge the condition of the sea bottom using sound waves. I did the same thing using my own body.

When I went out on deck, I'd check the color of the water and the height of the waves. I could see at a glance where the shallows were, where we were likely to touch bottom. Just by looking I could tell exactly how deep the river was, to the inch. Believe it or not, it's true. The bottom of the River Tone would be slightly different every single day, and if you didn't have the know-how to read the river, you had no business taking passengers anywhere. The Onagi wasn't as tricky, but there was an awful lot of traffic, and if you didn't keep a sharp lookout you'd have a collision. You couldn't doze off. I always went out on deck and kept an eye on things as we moved along.

The Structure of the **Tsuun Maru**

We talk about the *Tsuun Maru* as if it was one steamer, but actually there were thirty-eight ships by that name, each one a slightly different shape and speed than the rest. Still, they were all pretty much the same. The helmsman's quarters were at the front. Behind that were the first-class passenger cabins. They cost half again as much as the tourist-class cabins, so on the Tokyo–Sawara run the tourist class was forty-eight sen and first class was seventy-two sen. There was also a dock fee of five sen tacked on, for a total of seventy-seven sen. That's how much inns charged for the privilege of walking through their doors and across the dock to board the ship. It was highway robbery. Around 1915 the fare between Tsuchiura and Okijuku, or Sawara and Ushibori, was eight sen—plus another five just for crossing the dock.

First-class cabins were impossibly expensive, so passengers mostly went steerage. The first-class cabins used to go empty all the time, so the crew'd take them over. There were no crew quarters as such. The men ate and slept in the deluxe cabins; if those happened to be taken, they had to move down to the engine room or the hold. On the Tone route the crew consisted of thirteen men, but on Lake Kasumigaura it was only eleven. You needed the extra hands on the Tone because the ship might run aground in shallow water, and then the cargo had to be transferred to a baggage boat.

The galley was between the captain's quarters and the engine room. It was so tiny that if two people were inside working, nobody else could get in. We used water right from the Tone and from Lake Kasumigaura for both cooking and drinking. The Edo and the Sumida were dirty. Their water was unusable, so before entering the canal we'd store water from the River Tone in huge buckets. In Tokyo we got water from shore, and when we went back to the Tone, we used river water again. People on *takase* riverboats thought nothing of using water from the River Edo, but with the town of Noda on the upper reaches of that river, its water couldn't help being dirty.

There was no meal service on the steamer. Cooks were there only to serve the crew, and passengers had to bring their own food aboard. Before I was captain, there used to be something called the Steamboat Boxed Lunch, but it wasn't especially good and nobody liked it.

There was a bath just for crew members too. We'd fill a wooden tub just big enough for one person with water from the river and heat it with steam from the furnace. It was piping hot in no time. After the passengers had gone below, you'd soak in the tub and gaze at the moon reflected on the water; that was quite a refined way to take a bath.

In winter the space over the engine room was a popular place to go. There was a three-foot space between the machinery and the ceiling, and if you lay thin boards known as *sana* there and spread out, even in winter it'd be as warm as midsummer. That only stands to reason, since directly below was a roaring coal fire. Anyway, that space was very snug and pleasant. When a westerly wind blew and the mercury dropped, the men got lazy; if someone got the least bit chilled working outside, he'd contrive to head straight for the *sana* space. But if everyone did that, the steamer might end up capsizing, so I spent a lot of time and trouble chasing crew members out of there.

Two men were responsible for stoking the furnace. We burned about three tons of coal a day. In front of the smokestack was an airhole called an ent-cock, above the stoker's head. You could change its direction by hand, so when it got too hot inside the stoker would turn it to catch the wind.

Below the cabins was the hold. The ship's center of gravity had to be as low as possible, so that's where we kept barrels of miso and soy sauce, fish, saké, fertilizer, cement, and anything else. There was a spare paddle wheel in there too. Sometimes in stormy weather a wheel could fall right off. The waves never got too rough on the Tone, but being out in the middle of Lake Kasu-

The *Tsuun Maru* (in foreground) and *takase* riverboats

migaura when the wind was blowing from the west was like being out on the ocean. The waves were so high that sometimes the paddle wheels would just spin and then break. When that happened, you had to remove the broken paddle wheel, get the spare out of the hold, and attach it. All the while the wind would be blowing great guns, so it was a hell of a job. The ships were old, so they were always breaking down someplace.

The newest one was Model 38, the one that came out in 1871. They never made any more after that. Whenever one of them broke down, we had to take it over to the Takabashi factory on the River Onagi for repairs. The engines were old too, so once a year someone from the Maritime Department would give them a thorough going-over. If the pressure exceeded a certain limit, the boiler could blow up, you see; he'd determine what that limit was and set the valves so the pressure wouldn't go over the danger line. When the valves were open, no matter how much coal you burned, the pressure wouldn't go beyond that point, so there was no danger of an explosion—but you couldn't get much power either. That's why the older a steamer was, the slower it went. Towing *takase* barges back upstream in a head wind was hard work.

The Tone Route

The steamer went through a canal to enter the River Tone from the Edo. The banks were crowded with bars, inns, and brothels—it was a lively old place. There were laborers whose job it was to pull the ship through the canal. They'd each drape a line across their shoulders, get down on all fours, and tow the *takase* along. In Ohori there were men called *norimawashi*, "round-abouts," who'd pull the towlines. They'd ride a *takase* from Ohori and pole it along till it entered the canal, then get out, go up on the bank, and all pull together. If it was a little boat manned only by a man and wife, then the man had to get up on the bank and pull for the entire five miles while his wife took the rudder. It took muscles to move boats through the canal.

Besides the canal, the River Tone had plenty of troubles too. When it rained, the flow of the river would change. Overnight, new shallows would appear. With a hold full of cargo and a boatload of passengers, naturally we'd be riding low in the water. So when the rain created new shallows, time and again we'd get stuck. Then the crew would lug out the cargo and set it on the *takase* barges behind us, to lighten the load. That's why every steamer on the Tone always had a couple of *takase* in tow. When the draft was shallower, sometimes we could get through. Other times, so much sand would have washed downstream that you couldn't get past the canal entrance. The only thing to do then was sit and wait twelve hours, or twenty-four, till the river bottom changed shape again. At either end of the canal, there were always dredgers at work, but if there was a particularly hard rain and too much sand piled up, sometimes a run was canceled.

The most prosperous place on our route would have been Sawara. It's fairly deserted today, but back then it was humming. That was our base. Every steamer from Tokyo unloaded all its passengers and cargo there. Whether you were heading for Lake Kasumigaura or on down to Choshi, you transferred at Sawara. There were no direct runs from Tokyo to the lake. Everybody went via Sawara. Besides the *Tsuun Maru*, there'd be every kind of boat there, big and little—freighters, riverboats, lighters, fishing boats, couriers, you name it, dozens of them crammed together at the harbor in Sawara or along the banks of the River Ono that wound through town. Inns, shops, restaurants, and brothels were jumbled together, and people came from all over. From other river towns, naturally, and from everywhere on the lake: Ushibori, Aso, Ukishima, Abasaki. For the courier boats, it was closer to row down to Sawara for shopping expeditions than to go to Tsuchiura. So they'd spend half a day

rowing to Sawara. The banks were lined with hundreds of boats that belonged to shoppers.

Working on the Lake

I transferred from the Tone route to the Lake Kasumigaura route in early 1919—about when the Inland Express Agency decided there was no future in water transport and switched to overland. After my experiences on the Tone, Kasumigaura came as somewhat of a relief because there was no current on the lake, and the water was deeper. On the other hand, the lack of time off was a hardship. We never got a day off, not even at New Year's or the summer Obon holiday. Back then everybody from farmers to shopkeepers worked so hard, you can't even compare it with the way people work today. Boatmen worked flat out every single day, day in and day out, barring a typhoon or some such disaster. New Year's Eve, New Year's Day—the boats ran.

There were jetties in Tsuchiura and Ushigome, but most steamer inns didn't have them; the steamer would stop offshore, and the inn would send passengers out on a lighter. The lighter pitched with the waves, so stepping from it to the steamer was a bit dicey. We had to keep a tight hold on the lighter to keep it from drifting away while passengers were getting on board. To do that, we used a long pole with a hook on one end, which we'd hook around the gunwale. Middle-aged women had a hard time of it because they wore a *koshimaki* underskirt that hampered their movements and got in the way. Sometimes we'd give them a hand and hoist them up from behind, but no one ever fell in the water. I never lost a passenger.

In summer kids would crawl all over the steamer. They weren't passengers; they'd be playing in the lake, swim out to where we were anchored offshore, then climb aboard when no one was looking. Kids back then were stark naked, boys and girls both. The second you looked away they'd shimmy up, quick as a wink, and go round to the cabins, dripping water. The passengers were mostly bored anyway, so they'd give them sweets and talk to them. "Where are you from, little boy?" That sort of thing. It wasn't long before a crewman would catch sight of the kids and chase after them, hollering: "You rascals! Up to your tricks again, are you, dripping water all over everything?" The kids would jump back into the water like a swarm of locusts and race for shore.

There was another steamboat besides the *Tsuun Maru*; it carried ocean fish from Choshi, at the mouth of the Tone, to market in cities like Ushibori and Tsuchiura. I never did that, but I did transport freshwater fish to market. Sometimes as I was steaming out towards the middle of the lake, I'd find a fishing boat waiting offshore. "What can I do for you?" I'd holler, and the fisherman would holler back, "Take my catch in to Tsuchiura for me, would you?" I'd slow down and wait for him to approach me and pass me his catch—smelt, or carp, or crucian carp, like as not—in buckets or baskets. I'd pile them on deck and when I got to Tsuchiura I'd take them to the dealer for him. If the dealer paid cash, I'd hold it for him; if there was any question about whether or not the catch would sell, I'd just leave it there. In those days you could catch ten or twenty pounds of fish every time you dropped your net in the water. Fishing was *too* good—it meant that fishermen ended up poorer than ever. Sometimes they caught so much, the dealers didn't know what to do with it.

How many years since I captained a steamer? I don't even know. The *Tsuun Maru* was gone by 1930, and everybody who knows it ever existed is old now.

4

TOWN LIFE

Tsuchiura, City of Water

Mr. Fukusaburo Takagi (1898–1981)0

Tsuchiura today has very little connection with water, but prior to the war it was a proud water capital. Everywhere you turned was another river, or pond, or canal—all interconnected, so that if you had a little boat, you could easily get from one corner of town to another.

The area east of Tsuchiura is Tozaki. Until around 1925 it used to be a small village, half farming and half fishing. Just one road went there from town, leading past the theater, and for miles around there was nothing else but paddy fields. The theater was built on an old execution ground. I used to work there, and I saw mounds of human bones with my own eyes. You couldn't build normal houses near a place like that. They put up that theater to comfort the spirits of the dead.

The Joban Railroad runs east of Tozaki, along the lake, and alongside the tracks there used to be an enormous pond extending I don't know how many miles, all the way to Kidamari. It was left after they dug up the earth they needed to level the ground for the tracks. There were no trucks back then for hauling dirt on construction jobs, only carts and *mokko* [straw baskets on poles]. You had to use whatever lay handy by the building site. Anyway, that pond stayed there at least till 1965. It was run by a fisheries experiment station.

Tsuchiura is built on wetlands, you see. Every time it rained, the lake would rise and the town would be flooded. The railroad served as a kind of dike. It wasn't enough to stop the flooding entirely, but it helped. We used to say it flooded every time a frog peed. The least bit of rain, and roads turned to lakes. Puddles formed in the dirt-floor entryways of all the houses. Shopkeepers who could afford it would buy the adjoining property, dig it up, and use the dirt to raise themselves above flood level. You could tell who had money at a glance: their house would be higher than everyone else's, and out back would be a pond filled with carp.

All the ponds and streams and canals gave the city its own charm, but there were drawbacks. What I'll never forget is the mosquitoes. With open sewers everywhere, the mosquitoes were something fierce. In the summer when you came home at night, the second you started to say, I'm home, five or six of 'em would fly right in your mouth. They clung to the ceiling in the day and came out after dark. Without a mosquito net you were doomed. In front of the tenement houses, where people did their cooking and the ground was moist, big black columns of mosquitoes used to hang in the air, giving off a constant whine. A lot of people were so desperately poor that they even pawned their mosquito netting, and without that, sleep was impossible. As a last resort they'd pick mugwort along the riverbanks and burn it to smoke the mosquitoes out.

The Geisha Tamafune

There was one section of town where three waterways came together; it's all been filled in now, but back then you could only get there by boat. There was a splendid two-story house there, right next to a big pine—all that remained of the pines that had lined the outer moat of Tsuchiura Castle. Gihei Okamoto, one of the richest men in town, built that house for his mistress, even though he had to tear down the banks of the old moat and level the ground to do it. His mistress was the former geisha Tamafune, a knockout beauty. The only one who could hold a candle to her was Kofuji, who no less a man than Isoroku Yamamoto fell in love with—he was the commander in chief of the Combined Fleet during World War II. Anyway, Tamafune was a rare beauty. Okamoto built a second home for himself made entirely of the finest cypress—a real palace, it was. Later it was made into a maternity hospital. Supposedly he built it to entertain important guests from Tokyo, but people whispered that the real reason was to impress Tamafune.

Okamoto loved to entertain in grand style. He had a special houseboat

Sunoko Bridge

built to take guests out on the lake—something like a deluxe yacht today. He'd take along several geisha to sing and dance, and hire a chef to cook up delicious meals for everybody to eat while they watched the entertainment. He was a big, fine-looking gentleman with a splendid mustache, and everybody in town looked up to him, including the mayor. But it didn't last. He overplayed his hand and went bankrupt. In the end he had to slink away under cover of night to escape his creditors, and only Tamafune went with him.

Sunoko Bridge and Debtor's Bridge

Sunoko Bridge ran through the center of town. It got its name because originally it was made of *sunoko* [woven bamboo] and could easily be set on fire. That was to protect the castle from enemy attack, back in the old days. At one end of the bridge was a cartwright's shop, where iron hoops were fitted on the wooden wheels used on rickshaws and carts. The iron went on hot and shrank as it cooled so it made a tight fit. When I was a boy, wheels were all made of plain wood, but as the shrinkage technology spread, more and more wheels were coated with iron. Rubber tires didn't come into use until quite a bit later, around 1925 or so. Those didn't rattle and they cushioned the ride, so they became hugely popular. Word quickly spread about which doctors had switched to rubber tires for their rickshaws. But till around the 1920s, rickshaw tires were all made of cast iron. They made an enormous racket, and they gave you a jerky, bumpy ride.

The cartwright was the equivalent of today's auto repair shop. There were several of them scattered around town. One was called "Maniawaseya" [The Patch-It-Up Shop]. The owner was a clever fellow who could generally get a broken rickshaw rolling again within the day, so that's how his shop got that name.

Across from the cartwright was a popular fish shop called "Hokotaya" that sold fresh sea fish. (The shop later moved just a little ways away, and the site is a parking lot now.) Of course, there was no ice to be had back then, so keeping fish fresh was no easy matter. Even though the fish came up from Choshi every morning in barrels packed in brine, it would often start turning bad on the way. After it arrived, it was auctioned off at the Tsuchiura Fish Market and then trundled off to the various fish shops. Hokotaya also made *kamaboko* [steamed fish paste]. The workers sat in front of thick wooden boards and pounded the fish rhythmically; the sound—a pleasant *tontoko tontoko*—carried all around town. After that the fish was ground to paste in a stone mortar. You could watch the whole process from the street. They served meals at Hokotaya too. It was a popular place to eat because of the fresh sea fish.

After the fish arrived at the fishmonger's, someone would carry it around town in a couple of baskets or buckets attached to a pole across the shoulders—so you can imagine that by the time it reached the customers, it could sometimes be pretty ripe. You could easily get food poisoning if you didn't watch out. Happened all the time. "Yesterday I got drunk on bonito," somebody'd say. That's what we called it—getting drunk. Why? Because after eating tainted fish you'd break out in a rash and your face would turn bright red, just as if you'd been drinking saké.

Across the street from Hokotaya was a large saké shop run by a man named Seinosuke Noguchi—the first person in Tsuchiura ever to manufacture and store ice. Noguchi dug a pond on a little mountain outside of town, and in winter it froze over. At first the ice wouldn't be very thick, but he hired someone to pour water on the pond day after day till a solid layer built up, a good seven or eight inches thick. Then he had the man carve that into blocks with a handsaw, wrap them in straw, and haul them off to his cellar. In summer, fish sellers and people looking after sick relatives would come to buy it. It was a

Debtor's Bridge

primitive method by today's standards, but what else could he have done?

Noguchi also was the first to store seed-papers for silkworms. Tiny silk-worm eggs attached to paper strips. Noguchi's ice-cellar was the perfect place for storing them until they were needed. The silk raisers' union persuaded him to store seed-papers for all of Tsuchiura and the surrounding area.

Behind Sunoko Bridge was a smaller, shabbier bridge known as Debtor's Bridge. Nobody christened it that, the name just gradually stuck. That bridge was handy for anybody who had too many debts to walk openly down the main street and wanted to sneak round the back way instead. You see, in those days, people hardly ever paid cash for anything. Whether for rice, miso, soy sauce or a doctor's bill, you were expected to pay up on New Year's Eve. Or you could pay in two installments, first at the summer Obon festival and then on New Year's Eve. For those who were really hard up—day laborers and arti-sans, for example—it was different; there, the husband would hand over his day's earnings to his wife, and she'd go out and buy a handful of rice for sup-per. But mostly people shopped on credit. Which is of course another way of saying they were in chronic debt. If you paid off your debts as you went along, good enough; but let things slide, and you could end up too deep in debt to get out at the end of the year. The last thing you'd want to do then is walk in front of a store where you owed money. On the main street, the biggest shops in town were lined up one after another, which was certainly inconvenient if you owed money everywhere. Having to stop and make excuses every few feet was a terrible nuisance. Naturally, people took to using back streets where they wouldn't have to face their creditors.

You see, times were different then. Nowadays if you do business on account, the bill collector can come around any time he wants to, but not back then. Nobody ever went out collecting except at the two regulation times of year—

The River Tamachi

it just wasn't done. So even if you were hopelessly in debt, as long as you could make it past New Year's Eve, you'd automatically have six more months of grace. People were naturally desperate not to be caught on New Year's Eve. They'd sneak about from place to place, trying to avoid being seen. But once bells began ringing at midnight to usher in the new year, you were home free. Then if you ran into a creditor, all you had to give him was a cheerful "Happy New Year!" There's a famous *rakugo* comic monolog about it. You couldn't help feeling a bit guilty the rest of the year, though, even if you weren't being dunned, so Debtor's Bridge filled a definite need. People were only too glad to use it.

The River Tamachi and Amida Hall

Amida Hall fronted on the River Tamachi, which used to serve as the outer moat of Tsuchiura Castle. Next to it was a public bath, and then a statue of Jizo, and then tenements where cart-drivers lived. After that was the House of the Rising Sun, a brothel where three or four girls worked. There were other brothels nearby as well, some of them quite big. A lot of the girls were as young as sixteen or seventeen, sold into the business by families without any means. Later the brothels were all ordered to relocate in Sakuramachi and the neighborhood kind of died, but Amida Hall is there even now.

It used to be surrounded by graves, many of them deserted, with no known relatives. It was decided to transfer the rest to a different temple. I was one of those entrusted with the task. That's right, in those days scaffolding-builders didn't only build houses and bridges—we did things like move gravestones and graves too.

Burial was the rule then, not cremation. The bodies, or what was left of them, would be buried in a sitting position inside a big jar or, more commonly, a wooden coffin. I personally moved seven or eight remains, and it was amazing how well they were preserved. Must've had something to do with the high water content of the soil. The bodies were actually preserved in water. When we dug down and opened the lid, the body would be sitting there as if it was still alive, the skin still firm. Bodies preserved with lime were in even better shape.

The second that the wind blew in, though, the bones would sink to the bottom, the water would turn muddy, and the skin would rise to the surface of the water. The air set off some sort of a reaction, I guess. The burial kimono was always rotted clean away; you couldn't make out any pattern or anything. The muscle and fat tissues would be clean and smooth to the touch.

Commoners were all buried sitting up. To be buried in a reclining position you had to be a member of the samurai class, and townspeople didn't qualify. In the old days, people weren't even equal after death.

Well, I've been very frank about what I saw, and I know it sounds strange but it was just a job. I worked hard at it every day, the way I would any job I took on. Once you made up your mind to do that, there wasn't anything to it.

The River Tsukiji

The Tsukiji used to be a big, beautiful river, over sixty feet wide, with willow branches trailing in the water on either side. It was a gorgeous sight. Facing the river were Nakazawa Photo Studio, Myokenji Temple, and the mansion of the first mayor of Tsuchiura, Mr. Hiyama. There was also a restaurant called the "Koyokan," and a junior high school.

This river was the outer moat of the castle, and for defense purposes sand had been dumped on the riverbed every twelve or fifteen feet, to make it shallow enough that in case of enemy attack you could escape to the other side without using a boat. That made it a wonderful place for children to play, right down through the mid-1920s.

The River Tsukiji

You may wonder how a river so wide and beautiful could have wound up as narrow as it is today, and there's actually a rather interesting explanation. There were houses all along the banks of the river, each with a wooden fence to shore up the bank. Being made of wood, the palings didn't last ten years. Every so often it was necessary to replace them with new ones, but that was never done in the same place. The new fence always went up a foot or two farther out into the river. People would dig up dirt from the riverbed to fill in the intervening space, and use it to plant vegetables or something. This was actually a subtle way for people to increase their landholdings, you see. So as twenty, thirty, forty years went by, the width of the river was narrowed by several feet from either side. The riverbank gradually became uneven too, since some people worked harder than others to increase the size of their land. Anybody who put up a stone wall to shore up the bank by his property was a laughingstock since that would make the borderline too clear and make it impossible to extend the property.

Most people owned one or two boats. Nobody ever stole the boats, but sometimes a thief would borrow one to make his getaway. The next day it would turn up somewhere down the river.

Boats were used for lovers' trysts too. One night when my grandfather was keeping watch there was a clatter out back where we had a number of boats tied up. I was just a little kid, but I wanted to know what was going on, so I went out back with Grandfather to check. There was a big old moon reflected on the water, and a young man was slipping one of our boats from its moorings. A girl had lifted up the skirts of her kimono to keep them from getting wet, and she was about to step into the boat. They were going out on the water for a little romancing. My grandfather took one look and yelled, "Hey!" The young man was so surprised he lost his footing and sent the boat flying. The girl had one foot on shore and the other in the boat, so she lost her balance and tumbled into the water. My grandfather shook his fist and yelled, "Serves you right, you hussy!" I remember she was a very pretty thing. But too old for me, unfortunately.

Fishing with a Pole and Basket

Today only old people know the word *shippiki*, which means fishing with a pole and basket. It used to be quite common. The edge of town was all muddy rice fields, separated by channels maybe ten feet across, and those channels were full of fish. In winter, if you stuck even your bare hands in the water and poked around a little, you could catch crucian carp. There were plenty for the taking. The water was so cold they lay in a kind of suspended animation and made no attempt to get away. Men out of work, construction workers and other day laborers, and tenant farmers all used to supplement their meager diet by coming out to do *shippiki*. Sometimes they took the fish they caught home for dinner, and sometimes they sold them for cash; either way, it helped tide them over.

Here's how you did it. You'd take a bamboo pole twelve feet long, fasten a sort of basket at one end, and probe the muddy water for fish to scoop up. Why not use nets, or some other more efficient method? No one could afford any such thing as a net. Besides, the fish were so plentiful that *shippiki* worked fine. The only trouble was, this was the coldest time of year, and standing all hours in the icy north wind, you'd get frozen to the core. The rivers were always covered with ice an inch thick. Even Lake Kasumigaura used to freeze over. After a day out in that awful wind, your whole body would be frozen stiff. The only way you could stand it was to gather dry reeds and make a fire to warm yourself now and then. Those fish were good eating, though. They had no strong fishy taste. We grilled them on skewers, or ate them sweet-boiled. They tasted heavenly.

Shippiki fishing

Poverty

There was a lot of poverty in the tenements near where I grew up. People today can't even comprehend the level of poverty back then. There was no welfare system, so many people were literally penniless. If they got sick, there was no money to pay a doctor so about all they could do was go lie down. The weak soon died. On the main street there was a row of prosperous shops, brightly lit at night, but just a few steps around to the back was a different world. Tenements had a common well and toilet facilities. People didn't even have indoor kitchens. They lit cooking fires outside by the front door instead. Not that there was anything to cook—a handful of rice per person mostly. If there was a bit of grilled fish to go with it, that was a treat. That's the way so many, many folks lived.

No work meant no rice for that day. So in the morning the men would go to some rich man's house and ask politely for a job. There might be work in the garden, or chopping firewood, or some such thing. That was better than nothing. When there was no work to be had, people scooped up fish by *shippiki* to ward off starvation.

Day laborers had no tatami mats in their houses, and the roofs leaked. When small planks blew off the roof, they used thin straw matting to cover the holes. Often you could see the moon through the holes in the roof. Landlords didn't want to make repairs for tenants who couldn't be counted on for the rent.

Day laborers and their families mostly had no clothes but what they wore on their backs. There were certainly no extra clothes to put on in winter. Tenant farmers were equally bad off. Often a man would work flat-out in the fields from three or four a.m. till nine or ten at night, with barely time to splash water on his face—all without earning any rice of his own. At the same time, landowners lived high on the hog, had storehouses piled with thousands of bags of rice, and dressed their children in the finest silk. I swear, they lived in a different world from everyone else.

Farmers couldn't afford to keep their children—they had all they could do just keeping food in their own mouths. Children were openly bought and sold. I couldn't begin to tell you how many girls from my area alone were sold off to geisha houses in the latter half of the nineteenth century and the beginning of the twentieth. Boys went to work for the landowner as often as not. Around 1910 they earned one measly yen per year. Even then the family was happy that there was one less mouth to feed.

Tenant farmers didn't have baths at home. In town anybody could go to the public bath, so even the poor people could have a hot soak, but there was no such thing in the country. The only thing to do was go to the home of a well-off farmer and ask to use his bath. Why didn't they build themselves a bath at home? That's easy—no firewood. Once you bought a bathtub you could use it for years, so that would have been a good investment, but without some sort of fuel, what good was it? Tenant farmers didn't have a scrap of land to their names. To light their cooking fires, they asked permission to forage for dry pine needles and fallen branches. There was never enough to heat a bath. But a bath was considered a luxury anyway, so a lot of people couldn't have one out of deference to their landowner. Using someone else's was a normal way of life. Stepping into clean hot water in your own home, like everyone does today, didn't happen till several years after the war.

There were all kinds of landowners, but just to give you some idea of the way things were, here's a story. Once I entered the home of a wealthy man to do some work for him, and I noticed a small room toward the back of the house that was like a prison cell, except instead of locking from the outside it locked from inside. I asked one of the servants what it was for. He told me the family all slept in there at night. Why go to so much trouble? I asked. Appar-

Doing laundry outside a tenement house

ently there'd been an attack once by an angry tenant farmer out for blood. This was a precaution just in case anybody ever tried the same thing again. I looked in and saw an alarm bell hanging from the ceiling. It was all arranged so that if anyone ever attacked them they'd strike the bell and bring the police running. That's the kind of world it was.

I've lived in Tsuchiura for over eighty years now. I've watched the city change and I have to say, this is the best it's ever been. There are always problems, but the difference between living conditions now and the way things used to be is like day and night.

Lakeside Kids

Mrs. Ko Hisamatsu (1911–1986)

When I was a girl I lived in the Tozaki section of Tsuchiura. Of course it's completely changed. Now there are houses everywhere, but there used to be nothing but rice paddies around where we lived. In fall when the rice was ripe, the paddies would turn black with sparrows. We put up a string all around the edge of the paddy, with cans hanging from it so that if you pulled on the end of the string the cans would crash together and make a loud noise. We ran the end of the string all the way back to the house, so you could sit in the living room and pull on it any time sparrows came. The noise of the cans scattered them into the air like sesame seeds. This was back in the days when children fell asleep listening to the steam locomotives go by, counting how many wheels they had by the sound.

On summer nights I remember the light of the fireflies. They flitted criss-cross over the rice paddies, on and on as far as you could see, filling the sky. My, what a sight that was! After dark we'd all go out by the water's edge, fan in hand, to see them gathered motionless on the willow branches, shining on and off. Every tree would be covered with numberless fireflies clinging to the branches and just breathing quietly, shining their lights in unison, on off, on off, on off. It was so beautiful. If you hit them with your fan they'd tumble to the ground and just lie there, shining. You could sweep them up into a bag, take them home and let them go inside a mosquito net, and they'd go on shining all night. They were prettier on dark, moonless nights than when the moon was out.

Speaking of the moon, it was thought to be especially beautiful on the night of November 23, when it was supposed to shimmer as it rose in the sky. Folks would stay up late to see it and invite each other out moon-viewing. We'd prepare special food for the occasion. Everyone trooped up to Eagle Shrine on top of the mountain to wait for the moon to come out. It was always bitter cold. Around eleven p.m. it would happen: first the lake would get brighter, and then the moon would slowly peek out and sail up into the sky

over the lake, shimmering as it rose. The air was never so sharp and crystalline as it was then, the moon never so divine and holy. We'd press our palms together and pray for good health and a bumper crop of rice. Everyone in Tozaki would stay out till past midnight.

There used to be so much damage from floods that the rice crop hardly ever amounted to much. In September it would rain. Water built up in the river—"fall water," we called it—and spilled over into the rice paddies. People were always shaking their heads over the ruined crop. A good crop of rice happened only once every four or five years.

After the war our river turned into a sewer ditch, but it used to be sparkling clean and pure. You could catch killifish, crucian carp, and bitterling. You could look down from Yachiyo Bridge and see them plainly, swimming in the water. It's a parking lot now. Used to be the best fishing spot around. When you traveled by boat, you could see the river bottom plain as day.

My friends and I used to row out to the shallows at night after supper, when it was cooler, and go for a swim. Rowing was second nature to all the children, even girls. The water there was so clean and beautiful under the moon, you wouldn't believe it. You could sit in your boat, look down into the water by the light of the moon, and see just where the bottom was rocky, where it was sandy, or where it was covered in little stones. You could see the seaweed waving in the water. Seems like a dream to me now.

There was something near here called Paradise Paddy that stretched all the way to the back of Mr. Nagai's soy sauce shop. I suppose it got that name because it was covered with lotus blossoms that were so beautiful. It's all built up with houses now. Back then it was wetlands, too moist and squishy to walk on. There were places where you'd sink down in mud clear to your hips, even if it hadn't been raining. You had to take a big detour to steer clear of them. The boys liked to play games in Paradise Paddy—the ground was soft, and

Lotus blossom

they'd run around yelling at the tops of their lungs and getting mud all over themselves till it got dark. It was a good place to fly kites too, because there weren't any utility poles to get in the way. The kites would really soar.

The fishermen all went through Paradise Paddy to get home after work. There was a waterway down the middle that branched off in all directions and connected with the dock at the back of everyone's house. They'd come through the lock gate after fishing, paddle through Paradise Paddy surrounded by lotus blossoms in summer, and get home without once setting foot on land.

Neighbors

People used to get along with each other like family. It was always, "Come on over for tea, why don't you?" or "Have a bite to eat before you go." People cared about each other, and nobody locked their door. Doors didn't have locks on them. People treated other people's kids just like their own too—fed them, even gave them baths. Adults were busy but kids never studied, they just played and played and played. It was all so different from now.

Girls played just as hard as boys did. When it rained and the water level went up, fish would be swept down to our area, so as soon as we saw the rain clouds come out we'd run home and get shrimp traps, and then scoot to the paddies. There was a narrow channel between the waterway and the paddy where you'd set up your trap, weighting it down with a little dirt. Then you'd take shelter somewhere till it stopped raining. Later when you went back to check, you'd find the trap full of mud-loaches and shrimp. We could catch shrimp and carp and crucian carp in the paddies too, especially in the early spring when they set out the rice seedlings and flooded the paddies. There were so many we could catch them with our bare hands. It's amazing to me now.

Lots of times we'd drain a stream. We'd wade out in it barefoot with our

kimono skirts tucked up, boys and girls alike, and stop up the water flowing in. Then we'd scoop out the water with a bucket or a scoop until it got so low that the fish were thrashing around. We'd go after them with our bare hands and put them in buckets to take home, all we could carry. Eels too.

Early in spring before the new growing season got underway, if you looked under the rice stubble you'd find holes, and if you dug down in those with your hands, you could always catch a mud-loach. Nowadays if you went into a stranger's rice paddy and started filling it with holes you'd catch hell for sure, but when we were kids nobody said a word. People started getting snippy about things like that after the war—1965 or 1970, I'd say—and kids stopped playing outdoors so much. Things used to be a lot warmer and friendlier.

The best time to catch mud-loaches was at night, around the time the rice seedlings were set out. Each child would soak a cloth in pine resin, fasten it to the end of a stick and light it to make a torch, then wade out into a flooded rice paddy. We went in groups of ten. There'd be clusters of children everywhere, bent on catching loaches. When you shone your torch down you could see the loach sleeping at the bottom of the water, all stretched out, as lazy and comfortable as could be. Then you'd spear him. I can't helping feeling a little sorry for the loach, now that I think of it, but we were children and we speared them one after another. They sold the spears at any candy store, so you see it was the most natural thing in the world for us to do. The mud-loaches then weren't horribly fat like they are now, and they weren't bad for you. They tasted wonderful. Anyway, the sight of torchlight wavering here and there in the darkness was beautiful.

In the fall we'd catch locusts. When you walked along the path between two rice paddies the locusts would scatter and leap up in front of you with a dry whir, more than you could possibly catch. After rice farmers started using chemical fertilizer they were gone, just like that.

Kids would fashion bags out of paper to hold the locusts they caught. The insects jumped around inside hard enough to break the bag, so some kids would bring a beer bottle instead. It was a race to see who could get the most. A big beer bottle filled right up in no time. When you'd caught as many as you could, then you'd take them home. Mother would fry them up in the frying pan with a little oil, and we'd have them for supper with our rice. They're good for you, you know. I believe they're good for the liver.

Life in the old days was hard, especially in winter. Fishermen had it especially tough because it got colder then than it does now, and the rivers would freeze solid at night. On a cold day it would be frozen all the way to Okijuku. Both the Kawaguchi and the Tazaki would be covered in a good inch of ice. The fishing boats always set out after midnight, so they'd set a lamp in the prow and have one man stand there and smash the ice with a bamboo pole as the boat inched forward. Everything was done by manpower. Just getting through the ice to reach a fishing spot meant hours of backbreaking work.

The hard work they did in the bitter cold explains why men all died so young. There weren't any men in their seventies or eighties. They all died at forty or fifty. The town was full of widows. While the men were out fishing in the cold and ice, the women sat around the fire sipping hot tea, as cozy as you please, chatting about one thing and another. Of course they outlived the men! Women had their share of hard work in the day, out in the rice fields, but men had to work at night too. It was a harsh life.

Anyway, one thing I'll never forget is the sight of bitterling laid out to dry in front of every house in Tozaki. You don't see them anymore, but back then we caught more than we knew what to do with. You couldn't give them away. All the houses hung them out to dry and kept a constant supply on hand for kids to munch on as snacks. When you threw leftover rice in the river after supper, bitterling would swarm up to eat it. Now they're gone, along with the rivers and the paddies.

The Eagle Shrine and the Jakamokojan Festival

Mr. Isamu Hisamatsu (1904–1990)

As kids, my friends and I spent a lot of time up at the Eagle Shrine. We climbed all the pine trees, did sumo wrestling in the courtyard, played tag and hide-and-seek. Looking out from the hilltop, there'd be nothing for miles around but deep green rice fields, and white sails out on Lake Kasumigaura. You could see steam locomotives puffing along the shore in the distance.

In the approach to the shrine, there used to be a bronze eagle. The town took up a collection once, around the turn of the century, and had it made. It was a grand thing, with eyes of real gold. Of course, a thief came along in no time and helped himself. After that the shrine took down the eagle so now only the pedestal is left. You have to remember, we were on the gold standard in those days, so gold wasn't all that unusual. You could always cash in bills for an equivalent amount of gold, and the five- and ten-yen coins were made of gold. When I was in primary school, one *monme*[1] of gold was worth five yen.

Anyway, one day we were playing there as usual, and along came a bunch of tattooed fishermen wearing flashy padded jackets. None of us had ever seen anything like them before. There were seven or eight of them, come to worship at the shrine. We just stood and stared, our mouths hanging open. Later I heard that they'd been shipwrecked out at sea. One day a big eagle appeared above them in the sky and led them safely to shore. They were convinced it was from the shrine, so they all came together to give thanks. I'll never forget the sight of them in those outlandish getups.

Funny thing is, despite its name, the shrine wasn't really dedicated to eagles. It was consecrated to Ame-no-hi-washi-no-mikoto, the god of farmers, who just happened to have the word *washi* ["eagle"] in his name. He was a peaceful god, the exact opposite of Hachiman, the war god. There was an Eagle Shrine in Tamura too, and the theory was that when people from Tamura moved to Tozaki, they brought their god right along with them.

The Eagle Shrine

On the way into the shrine, on the left there used to be a restaurant called the "Kogetsu" that my father often visited. It was built right out onto the water, so you could gaze out at the moon reflected in Lake Kasumigaura while you sipped your saké. It must have been wonderful.

Speaking of the shrine reminds me of the professional sumo wrestling matches that used to be held there. The wrestlers traveled all around Japan on tour. Back then their only regular tournaments were at New Year's and in May, so they had time to visit even out-of-the-way places like our town. Everybody and his grandmother turned out for the occasion.

The water in the canal surrounding the shrine was very clean. There were lots of big, brightly colored carp in it, I remember. We'd stand on the bridge and look down on them in the water. We also liked sailing boats, making dams, and catching fish.

Here's a funny song we used to sing as we played:

Atto awameshi chazuke ni koko	A bowl of millet, tea on top, with pickles
Umakunakutemo takusan agare	Tastes no good but help yourself
Agakkara motteko	I'll help myself so bring it on
Motteko sutteko	Bring it on, there you go
Ana hotte tsunmugure	Dig a hole and jump on in
Tsunmugukkara anaa hore	I'll jump in so dig the hole
Ana honnaa gotaigida	Digging holes is boring
Gotaigibushi kakkuree	Boring, hide!
Kakkuraakara motteko	Okay I'll hide so bring it on
Motteko sutteko	Bring it on, there you go
Anaa hotte tsunmugure	Dig a hole and jump on in

Oden stall

The Jakamokojan Festival

No one knows for sure when the Jakamokojan Festival got started, though it definitely goes way back. It probably went along with community recitations of the Buddhist *nenbutsu* invocation; the word *jakamokojan* could have been a chorus that did the singing to accompany sacred *kagura* dancing.[2] Anyway, it was a popular festival in my boyhood.

On January 15 by the old calendar, they'd set up five or six stalls on the temple grounds where folks would sit on straw matting and eat hot *oden*—or rather, to give it its proper name, *dengaku*. It wasn't like today's *oden* stew, with hard-boiled eggs and all sorts of goodies in a hot broth. There were just three ingredients: grilled tofu, slices of *konnyaku* [devil's-tongue jelly], and taro. We ate them on bamboo skewers with a sweet, sticky miso sauce.

The stalls weren't just in the temple grounds. Ordinary folks made *oden* too, and set up shop selling it from one end of town to the other. Everybody came streaming out for the occasion, dressed in warm clothes because it was so cold. We kids went barefoot, but we had on leggings and long sleeves. Our cheeks and hands and feet would be bright red. Then after visiting the shrine, we'd wolf down hot *oden*.

The sizzle and smell of grilling food was everywhere. Theaters did a brisk business, and the sound of flutes and drums added to the liveliness. After dark some of the stalls would be strung with carbide lanterns, and the light was dazzling.

Besides *oden,* there used to be sweets for sale called *kinkato.* They were made by boiling white sugar and setting it in molds, then cooling them with water to make white, hard candies. Then the candies would be decorated with red or purple food coloring. They were really eye-catching. They came shaped like foxes, or the god of wealth, and all sorts of things. Big ones were five or ten sen, little ones just two.

Preparing *dengaku*

There was another kind of sweet too, called *oshinko*. The maker would knead rice and sugar together, then use his fingers and chopsticks to fashion it into different shapes—chickens, rabbits, all kinds of animals. We kids would watch with our mouths wide open, as if it were a magic show.

Eating festival *oden* was supposed to protect you from sickness all year. Folks who braved the cold to hike up the mountain were a hardy, healthy bunch, I'll say. Children loved the Jakamokojan Festival. We used to tick off the days till it came. It started losing steam with the coming of the war, though, and afterwards there was so little food to go around that it never got going again till 1955, when the war widows took it over. It never really caught on, though. Now the young people and the women in town are trying to revive the festival. It's a great old tradition, simple and rustic, and as for me, I'd like to see it go on forever.

Festivals and Feast Days

Mr. Michizo Tamura (1912–1998)

Festivals and feast days[3] today are nothing like they were in the old days. Back in our time they got celebrated in style. These are the feast days every month: the fifth is "Suiten-gu," the tenth is "Konpira-sama," the twenty-third is "Sanya-sama," the twenty-fifth is "Tenjin-sama," and the twenty-eighth is "O-Fudo-sama."[4] On those days storekeepers would string lanterns out in front of their shops, and people would set up outdoor stalls selling everything under the sun. There weren't many amusements back then, so we kids got a real charge out of feast days. Nakajomachi, where I was from, was downtown Tsuchiura, so it was always the most crowded. On the feast of Tenjin-sama they'd set up an outdoor theater on an empty lot to show motion pictures. Then the place would be so crowded you could hardly budge. Mostly they showed swordfight pictures, from seven till ten at night. Since the show was outdoors, the screen would flutter in the wind, so you could see the picture even from behind. There was no charge, of course. Street vendors were everywhere. The smell of carbide and the sound of it crackling added to the atmosphere and made everything that much more festive.

There were special treats to mark the occasion too. *Fukujin-yaki*, for one. Those came shaped like trains or treasure ships or almost anything, and they were delicious. I remember buying piles of them. There were special griddle-cakes just for children as well. Those you could buy around town on regular days too, not just festival days. Children would crowd around, each one clutching his five sen, while the man poured batter out onto a hot plate. When a pancake was nicely brown he'd add sweet bean jam and roll it up like a trumpet, or cut-up meat and onions and slather it with sauce—or he might add shrimp, or whatever you wanted. In cold weather those tasted so good, hot off the griddle.

Another snack we children used to love was *shinko-zaiku*, little rice-flour pastries in different shapes. They used to sell those till recently. The vendor

Festival at a temple

would ring a little bell to let you know he'd come round. Ever heard of *fuki-tofu*? Boiled broad beans, peeled and stewed with sugar. Mmm, good! Then there was *budo-mochi*, with a thin crust and plenty of bean jam inside, which you could get at a shop just around the corner from the fishmonger by Manabe Hill. As soon as I came home from school I'd get on my bike and pedal over there as fast as I could to buy some. Twenty or thirty sen would buy more than enough for the whole family and all the workers in our shop.

In April we went cherry blossom–viewing. Mother used to take me up to Komatsu for it. We walked through rice fields to a stone staircase, and at the top the vendors would have their stalls set up, where you could buy things like sweet dumplings on a stick. From up there you could see the whole Tsuchiura Basin at a glance, fresh with new leaves, and Lake Kasumigaura off sparkling in the sun. What a grand view it was.

In summer Suijin-sama and Gion festivals were the big ones. And at the midsummer Obon festival, we floated lanterns on the river. That day everyone wore yukata with a fan tucked into the sash at the back. At night we would set offerings in straw mats and float them down the River Sakura, to see off the spirits of the dead. The sight of the flickering candlelight reflected in the water was so beautiful. That was the moment when it really felt like Obon. There was always a big turnout for the occasion. People brought wicker furniture and benches to sit on and enjoy the cool of the evening while they watched. Up and down the riverbanks were playhouses where singing and playacting went on.

In the fall, around November 15 was something called "*machi*," a harvest festival that took place after every farm family had finished gathering in the year's crops. The original purpose, they say, was bartering, but when I was a kid it was all about sumo wrestling. The strongest young fellows for miles around would gather and compete, with a prize going to the winner. Everybody got caught up in it and rooted for their favorite. The grownups would get together with friends and drink saké. The kids were given *amazake* [sweet saké].

As the year came to an end we'd be busy with housecleaning, getting ready for New Year's. Everybody in town looked forward to New Year's more than anything, children and adults and workers and everybody. That time of year was special. On ordinary days the store would be open till at least ten p.m., so workers were usually in bed by midnight. But for the first week or so of the new year we closed at five.

As soon as supper was over, we'd all play card games or *sugoroku* [a form of parcheesi], the family and the shopworkers together. That went on till eleven, twelve, one in the morning. For prizes there'd be tangerines or peanuts, or a kind of cheap sweet that looked like a woman's hairstyle. There was a cheap sweet shop in Honmachi where five sen would buy a mountain of goodies. First prize would be something really good, say bean-jam buns from one of the best shops in town—when it was announced, people would get fired up and do their best to win. Good sweets were rare back then, so something like that was a real treat. We'd eat tempura soba too—the one time in the year when we did. Now you can go to a restaurant and order it any time you want to, but back then it had to be a special occasion. Come to think of it, our lives were about as simple as they could be. All the more reason why we looked forward so much to festivals, ticking off the days on our fingers.

Two Counting Songs

    Number one is Ichi Shrine
    Two for the shrine at Nikko
    Three for Songoro in Sakura

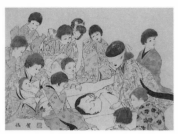

A game played at New Year's

Four for Zenkoji in Shinano
Five for the Grand Shrine at Izumo
Six for the village gods
Seven for Narita, god of fire
Eight for Hachiman, god of war
Nine for Kukai on Mount Koya
Ten for Tokyo's Sengakuji
Visit every one of them—
You still won't get well!

One for the chick who loves the sun
Two for the big-headed dwarf
Three for soybeans to make miso
Four for the bride and groom.
Five for the doc and his medicine box
Six for the girl and her sewing box
Seven for the hungry baby.
Eight for the monk who lives in the mountains
playing his conch-shell trumpet
Nine for the monk who begs for his supper
playing his bamboo flute
Ten for the lord in his castle.

Around the River Tsukiji

Mr. Tamotsu Iisaka (1894–1976)

Tsuchiura used to be a city of interconnecting rivers. The River Tsukiji ran behind my house, and on the opposite bank was a big storehouse with white walls that belonged to an old family of tatami mat–makers named Matsuyasu. We kids would row past that storehouse to the River Tozaki, then to the River Kawaguchi, through the lock, and out onto Lake Kasumigaura. All the houses had boats tied up in back.

My family was of samurai stock, so we had a little dock for our boat, with a roof fixed up to keep the rain off. Everybody used boats to get around; kids used them to go off and play. The water wasn't all that clean, but we could play in it, naked except for a loincloth.

To the right of the storehouse was a fish shop that sold sea fish, fresh up from Choshi every morning on the *Asahi Maru*. Next to that was a temple where you could hear the sound of sutra chanting in the morning. It's still there.

Across the river, between Nakamachi and Takajomachi, was a gate called "Akazu" [Won't Open]. It was put up centuries ago to separate the two quarters—one for merchants and the other for samurai. They were mighty strict about the separation policy back then. There used to be other gates all around town, everywhere the samurai lived, but around the middle of the nineteenth century they gradually took them down. Merchants lived in far more imposing residences than samurai. The streets were lined with live-in stores that had great high roofs and large storehouses attached.

I remember a place belonging to a very wealthy merchant, called the "Watakan." The owner dealt in soy sauce, grains, and fertilizer, and he was a big landlord besides. Every fall a long line of tenant farmers formed in the street, bringing him bags of rice by the cartload. That man must have had a thousand bags of rice in his storehouse all the time. He employed over a dozen servants. His courtyard was big enough for him to host enormous cherry blossom–viewing parties. Even places that weren't so big made money hand

The River Tsukiji

over fist. On feast days they set up tables in the streets selling all kinds of stuff. Everything seemed to sprout wings and fly away, it sold so fast. Some of my friends were merchants' kids, and I heard their parents used to stay up far into the night counting all the money they'd made. There was just no comparison with samurai families, who had a very frugal, simple lifestyle. Samurai houses had dilapidated thatched roofs, with shepherd's purse waving in the wind on top.

Men of samurai stock all went to work. They became bank clerks and policemen. But generally their lives were far from easy. Going down the river in that part of town, everywhere you looked you'd see rows of old clothes and grayish diapers flapping in the breeze.

There were lots of geisha houses and restaurants in these parts too. The best known was the "Koyokan," where five or six geisha worked. When I was a boy I would hear the sound of drums and shamisen coming from there. It was about where the conference hall is now. There were other, smaller places too: I can remember the "Kadomatsu" and the "Shinhama." Somewhere, a shamisen was always playing.

Around the Castle

Mr. Takanobu Seki (1896–1984)

On the south bank of the canal by the ruins of Tsuchiura Castle was Kamoshimo Hospital. It used to be a private mansion, and my family used to live on the estate grounds. When I was born, the main house was occupied by a man named Hitoshi Hiratsuka, who was the district headman. The main house was transported to Tsuchiura from Azabu in Tokyo. Let me explain. For generations, men from my family served as master of firearms for the Tsuchiya fief; after being sent to Edo to serve, eventually the family had part of the house they lived in there dismantled and transported here by boat. Apparently that included even the stone foundation. This was in the 1880s.

Including Hiratsuka, three generations of district headmen lived in that house. It's strange, but none of them ever had a telephone. Other important men lived around the castle—judges, lawyers, government officials—but none of them owned a telephone either. There was no phone in the school or in the courthouse. Probably the only places in town with telephones were the large shops. In case of an emergency, people relied on express messengers. There were couriers who lived in the homes of the supreme court justice and the district headman, and whenever the need arose, off they'd fly with a written communication to deliver to someone. Of course you never knew when an emergency might come up, so they had to be on call twenty-four hours a day. The only means of communication back then were face-to-face verbal communication and letters, so it was definitely inconvenient—but then that was a slower, more relaxed time than we have now. The courthouse didn't get telephone service till around 1920.

I was about fifteen when the town got electric lights. Until then there were no utility poles, which was certainly handy if you wanted to fly kites. The year before, my class went on a school trip with our teacher, from Nikko to Takasaki. When we stayed in the barracks of the Takasaki regiment, that was the first time in my life I ever saw electric lights. They were so bright, I was bowled over.

Before electricity the streets were lighted with oil lamps. Every night a man with a stepladder made the rounds of the town, putting oil in the lamps; there weren't very many in all. Often there'd only be a lamp outside the house of someone important. At night the town would be ink-dark; you could barely see a few feet ahead. If you went out on an errand after dark you had to carry a lantern on a pole out in front of you, but even then about all you could see was your own two feet. After it rained the ground would be muddy and treacherous, and walking was a terrible chore.

Out towards what is now Route 6 were the fields of Tsuchiura Prison. Men in red prison uniforms worked there, chained together two by two. There was a huge night-soil reservoir in the middle of the field where they carried all the human waste from the prison and left it to decompose. There used to be a cow shed in another field separated from the prison field by a fence, and farmers would come in carts with ladles every morning to scoop up night soil from that reservoir. Whether it cost anything or not I have no idea, but night soil was a valuable commodity, and some people were obviously willing to travel long distances to get it.

Tamotsu Takada [later a successful playwright and novelist] was a year ahead of me in school, but we were good friends as kids. We used to do all kinds of things together. One place we liked to play was the park, which looked quite a bit different back then. The western turret is gone now,[5] but there used to be a perfectly enormous fir tree there. It was the tallest, most imposing tree in all Tsuchiura. It looked as if it went all the way to the top of the sky and beyond. My father used to take me to Lake Kasumigaura for swimming and fishing, and I swear I could always see that fir tree from there. There were pine trees in the park too, and I used to climb them to the top and look off at the blueness of Lake Kasumigaura in the distance.

I always liked the view from high places; I must have climbed every tree there was. There's an oak tree that became a natural monument, but it wasn't very tall. To the east of that tree was a pond. Where the sandbox and bars are now used to be a big mulberry tree that all the children climbed. We'd race each other to the top and stuff ourselves with mulberries.

Gourd Pond is relatively new. That used to be a big field of rape blossoms. There were nettle trees there too, but their trunks were still thin; I'd grab one with both hands and shake it till jewel beetles fell to the ground.

On the banks of the canal directly behind my house was a kingfisher nest. Now there's a pretty bird. It would skim over the water to catch fish. When I was little, I wanted to capture one so much that I crawled out on the bank and stuck my hand in the nest, but it was so deep that I got nothing for my pains.

My grandmother used to say that when she first moved there, back around 1850, she'd hear foxes by the castle night after night. There were no houses or people in the vicinity back then, so the foxes had a free run of the area. No doubt they used it as a base to raid the chicken coops in town.

Fishing by Zenikame Bridge

Mr. Kozaburo Sato (1924–1994)

Fishing for recreation with a square dip net is an old, old tradition in my family. Ours was huge, fifteen feet square. Both my father and my grandfather liked fishing with the scoop net better than eating. It was located down the river from Tsuchiura Bridge, towards Zenikame Bridge. My grandfather would sit by the net from morning till night, inside a little wooden hut six feet square. Everything he could possibly need was there in the hut—a *hibachi*, tobacco, a lantern, and so on—and somebody'd bring him all his meals. He'd just sit there and drink hot saké, or play a game of *go* with his buddies. You know, it really was a great life for a man, free and easy, far removed from the cares of the world. The river was clean back then too, and my grandfather caught more fish than he knew what to do with. Sometimes it was just unbelievable.

One day late in March, the wind was blowing from the south, and then it suddenly shifted and came in from the west. That was the start of a big storm. My grandfather had had no warning, and he couldn't raise that net in such a storm, so he just left it lying there one entire day. Then, as the saying goes, the sun went down and the wind stopped. The water had gotten stirred up quite a bit, and my grandfather was pretty sure there would be junk caught in the net, but he went out and began to winch it up anyway. Before he could work it all the way up, the net got terrifically heavy, and he could hardly budge it. He kept at it, slowly working it up until he could just about make out the edges of the net. Then it was just too heavy and wouldn't move any more. Finally he started to see fish jostling in the net. In the end, after he got them all counted, he told me there were over three hundred *sai* [bony fish about two feet long] in that net. That wasn't the only time he had a haul like that either.

To give you some idea of how clean the water was, he used to catch a lot of smelt, good-sized ones too, especially around the end of April. I remember when I was about five, he'd bring around the smelt he'd caught and show them off proudly. "Here, sonny, take a whiff," he'd say. "Smells just like watermelon."

Near Zenikame Bridge was a store selling arrowroot-starch cakes called "Fuya," and across from that was a store called "Takeya" that had piles of bamboo along the riverbank. The owner made bamboo brooms and things like that, but he was a great fisherman too. Often, in the river out in front of his store, he'd set baskets of *yamabe* [trout] he'd caught, to keep them fresh. There used to be a lot of those around here. Anyway, we kids would swim underwater and dump them out for a prank. He used to get boiling mad.

One door down from there was a fellow who—well, to put it bluntly, he was a pimp. Women wearing thick white face powder were always going in and out of his place. There was a kind of seedy atmosphere about it. But he was another one who loved fishing; he was a master of trout fishing, with his own special spot staked out under Zenikame Bridge.

A Mr. Asa also lived by the bridge, in a house with a peaked roof; he was a highly skilled artisan who made winnowing tools out of bamboo, and just as crazy about fishing as the others. Come to think of it, that whole neighborhood was full of men who'd as soon fish as eat. Funny thing is, all of them lived in houses that flooded any time it rained. The houses were built on a dry riverbed, so what could you expect? I guess people were pretty casual about such things back then. Somehow they got away with it. Mr. Asa stayed on in his place a good long time; no matter how many times he was flooded out, he wouldn't hear of moving. His house stayed standing till the wartime, when they repaired the banks of the River Sakura.

As a kid I always played in the water there. It was so clear I could see shrimp walking on the sand at the bottom. I'd reach out to catch one, and it'd dart away and disappear. Fish used to swim right up alongside me, plain as day. I never could get hold of silk thread to attach a fishhook to, so I used horsehairs instead. There were horse-drawn wagons all over town, you see, so

Fishing at Zenikame Bridge

we'd sneak up behind a horse as it was swishing its tail at the flies, watch for a chance, and yank out a hair or two. There was a superstition that horsehairs brought luck, but it depended on the horse. Some had just the right elasticity, but others were too stiff to be much use.

We'd be out playing all day long, running around barefoot in the mud, our faces and arms black with dirt. In cold weather my hands and feet would freeze till I couldn't take a bath—getting in the hot water hurt too much. But I was always healthy. Never sick a day.

One game we played was called *genkobuchi*. We'd whittle sticks from willows that grew in the rushes, then stand them in the mud and try to knock each other's over. We whittled bows for ourselves too, and fashioned reed-arrows to shoot back and forth. We were always doing the kind of things that made our teacher yell at us in school.

The best place for swimming was around Shorinji Temple. In a hard rain the temple cemetery would flood, so even the gravestones toppled over. The riverbanks were steep, and coffins stuck right out of them. People didn't practice cremation in those days, so there they'd be—the bones of the dead—washed clean in the river water. We used to sneak up as close as we dared, half afraid to look, half unable to tear our eyes away, till it got too scary and we ran off. Now that I think about it, they did a pretty lousy job of managing that cemetery. The temple was torn down later, during reconstruction of the riverbanks; it used to have a lot of parishioners.

Fishing on the River Sakura

Nowadays there are hardly any fish, and you never see anyone fishing in the river, but back in my day there were endless styles of fishing. For one thing, there were any number of square dip nets around what's now Gakuen Ohashi

Bridge. Before the war, come spring there'd be flowering cherry trees and fields of yellow rape as far as Mushikake Dam, with larks soaring up—a beautiful age, that's what it was. *Sai* were in their prime just when the cherries came out, and that's when you saw the most square dip nets.

I myself was partial to fishing with triangular scoop nets. We used to call them *kakkui* around here. You'd aim for a school of fish that was swimming along vigorously, the way they do after a heavy rain. The sensation of scooping up a fish like a carp was indescribable—you could feel it hit against your arm with a satisfying *zam!* I liked it so much, I did it all the time. One evening I filled bucket after bucket with carp, crucian carp, *sai,* and other kinds of fish.

After May, it was *demizu-ami,* flood-net fishing. That's a smaller version of a square dip net, and we used it to catch carp. Other kinds of fish got so thin and scrawny after April, once the breeding season was over, they weren't worth eating. But carp you could go for year-round.

At the beginning of fall we did plenty of *nobenawa* [longline fishing]. The boat would draw a long fishline, six hundred to twelve hundred feet long, with baited lines attached every six feet. We'd leave the lines in place overnight and haul them up the next morning. You'd think a line that long would catch on snags and get into a terrible snarl, but we knew what we were doing and we could always get it free.

We went fishing for catfish in the fall too. The method we used was a fish trap called *takappo.* It involved cutting off three feet of bamboo and taking out the nodes, then tying the bamboo sections together in pairs and submerging them in water in the springtime. By fall, you see, they'd be thoroughly water-logged and heavy. Then we'd drag the trap by boat to a spot we'd targeted and lower it into the water, leaving a marker. It had to be someplace in deep water, where the riverbed was firm. Raising it up again was a tricky proposition. It'd be full of catfish or eels or, if there were no more catfish, a

Higai

school of *higai* [a fatty fish about six inches long]. Catfish were one of the first kinds of fish to disappear, so this method was abandoned years ago.

In winter we used *makiami* [round haul nets]. We'd find some place where fish naturally congregated in the winter months, deep in the lake, and surround them with a net. Then, using a stick that was blunted on one end like a practice spear, we'd go around poking the cluster. Till then, the fish would just hang perfectly still in the icy water, in a kind of suspended animation, but that activity would scare them into rushing out straight into the net. This worked for catching *sai*, dace, carp, and crucian carp. The lake used to freeze over in the winter; when you broke the ice and lowered a net, sometimes you'd come on a school of eels weighing hundreds of pounds. You may not believe it, but it's true: we used to get hundreds of pounds of eels at a time.

There was also something called *ebidaru* [shrimp traps]: narrow, delicately woven tubes of bamboo, baited with crushed mud-snails. Eels used to get into them a lot too.

Bindaru [fishing with glass pots] was another technique that we used from November to January. You'd put chrysalis powder in a special glass pot with a hole in the top and submerge it in the water to catch bitterlings. Those would be skewered and broiled with soy, and sold in Tokyo as *suzume-yaki*.[6] To come out ahead, all you needed to catch was sixteen or seventeen pounds—but that meant raising and lowering the traps in midwinter, in a raw north wind. It was a very tough undertaking. People still fished that way until I guess I was in my forties or so.

There were plenty of other kinds of fishing too. The reason there were so many different techniques is simple—the fishing was that good. After I came back from the war I went fishing again by Zenikame Bridge, and I'll never forget what happened: in just over three hours I caught sixteen crucian carp a foot long, and a bucketful of smaller ones to boot. That's the stuff of dreams now.

Ujo Noguchi and the School Song

Mr. Gunji Komori (1898–1988)

Up to the 1930s, Tsuchiura Primary School had no school song. But I taught in Tsuchiura, and I was determined to see that our school had a first-class song, one we could all be proud of. I proposed to the principal that we ask the famous poet and lyricist Ujo Noguchi to write the words. The principal was all for the idea, but he couldn't believe such a famous man would agree. "Don't worry about that," I said. "Noguchi was born in Ibaraki. If we ask him, he's bound to say yes." And so it ended up that the job of asking him fell to me.

I went to call on Noguchi in spring 1935, at his house in Kichijoji, in Tokyo—by appointment, of course. Way back then Kichijoji was a lonesome stop out in the country, with nothing but a few farmhouses, and here and there a shop selling dumplings or cheap sweets. It took me ten minutes to reach Noguchi's house, where he lived quietly with his wife and children. It was a very tasteful house, with an inner courtyard. He had no live-in pupils serving as houseboys, the way so many writers used to do.

Well, he was as gracious as he could possibly have been. There he was, one of the finest poets in all Japan, but he didn't put on any airs with me. He chatted straight off as if he'd known me for ten years. I don't think I ever met anyone with so much warmth and charm in all my life.

He had a large garden, but no bonsai. Instead he had something called *bonseki*, which was nothing but natural stones displayed in water-filled trays. He said he watered his stones every day. They were of various colors—blues, pinks and reds, white—and the moss growing on them produced flowers and thread-like filaments of great beauty. He told me with a smile, "I like nature. When I study rocks, the most basic part of nature, all sorts of ideas come to me."

He came to Tsuchiura on a glorious day in May 1935. I went to meet him at the station. There were rickshaws and taxicabs lined up, but he told me he'd rather walk into town and have a good look around. We went across Sakura Bridge into Honmachi, then through Nakamachi, Tamachi and Yokomachi, and up Manabe Hill. From Dochu we went around to a high spot overlooking Lake Kasumigaura. He let out his breath, I remember, and said softly, "How beautiful!" Then he was silent, just looking and looking. Unfortunately, the view of Mount Tsukuba was cut off from there. Afterwards we walked all the way down to the edge of the lake. The reeds and wild rice were growing thickly, and we could see water birds among them. People on houseboats were resting comfortably, or puttering around doing laundry or other chores.

"This is a good place," he said to himself. He walked around, stopping now and then as if thinking about something. In town it was the same. Every so often he'd ask me a short question. He wanted to know about local history, people's lives, all sorts of things.

Then we went back over Sakura Bridge, turned right onto Naval Road, and walked up Suikosha Hill to where the city hall is now. When we got there, he suddenly cried out.

There in front of us were the white-sailed fishing boats, gliding gracefully over the water, and the endless deep blue of the lake. Dejima was wrapped in mist, and off to the west Mount Tsukuba glowed a soft purple. Curving through the wide expanse of green rice fields was the River Sakura. The town spilled from the castle site down to the shore of the lake.

When he spoke, his voice was filled with emotion. "This is a place of exceptional beauty," he said. He added that, in his judgment, being surrounded by such scenery made the residents of Tsuchiura some of the luckiest people in all Japan.

He stood there for a long time as if in a trance. I can't tell you what a moving and humbling experience it was for me to see our country's leading poet stand lost in thought on that hill, under that perfect spring sky—all for the sake of our local primary school.

That night he stayed at the Matsusho Inn—a hotel that's been there for

centuries, next to where the Sanwa Bank is today. The following day he said he preferred to wander around town alone, so I left him to his own devices. He stayed one more night in the inn and then went back to Tokyo the next morning.

It was about a month later that he sent us the finished song. The composer was his personal choice—Kinshi Hiraoka. The daughter of the Owada Hospital chief of staff made a recording, and there was an all-school assembly in the gymnasium to formally introduce the new song. I suppose we rehearsed it ahead of time, but I don't remember anything about that. Anyway, everyone from the principal on down was tickled pink. I felt a huge sense of relief at having carried out my great task. I felt some pride, yes, but more than anything it was a load off my shoulders.

The School Song of Tsuchiura Primary School

In the sky at dawn, veiled in faint purple
It rises through the mist—Mount Tsukuba.
Crimson deepening, gracefully it winds
Through blossoming spring—the River Sakura.

The peaceful waves of Lake Kasumigaura
Continue on forever, far as the eye can see.
Its glory ever increasing, Kame Castle goes on
In silent reminder of ages now gone by.

May our school badge circle carry on
Through the years, nothing added, nothing lost,
Like nature's blessings–an emblem everlasting
Of this enduring reign.

Training as a Geisha

Mrs. Taki Nose (1895–1999)

Until I was ten—around the time of the Russo-Japanese War—we lived in Tajuku, near a big pond. Around the corner from the cabinetmaker, where the community center is today, was the pawnshop "Minakawa"; next door was a tatami mat–maker, and off to one side a ways was a grand house belonging to Mr. Hirose, the head of the post office. Mr. Hirose dug up dirt to raise the foundations of his house and guard against flooding, so it stood head and shoulders above the other houses in the neighborhood. The hole left afterwards eventually filled up with water, creating a nice big pond. We kids used to splash around in it barefoot. West of the pond there was nothing but rice paddies, with the old school building off by itself in the distance, and beyond that Mount Tsukuba.

We had no toys to speak of. Instead we wove grass and flowers into necklaces, made mud pies, played hide-and-seek and tag and other games. Our clothes were very plain and simple. Boys and girls dressed just alike, in short striped kimonos. Only young ladies from families rich enough to have a storehouse wore muslin. You could tell poor children from the rich ones at a glance; even their hairstyles were different. Most children wore their hair pulled back as tight as could be, with a hair ornament of one kind or another. *Takenaga* were inch-wide ornaments made of paper with pretty designs. Girls who couldn't afford them used *ogoma* instead, which consisted of wood shavings they picked up and painted their own designs on in red and purple. That's how girls who never had two coins to rub together were able to make themselves look pretty.

Girls from better families generally wore their hair in braids. It was true of everybody, not just children—you could tell someone's station at a glance, from the way she wore her hair. Servants and the mistress of a household had completely different hairstyles. Even among housemaids, those who cooked meals were lower in status than those who cleaned the rooms, and they wore their hair differently. You could generally tell what sort of work people did just by look-

ing at their hairstyles and kimono. Only children from the best families wore
geta. Mostly, people wore sandals made of bamboo or straw. Nobody in town
went barefoot, but in the countryside everyone did, children and adults both.

One thing I remember from those days is an eating-place called "Katsu-
bushiya" that sold something called "iris dumplings" [dumplings in the shape
of irises]. They were scrumptious. The old man there would carefully split the
end of a piece of bamboo into five or six narrow prongs and then spread
them out like fingers on a hand; then on each prong he'd skewer one little
dumpling the size of the tip of a baby finger, flatten them out, and grill them
one by one over hot coals. When they were done, he slathered them in honey.
One set of those was five sen.

Another treat was *botchirayaki*, griddle cakes made from slightly sweetened
wheat flour. They had the most wonderful smell—just walking near them
would make your mouth water. If I had a little extra spending money, I'd buy
a bull's-eye and put it on top of one of the griddle cakes while it heated, so that
the candy would melt all over it and form a dark, sweet syrup. That was unbelievably delicious. It was too good just to gobble up—that would have been a
shame. We kids used to take hold of the melting bull's-eye with our chopsticks
and move it around over the *botchirayaki*, drawing pictures for fun—a dragon-
fly, say, or a turtle or a fish—and then we'd take our time eating it, savoring
every bite. I think those were two sen apiece.

On the twenty-eighth of every month, the feast day for O-Fudo-sama, a
priest from Ryusenji Temple in Maekawa would come and chant sutras. The
altar would be covered in candles, and huge crowds of worshippers always
turned out. On days like that the streets would be jammed with stalls selling
children's toys, wooden *geta* clogs, tools, almost anything you can imagine.
Stallkeepers would chant rhythmically to attract customers: "Come on over,
buy a little something, everything here is only ten sen! Step right up and buy a

little something, buy yourself a little good luck!" Someone else would spread out an old scroll painting and announce, "This fine work of art dates from the Kamakura period. Step right up one and all, come take a look!" You can't begin to imagine what a swirl of noise and activity it was, and what fun!

Tai-yaki [fish-shaped pancakes filled with bean jam] were two sen. They used to make them this plump and big, with bean jam all the way into the tail. On other festival days there would be stalls lining both sides of the main road in Yokomachi and Tamachi, with amateur theatricals too. A candy store called "Tsukaji" used to sell bags of broken candy for five sen, with all different kinds of sweets inside. We looked forward with such excitement to getting them. I love to remember those days. It was a happy, happy time.

Here's a song we used to sing while bouncing a ball:

> *Teteshara, mameshara*
> Monkey loves his red coat,
> Went out on the town last night.
> What did he have to eat?
> Horse mackerel soup, crucian carp boiled in soy.
> One bowl, slurp! Two, slurp slurp!
> The third place served no fish at all
> So he got hopping mad.

Training

When I turned nine, I went into training at a geisha house in Honmachi called "Fujimoto." The training was extremely rigorous. Few geisha nowadays can play the shamisen, but back then you were expected not only to master the shamisen but also to learn to dance and play the hand-drums, or *tsuzumi*. As a

Shamisen lesson

geisha, you made your living by entertaining clients with your artistic abilities, and it took at least three years before you were worth your salt. So as I say, the training was severe—far beyond what people today could imagine.

Mind you, any kind of apprenticeship was an ordeal in those days. Before any carpenter or joiner could go out on his own, he had to put in time as an apprentice, getting yelled at and hit—and every time he made a mistake, his master would call him names: "you damn fool," "you numskull." The world of geisha was no different. Play a wrong note during your lesson and the teacher would strike your hand with her big ivory plectrum and draw blood. Even then you had to apologize humbly and beg her to go on teaching you. Then it was just grit your teeth and get on with the lesson. We were able to stand it because we were so determined to learn. You see, if someone gives you something, why, you never know—some day they might ask for it back. But once you've mastered an art, it's yours till the day you die. The more you hone your skill, the finer it is. So we kept on at any cost.

What sets a geisha apart is the level of her art. If it doesn't amount to much, and she only flirts with clients or sells her favors, she's no better than a prostitute. Tsuchiura had its share of brothels, or "powder houses," as they were called. There must have been a hundred establishments that tried to lure unsuspecting clients in—but a geisha house set out to entertain its customers in an entirely different way. Every geisha had to play the shamisen and sing, know dances for every season, and play hand-drums—both the large and smaller ones—as well as the gong and the *koto*. If she had a mind to go into business on her own, she needed to learn flower arranging and tea ceremony besides. When a customer hired a geisha, she had to be prepared to lead him away from mundane cares with her art, into another world. That's why the training was so rigorous, and why geisha took such pride in their work.

When I woke up in the morning, I got dressed and then put a towel over my head, tucked up my skirt, and helped scrub the house from top to bottom. After that it was time for the lesson. We'd hurry off to the teacher's house— before breakfast, naturally. "You can't learn on a full stomach," people said. The teacher wouldn't have had her breakfast yet either. In winter there was no heat, and my hands would get so cold I could barely move my fingers. It was bad enough just sitting in front of my teacher to play—I always got so nervous I froze, every time. That's how strict the relation was between a pupil and her teacher.

During the lesson, you sat and paid attention for all you were worth. If she taught you something three times and you still didn't know it, she'd bash you right across the fingers with her plectrum, like I said. Your fingers would be bleeding, and they'd hurt like anything, but if you so much as made a face she'd hit you again for being a weakling. It would never have occurred to her to go easy on us just because we were children.

It was the same with dancing lessons. One little slip and the teacher would yell "No!" and give you a slap. If you still got it wrong, she'd give you a kick that sent you flying. Then if you felt bad and started to cry, she'd turn her back and say, "Well, if *that's* the way you feel, you'd better quit right now. You obviously haven't got it in you to be a geisha. Go on, get out!" No matter what she said, I'd prostrate myself, with my forehead flat against the tatami floor, and beg her to take me back: "I'm sorry," I'd say. "I promise I'll do better after this, so please teach me again." Then she'd relent. "Well, all right," she'd say, "but you'd better straighten up and pay attention. Do it again, now, and get it in your bones!" I'd be so happy and relieved to get on with the lesson, I'd apply myself ten times harder than before.

I wanted so much to hear my teacher say, "Well done," that I used to say this prayer to all the gods and Buddha: "Please, please, please let me improve. I promise not to eat any dumplings or sweets until I learn this piece. So please help me do it." In short, all I ever thought about, waking and sleeping, was my lessons and what I was supposed to know. On the way home my head would be chock-full of what I'd just learned. I can remember using the handle of my umbrella as the neck of the shamisen and working my fingers up and down, trying to fix the notes in my mind as I went along. I didn't care one whit what anybody might think if they saw me. Nothing mattered except my lessons.

When I played the small hand-drum, I would heat it at the brazier and keep beating the tight drumskin for hours on end until it gave off just the right high-pitched sound. After a while my nails would split and my fingertips would bleed—the drumskin would be covered in blood. The blood would drip down and stain my kimono too, so I used to spread a handkerchief in my lap as protection, but I got in trouble for that. "You can't play properly with a thing like that in your lap," the teacher would scold me. I had no idea what I was supposed to do.

When I was little, I also had to work as a *hakoya*—that's the person who carries the shamisen in its box for a geisha on her way to or from an appointment. Sometimes I had to go out around midnight to a restaurant far away to accompany a sister geisha home. It was lonely and scary on the way over, believe you me. There were no street lights at all, so the lanes were pitch-dark. Hardly anybody was out at that hour either. I carried a lantern with me, but its light didn't reach far; actually, it only made the surrounding darkness seem blacker and scarier. Moonlit nights were a blessing. When there was a full moon, I'd gaze up at it again and again as I trotted off to meet someone.

Etiquette and deportment were other things that were very strictly taught. We were told to go up the stairs without making any noise. If a sister geisha listened at the foot of the stairs as I went up and could hear my footsteps, she'd grab the hem of my kimono and pull me back down for a scolding: "How many times do you have to be told?" she'd say. If you ever answered back, you

Young geisha

were in for it. You'd be slapped good and hard till your cheek swelled up. There had to be unquestioning obedience at all times.

Apprenticeship

After three years of this training, you were promoted to *hangyoku* ["half-jewel"], or apprentice geisha, which meant being allowed to accompany a full-fledged geisha on her engagements. There was another whole set of rules for that. In my day we had to sit perfectly still, like little princesses. The most important thing for us to remember was that it was our job to draw the customer away from the ordinary world to a finer, more beautiful place, one where he could forget the trials of life and just enjoy himself. So even if you were hungry or cold, you couldn't let on. You had to look utterly unconcerned. "I don't eat food the way others do, I don't drink saké, I don't go to the privy." That's the impression you had to create.

Your makeup was part of the effect. It had to be pleasing to the customer, so we took endless pains with it. The powder we used came in a little box, and it was rather granular. Powder from Kyoto was the best; you'd take seven to ten granules in your palm, dissolve it in skin tonic, and apply it to your cheeks and neck. Rouge we applied with the tip of the little finger, making a small red circle right in the center of the lips. Any leftover went on the earlobes.

I went to the hairdresser's once a week, but most of the time I arranged my hair by myself. There was a big array of combs in the makeup box, and I used them to do it up by myself, both sides and top. The boxwood comb was the best. I'd comb my hair again and again and fasten it just the way I liked it. It used to take a good hour. When I got my hair arranged just so and went off to an engagement, I'd come back and sleep with my head on a wooden box-pillow to keep from mussing my hairdo.

Hairdresser

The dances we performed varied according to the month. At New Year's we performed "New Year" on January 1, "Long Reign" on the second, and "The Isle of Eternal Youth" on the third. There was a different piece for every day of the first week. Then in February it was "Spring for the Plum," in March "The Four Seasons of Kyoto," in April "Cherry Blossom–Viewing Dance," and so on. We had to prepare something different every month, and besides, we had to be ready if a customer requested a certain ditty or ballad. In those days geisha weren't the only ones who studied music and dance—young masters of great establishments did too, and so did clerks and craftsmen. That made our job all the harder. If you knew so-and-so was learning such-and-such a piece, you had to learn it too, or suffer humiliation. We had to work hard to stay on our toes.

But there were a lot of enjoyable times too. We'd gather in a restaurant with the owners of the big stores in town, and we geisha would play the shamisen and sing. Everybody was a master of their instrument; those with no instrument to play would tie a towel around their head, grab a broom or dust mop and dance around the room, crowing, "Cleanup, cleanup," with all sorts of comical gestures and movements. We never stopped laughing. Such fun you never saw!

I was invited to a great many weddings too. Back then, whether you lived on a farm or in town, everybody had the ceremony performed at home, and the celebrating went on for days. I was invited for other events too, like ceremonies for the dedication of a new house—almost any formal, happy occasion.

So you see, we geisha had our hands full back in those days. Then the war came along and changed people's hearts—roughened them, if you ask me. After the war, geisha themselves changed, and so did customers' tastes. Remembering it like this certainly makes me miss that time.

The Restaurant "Sansuikaku"

Mrs. Misao Yamamoto (1906–1982)
(Professional name: Kokango)

Until the war, there used to be several big ponds in what is now part of Saku-ramachi, each one with carp in it. Alongside the ponds was a large, three-story wooden restaurant called "Sansuikaku." It used to be the finest place of enter-tainment in all Tsuchiura. I had free run of the place since I was a little girl, so I know quite a bit about it. My mother was a geisha, and a close friend of the landlady, who was a superb singer of *tokiwazu* ballads. She was a gorgeous woman with a voice that could just melt you. The owner fell madly in love with her on a trip to Shizuoka one time and brought her back with him as his mistress.

The first floor of Sansuikaku contained the kitchen and smaller rooms; the second floor had an enormous hundred-mat room and a stage, and the third floor, which was a bit smaller, had three or four medium-sized rooms. The famous painter Shinsui Ito stayed there many a time. Sometimes I'd peek in and see him with an enormous sheet of paper spread out on the tatami mats, painting some picture. Also the comic artist Ippei, who was married to writer Kanoko Okamoto, used to stay there with his friends, and I would get them to dash off cartoon drawings for me. Other famous people came too. Tsuchiura was known as a city of water, and they came to go pleasure boating on Lake Kasumigaura. I was only a little girl when Shinsui Ito came to stay, but I remem-ber going in his room and seeing him paint on fans. He dashed off scenes of chrysanthemums and autumn grasses in quick, light strokes—such lovely paint-ings that even at that young age I couldn't help staring in wonder. When I was a little older, I got him to paint designs on an obi and some other things of mine. All the geisha had him paint pictures on their kimonos and obis, but then in the flood of 1938, they were nearly all ruined. That was such a dreadful shame.

Naval officers were some of our best customers. They used to run a little wild at parties, though. The closer we came to war, the worse it got. They used to do something they called "digging for potatoes": they'd strip the tatami mats from the floor and hurl them out the windows into the pond in the

The Sansuikaku

back, pull down boards from the ceiling and throw them outside too, break all the ornaments … oh yes, quite a ruckus, all right! They were young and had more energy than they knew what to do with, I suppose. I think at the same time they must have been gripped by the thought that they were soon going to die. They used to get out of control—but back then naval officers used to lord it over everyone else, and we just let them do as they pleased. The naval authorities turned a blind eye, probably because the men never hurt anybody, and the navy quietly paid for all the damage.

Before both the May 15th Incident and the February 26th Incident,[7] they say the young rebel officers involved met in the Sansuikaku to make their plans. We geisha had no way of knowing what actually went on, but apparently there was some connection. After the February uprising, the military police increased their patrols, and there was a sudden drop in parties.

Not far from Sansuikaku was the Niihari Community Hospital, which is now the Tsuchiura Community Hospital. It was the best general hospital in town. I was treated there once for typhoid fever, and everyone was so nice to me that I popped in all the time to visit, even after I got well. The nurses would say, "Here now, we'll make you some red wine," and then they'd add some kind of red coloring to sugar water. I just loved it. I used to skip school so I could go to the hospital. The doctors would give me a hard time when they caught me, though: "What are you doing here, little lady?" they'd say sternly. "You belong in school!" But you see, I didn't want to go to school. From the time I was a little thing, I used to have my hair dressed formally to attend geisha parties. So when I went to school, the other children would laugh and taunt me, saying, "There goes the geisha kid!" That was bad enough, but then I caught typhoid and had to miss half a year of school, and even though I wasn't stupid, I fell behind until it was hopeless. I never liked school again after that.

Anyway, in those days becoming a professional geisha was really tough.

A restaurant kitchen

When it came to my lessons, my mother was a stickler, always flying into a rage over my lapses. If I had trouble getting the hang of my music or dancing, she'd grab me by the hair and drag me along the floor, or throw me right out of the house, or give me a flying kick. Those things happened all the time. I couldn't begin to tell you how many times I was locked out of the house in the middle of the night. But I have to say it worked: you couldn't help learning, and eventually, if you kept at a piece long enough, you would get it in your bones.

It took three to five years before an apprentice geisha could make her professional debut. That meant being able to perform a piece appropriate to the season of the year—dancing and singing both—as well as attaining proficiency on the shamisen and the hand-drums. Since being a geisha meant doing all that at the very highest level, customers always went away entertained and satisfied. There were lively goings-on every night at the Sansuikaku and the other restaurants—but now of course it's all changed.

NOTES

AUTHOR'S PREFACE

[1] A character from legend who saves the life of a sea turtle. One day several years later the turtle carries him to the magnificent Dragon Palace at the bottom of the ocean as a reward. Urashima Taro returns to his village after what he thinks has been just a short visit, to find the houses he knew gone and his friends and family long dead. He opens a box he was given in the palace as a farewell gift; a plume of white smoke comes out, instantly transforming him into a wizened old man.

PART 1

A CAPTAIN'S WIFE

[1] A unit of currency no longer used, the *sen* was 1/100th of a yen.

[2] The author's father, Dr. Susumu Saga.

OHORI, THE CENTER OF RIVER TRAFFIC

[3] The Tone Canal opened in 1888. Construction took two years and cost 590,000 yen. The canal was five miles long and measured 108 feet across at its widest point, 30 at its narrowest. Its average depth was 16 feet. Writer Sojinkan Sugimura (1872–1945) penned this affectionate encomium: "The word 'canal' may suggest a dry, unlovely waterway with walls of concrete, but this one is different. It is wide and curving, and as delightful as any country stream. The banks are lined with cherry trees, maples, azaleas, and golden kerria—trees and flowers that add color and beauty to every season. Waterfowl swim among the rushes. Bamboo rafts come floating down from the Tone. Atop the embankments, smoke rises invitingly from houses of entertainment, and banners of drinking establishments wave in the breeze. It is a peaceful and bucolic scene."

PART 2

A FISHERMAN AND HIS WIFE

[1] If a prospective groom drank tea served by a prospective bride in her home, in the presence of her parents and the go-between, it was a signal that he agreed to the marriage.

ANGLING FOR EELS SIDE BY SIDE

[2] Literally, "ouch-ouch" disease. In 1964–1965, patients with symptoms of mercury poisoning appeared in a rural district near the city of Niigata on the estuary of the River Agano. A factory upstream was found to have polluted the entire river basin, affecting river fish and poisoning hundreds of people.

PART 3

TWO EXCURSIONS ON THE *TSUUN MARU*

1 Dedicated to the spirits of Japan's war dead.

2 The making of life-size chrysanthemum dolls, *kiku ningyo*, is a centuries-old craft tradition. A frame is first made from strips of bamboo, and then plants with small flowers and long bendable stems are selected. The plants are dug up whole and their roots wrapped in moist moss. They are then braided through and tied to the frame to create a body completely clothed in flowers. Finally a head, hands and feet made of wood or ceramics are added. Each doll requires between 100 and 150 plants, and the flowers can live for as long as two weeks, during which time the dolls are displayed.

PART 4

THE EAGLE SHRINE AND THE JAKAMOKOJAN FESTIVAL

1 A *monme* is 0.132 oz.

2 The word "jakamokojan" is also thought to be onomatopoetic, representing the sound of the ancient *kagura* music.

FESTIVALS AND FEAST DAYS

3 Feast days (*ennichi*) are days considered to have a special connection (*en*) with Shinto or Buddhist deities, commemorating their birth, miracles, vows, and the like. Today they have little religious significance.

4 The feast days are named for various deities, several of whom are considered to be the protectors of sailors.

AROUND THE CASTLE

5 It was rebuilt in 1990.

FISHING BY ZENIKAME BRIDGE

6 Literally, "grilled sparrow." Its head intact, a small fish such as bitterling or crucian carp was split open and skewered, then broiled with miso and soy sauce. It got its name because it looked like grilled sparrow.

THE RESTAURANT "SANSUIKAKU"

7 Military uprisings. On May 15, 1932, young naval officers assassinated Prime Minister Tsuyoshi Inukai in an attempted coup d'etat. All quickly surrendered to military police. On February 26, 1936, several political figures were killed and the hub of Tokyo was seized by 1,400 troops led by junior army officers. Nineteen leaders were swiftly sentenced to death and executed.

(英文) 霞ヶ浦風土記

Memories of Wind and Waves
A Self-Portrait of Lakeside Japan

2002 年 5 月17日　第 1 刷発行

著　者　佐賀純一

訳　者　ジュリエット・カーペンター

発行者　野間佐和子

発行所　講談社インターナショナル株式会社
　　　　〒112-8652 東京都文京区音羽 1-17-14
　　　　電話　03-3944-6493 (編集部)
　　　　　　　03-3944-6492 (営業部・業務部)
　　　　ホームページ　http://www.kodansha-intl.co.jp

印刷所　大日本印刷株式会社

製本所　黒柳製本株式会社

落丁本・乱丁本は、小社業務部宛にお送りください。送料小社負担にてお取替えします。なお、この本についてのお問い合わせは、編集部宛にお願いいたします。本書の無断複写(コピー)、転載は著作権法の例外を除き、禁じられています。

定価はカバーに表示してあります。

© Junichi Saga 2002
Printed in Japan
ISBN 4-7700-2758-3

MITO

ISHIOKA

HOKOTA

TAMATSUKURI

TAKAHAMA

Kashiwazaki

Tabuse

Ayumizaki

LAKE
KASUMIGAURA

DEJIMA

Shitozaki

Ushiwata

Ukishi

Tajuku

Okijuku

Ishida

Hajiyama

Yog
Bay

TSUCHIURA

Magake

Ami

Kihara